THE ENROLLMENT PROBLEM

THE ENROLLMENT PROBLEM
PROBLEM
Proven Management Techniques

Ronald J. Ingersoll

American Council on Education • Macmillan Publishing Company
NEW YORK

Collier Macmillan Publishers
LONDON

Macmillan Publishing Company
a Division of Macmillan, Inc.
866 Third Avenue, New York, N. Y. 10022

Collier Macmillan Canada, Inc.

Library of Congress Catalog Card Number: 87-33356

Printed in the United States of America

printing number
1 2 3 4 5 6 7 8 9 10

Library of Congress Cataloging in Publication Data

Ingersoll, Ronald J.
    The enrollment problem: proven management techniques/Ronald J.
Ingersoll.
        p.   cm.
    Bibliography: p.
    Includes index.
    ISBN 0-02-915520-7
    1. Universities and colleges—United States—Admission.
2. Universities and colleges—United States—Administration.
I. Title
LB2351.2.I54 1988
378'.1059'73—dc19   87-33356
                                                              CIP

This book is dedicated to enrollment professionals, who deal with a changing field and have shown exceptional depth of character and excellence in coping with it.

CONTENTS

PREFACE

This book is for college and university presidents, vice presidents, deans, enrollment managers, and program directors who are concerned with the enrollments at their institutions. It encompasses concerns about new and returning students of all types: traditional, nontraditional, graduate, and professional. The book also will help those in secondary schools consider their options in terms of enrollment futures.

This book is drawn from experiences during twelve years of work with enrollment programs at all levels, and observing what works and what does not work in terms of positive efforts to impact enrollment in the short and long term. The book also draws from the fields of education, admissions, enrollment, organizational development, communication theory, and the best that is currently available about institutional climates. This will add to and bring together much of the current literature and practice in enrollment management for those who are experienced and for those who are just entering the field.

There was nothing like this available for me when I started in enrollment management in 1974. There were many things to learn through experience and through work with people who approached their problems in different and exciting ways. The approach that came to be called the Enrollment Management Matrix emerged as I and my associates encountered the variables preventing many schools from realizing their full potentials in their enrollment programs. As problems became more severe and complex, the matrix surfaced as a positive way to address productively the varying populations and areas of concern. This matrix is a way of sorting out the options available and creating the desired state that an institution needs for its enrollment. As with a Rubik's cube, the complex issue of putting all the faces in the right place is addressed.

The key to the use of this book is a willingness to address enrollment issues in a systematic and professional way. There is a need to bring together the primary areas of concern—including the product of the institution, the databases directed at enrollment, communication with the external world, management, and climate—into a productive total effort. The Enrollment Management Matrix presents this approach and uses it to address areas ranging from retention to market segmentation.

The first chapter develops the history of enrollment management from simple admissions work through marketing and finally to the stage of enrollment management. Admissions is a field that has changed dramatically in a short period of time, leaving many concepts and solutions in its wake. For schools that are involved in various stages of growth in the enrollment area, this chapter will help to put things in perspective.

In Chapter 2, the Enrollment Management Matrix is presented and various components of the matrix are defined. Relationships are highlighted so that the next few chapters are easy to relate to the total picture. It is important to grasp the issue of relationships among the various parts of the matrix as well as the importance of the attribute of content and the variable of attitudes and beliefs.

Attitudes and beliefs often form impediments to effective enrollment management, expecially if a great deal of change must occur. Often these changes can occur in connection with new "ways of doing business" that are very different from those currently in place for the organization. This is the essence of the content attribute of the matrix.

The product area is discussed in Chapter 3, using a model developed by Theodore Levitt. The focus is on product packaging and the development of a broader view of institutional product. Meeting students' expectations is not enough to succeed. In the future, there must be more to offer and a school must already be developing its future product in the present to be successful in the long-term. Several examples are used to illustrate content issues, and the critical area of institutional fit is addressed.

The product and the climate of the institution are likely to impact enrollment success heavily. Without one's attention to these areas, the fully successful organization will not be possible. Instead, there will be continual concerns about the institution's ability to meet its enrollment needs each year.

Chapters 4 and 5 address the data area. The focus is on developing an appreciation of the types of data that should be collected and the ways in which they can be converted into useful information. The use of focus groups is a special consideration, along with the principle of developing the most appropriate questions before proceeding with research of any kind.

A college or university must assure itself that it will be able to use data before beginning database development. If the belief that changes will result from collecting information does not exist, the use of funds and energy to collect data is inappropriate.

In Chapter 6, the critical area of communication with students and "influentials" (those capable of influencing the student's decision) is related to product and data. In this chapter, the most direct use of a causal relationship is developed in a communication formula. The formula can be tested, and it illustrates the use of information in terms of communication variables.

Chapter 7 organizes ideas for management of the enrollment process. A key focus is enrollment planning, and a three-step process is suggested that will lead to better understanding and application of the energies of those involved in enrollment programs.

Training and development of enrollment-related staff members will be critical in the future. They will need to go well beyond what is practiced today. This will require better knowledge in all areas including knowledge of the college, the student, the market, and ways of working professionally with students and influentials to balance the objectives of the student and the goals of the institution.

Chapter 8 may be the most helpful to overall success in enrollment efforts. This chapter stresses the role of the institutional climate in enrollment success. In essence, the climate determines the internal environment created by the organization and the likelihood of its being able to respond to its own needs and the desires of the student.

The climate is organized into three areas: the flow of information, political systems, and the culture, that is, the attitudes and beliefs of people in the system. It is these three areas that will determine the ease with which a desired state of enrollment can be reached. Often the poor flow of information makes life miserable for students in a large or small educational system. At the same time, entrenched beliefs and political systems can block even the smallest change for the better. Several ideas are suggested for approaching this area.

The task force concept is introduced in Chapter 9 as a way to develop a more positive climate and a better chance at involvement of a variety of people in developing and implementing enrollment strategy. The composition and preparation of the task force is essential to its success. This is presented along with other areas basic to task force and enrollment progress.

Chapters 10 and 11 present specific enrollment issues and use the matrix to address them. Market segmentation, retention, and approaches to various types of students are reviewed. In these chapters, graduate, nontraditional, and professional programs are discussed in terms of the overall concept. It has been our experience that the matrix works with each of these and can provide stability and success in enrollment for all types of programs.

Throughout this book, data has been cited that has come from a variety of sources, including the National Student Database, a resource of the Ingersoll Group, Inc. The details of this national study are presented in an appendix along with a copy of the survey used. Its data has been compared to other databases, such as those of the College Board, American College Testing Program (ACT), and the work of Alexander W. Astin at UCLA.[1]

The glossary and bibliography represent an attempt to define some common terms and literature with which to address the complexity of enrollment management. This set of references has been developed from books and articles used in addressing enrollment issues of all types.

This book will be helpful for individuals who are trying to identify the various options available to them in dealing with enrollment problems. It will help to highlight the options that might best be used now and to focus attention on issues that need to be managed in the future. Enrollment management clearly is a process that never arrives at a final answer. What will work today will likely not work five years from now. Dealing successfully with this uncertainty is the core of this book.

[1]Astin, Alexander W. Cooperative Institutional Research Program: American Council on Education, University of California, Los Angeles.

ACKNOWLEDGMENTS

I must pay my respect and appreciation to people who have read, edited, prepared, and discussed various parts of this manuscript: Doris Ingersoll, Tom Williams, Kim Bucklin, and Ruth Sims, of The Ingersoll Group, Inc.; Jim Miller and Phillip Tyler of Rochester Institute of Technology; John Klockentager from Buena Vista College; Eric Wentworth from the Council for the Advancement and Support of Education; and Brice Harris of the Kansas City Community College System.

I wish to express my appreciation to each president, admissions director, and staff member of the institutions with whom we have worked. Through their participation in our efforts, I have learned a great deal about enrollment issues and the people and processes involved in building effective programs. This has been especially true of the clients we have had over the years and associations with individuals in various organizations that support enrollment efforts. Among these are some people who stand out: Charles Dick, president of Westminster College in Salt Lake City; Jim Miller at Rochester Institute of Technology; and Christa Oxford and the people at Southern Illinois University at Edwardsville.

A special note of appreciation goes to Jim Murray of the American Council on Education and Lloyd Chilton of Macmillan. They and their staffs have handled this book in a most professional and helpful way.

–1–
THE EVALUATION OF ENROLLMENT MANAGEMENT

From Back Roads to Systems

There seems to be little doubt that, in the future, most educational institutions will have to be more organized to deal with enrollment issues. In the early stages of demographic and other restraining forces for enrollment, denial was a standard response: the school and its faculty might deny that the issue would affect them, and the resulting enrollment declines were blamed on directors of admissions and their staffs or on the outside world.

In some cases this perspective was true, but denial became increasingly difficult to justify as more and more schools had to face declines and the impact of societal changes on enrollments. More and deeper questions have had to be asked, and the answers involve the total organization in terms of a commitment to managing enrollments.

It is to the systematic process of dealing with enrollment issues that this book is directed—the movement of the enrollment effort through various stages, which in part mirror the history of enrollment management in general.

FROM SCREENING TO MANAGING

The way in which colleges and universities have treated enrollment issues represents a path of increasing complexity from pure admissions work to the evolving sophistication of enrollment management.

Some years ago at our colleges and universities, there were more efforts put forth to create enrollments in schools than was true of more recent periods, such as the fifties. At one time it was not unusual for presidents and faculty members to be on the road talking to students, ministers, parents, and others to keep the enrollments of their schools going. In this period, many schools were starting, and the president and the founder were likely to be the same. The success of the school was very close to the heart for many of these individuals, as the following comments of a retiring California school president indicate:

> My wife and I would get into the car on Monday and drive throughout the country talking with every student we could find. These conversations were in the home, the school, or sometimes, in the classroom.
>
> By the end of the week, we knew who we had and who we did not and we could start over again on Monday. We worked very hard to gain the enrollments we needed.

This president could not understand why there should be any enrollment difficulties. To a large extent, he expected the staff to function in the same way as he and his wife did. And to some degree he was right. If the staff would put in more time and be more enthusiastic about the school, better enrollments would likely be produced.

The most familiar, recent stage of this enrollment management history is the school that could not keep up with the paperwork and wanted to have only the best students possible. The function of the office was to screen the potential students as carefully as possible and keep out anyone the faculty did not want. This was the admissions stage.

This gave way to a period of recruitment. In this phase the concept was to fill the funnel as full as possible and hope that the same good quality of student as before would fall out the bottom. The issue was still screening, but with the additional step of filling the pool as fully as possible with the hoped result of the same number and type of student as before.

This evolved to the stage of marketing, which in many people's minds represented the idea that if you make people aware of the school, then students will want to come. A "hidden jewel" is still the concept held by many presidents and boards in regard to their enrollment issues, and the solution is advertising and awareness activities and little else. These marketing efforts likely involved very little product development and looked only superficially at the issue of fit with the student and consumer satisfaction.

Each of these steps may work for some schools, but it is becoming increasingly clear that the efforts by the enrollment staff and others need to be different today to cope with a very difficult decade of enrollment success.

The enrollment effort needs to be better developed, targeted, and coordinated, and the era of competition and strategy has now arrived. The enrollment of an institution must be truly managed in order for the student and the school to be satisfied with the results of the effort. It is to the present stage of efforts by institutions to manage their enrollments and to their future efforts that this book is directed—without losing sight of the fact that there still may need to be people driving the back roads each day.

CHANGES IN THE ENVIRONMENT

Changes in the environment are part of our existence and are likely to be found in three general areas: in society, in the students we deal with, and in higher education in general. Each of these areas will present challenges to the administration and faculty of the organization that will result in difficult and challenging decisions on the part of the school in regard to its enrollment future.

SOCIETY

The shift in attitudes of people to success in work and the changing nature of work will likely cause severe challenges. As the consumer demands preparation for a diversity of college outcomes rather than for graduate or professional schools, institutions will need to respond with new insights and beliefs.

Faculty who are unfamiliar with the vast amount of information on careers other than their own will need to prepare to deliver the education needed by today's young people—preparation that will likely need to be as educationally demanding as that required for any sort of academic experience. In addition, schools will be preparing people for new types of jobs wherein the skills, attitudes, beliefs, and knowledge required for success will, in part, have to be based on some very fundamental concepts, on new directions in behavior, thinking, and emphasis.

STUDENTS

Here the demographics have been the clearest indicator of problems ahead (Tables 1.1, 1.2). Also included in the issues will be changing expectations of colleges, changing views of what an attractive institution must be able to offer, and changes in the degree of competition that each school will face for students in the future.

TABLE 1.1. Changes in the Number of 18-Year-Olds: Percentage Change from 1981*

Region	1987 % Change	1988 % Change	1994 % Change	1999 % Change
United States	−14	0	−22	− 9
Northeast	−18	−16	−35	−30
North central	−19	−16	−29	−22
Southeast and South central	−10	− 2	−11	+ 3
Western	− 9	− 2	−11	+19

*This data represents an estimate of changes in the number of potential students available relative to the base year. *Source: High School Graduates: Projections for the Fifty States* (Boulder: Western Interstate Commission for Higher Education).

TABLE 1.2. Projection (Not a Prediction) of the United States Population, by Age Groups, 1976–2000 (in Thousands)*

Year	16–17	18–21	22–24	25–29	30–34	35 & Over	Total: 16 & Over	Total: 18 & Over
1976	8,397	16,771	11,395	17,806	14,238	89,718	158,324	149,927
1977	8,442	16,970	11,655	17,745	15,416	90,767	160,996	152,554
1978	8,425	17,106	11,874	18,055	15,894	92,183	163,535	155,110
1979	8,279	17,156	12,143	18,451	16,558	93,396	165,982	157,703
1980	8,157	17,117	12,346	18,930	17,242	94,554	168,335	160,179
1981	7,929	17,018	12,494	19,324	18,138	95,595	170,498	162,569
1982	7,549	16,875	12,483	19,775	18,086	98,747	172,428	164,879
1983	7,236	16,499	12,523	20,140	18,400	99,430	174,227	166,990
1984	7,056	15,988	12,491	20,405	18,798	101,172	175,911	168,855
1985	7,020	15,442	12,411	20,581	19,278	106,422	177,607	170,587
1986	7,151	14,871	12,212	20,771	19,694	104,687	179,367	172,215
1987	7,317	14,520	11,925	20,737	20,126	106,555	181,182	173,865
1988	7,092	14,470	11,497	20,631	20,487	108,484	182,660	175,568
1989	6,603	14,600	11,029	20,475	20,747	110,471	183,923	177,321
1990	6,345	14,506	10,641	20,169	20,917	112,503	185,082	178,737
1991	6,351	14,177	10,508	19,600	21,106	114,548	186,291	179,940
1992	6,382	13,685	10,555	19,017	21,068	116,710	187,418	181,035
1993	6,397	13,198	10,759	18,417	20,959	118,847	188,577	182,181
1994	6,555	12,971	10,622	17,919	20,800	120,939	189,806	183,251
1995	6,783	12,995	10,228	17,665	20,489	122,981	191,139	184,357
1996	7,074	13,184	9,680	17,691	19,914	125,060	192,603	185,529
1997	7,388	13,432	9,506	17,514	19,327	127,030	194,197	186,809
1998	7,644	13,888	9,463	17,242	18,727	128,906	195,872	188,227
1999	7,813	14,434	9,555	16,858	18,233	130,697	197,589	189,776
2000	7,924	14,990	9,663	16,469	17,981	132,298	199,324	191,400

*Source: United States Department of Commerce, Bureau of the Census. "Projections of the Population of the United States: 1977 to 2050," *Current Population Reports,* Series P-25, No. 704, July 1977, pp. 28, 37–60. Reprinted from *Adult Learning, Higher Education, and the Economics of Unused Capacity.*

TABLE 1.3. Trends in Attitudes*

Objectives Considered Essential or "Very Important"	% Who Said "Very Important" 1972	1985
Become accomplished in one of the performing arts.	10.1	9.9
Become an authority in my field.	64.8	73.1
Be well-off financially.	50.6	75.4
Develop a meaningful philosophy of life.	67.3	43.6
Obtain recognition from colleagues for contributions to my special field.	41.2	57.1

*Source: Alexander Astin, Kenneth Green, William Korn, *The American Freshman: Twenty Year Trends.* Cooperative Institutional Research Program, University of California, 1987.

Major changes in students' attitudes are indicated in Table 1.3. It is also indicated, by the same authors, that participation rates, at least out of high school, are likely to fall.

COLLEGES

Our educational institutions will face a difficult future with many challenges that come from declining facilities and people that have been ignored and allowed to drift. Dealing with faculty and staff development along with needs to improve facilities and programs will come at a time when other pressures have accumulated both inside and outside the institution.

A great many negative forces are building that could confront colleges and universities in the near future. At the same time we are developing the energy and expertise required for dealing with these issues. Institutional leadership has become a general topic of presidents and boards of colleges and universities. The many options available to schools are still open and can be addressed by utilizing talented and energetic people who want to do well for their schools and themselves. With careful attention to new approaches while not ignoring the fundamentals of the past, any institution can still do well. But it will certainly not be business as usual.

ISSUES AND RESPONSES

These various examples of the enrollment issues mentioned have many dimensions that should cause concern:

- The issue affects all types of schools: public, private, liberal arts, technical, professional, large, small, metropolitan, and rural.

- It threatens jobs and the personal security of people who work with colleges and universities.
- It has the potential to impact the quality of our institutions negatively as people deal with survival issues and the quality of the students who graduate.

VARIETIES OF REACTIONS

The enrollment situation, when it is developing or has arrived, may produce a variety of responses: denial; recognition, but heavy emphasis on a promotional response; passing the problem on to someone else; the marketing response; hiring and firing of personnel; some research and data, or vast reports by prestigious organizations advising a return to what worked before. This may produce some short-term successes, but rarely is the problem gone.

DENIAL.   There may be clear evidence of present or potential problems in the marketplace. This may be a situation where, for example, the demand for a particular program is decreasing, the demand for graduates decreases, or the competition increases. Yet, in a denial situation, the people involved will either ignore the problem completely or will say it doesn't matter.

This response is well illustrated in many professional schools. For example, problems have clearly been evident in the law school area for several years (Figure 1.1). Early on, data on law enrollments indicated that problems were developing and that people knew what some solutions might be and even knew how to implement them. Because of huge increases in the number of women interested in law and, to some extent, increases in the number of minorities studying law, the most serious problem has been delayed. But the crisis is now here.

When there is no longer mass denial, there may be partial or complete recognition that there is a problem, but the responses can vary. The reaction may be to give the problem to someone else, get a new director, or create a new set of publications that will be flashier and bigger than the previous set.

PASSING THE PROBLEM ALONG.   This is a strategy frequently applied by presidents and other senior administrators. They know there is a problem, but they pass it along to another senior person, commonly the director of admissions or outsiders such as consultants. These individuals may be expected to solve the problem without much help. In fact, the only things the president wants to hear, in this case, are positive results or, at the very least, positive signs that the problem may be solved. It may surprise the top people when, in the end, the enrollment situation

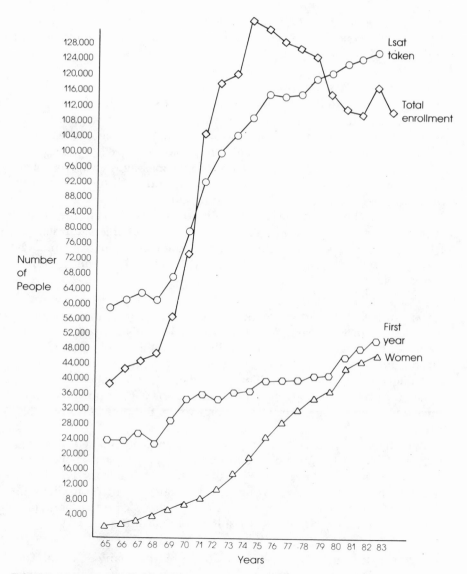

FIGURE 1.1. LAW SCHOOL DATA.

is not so good. Cover-ups and restricted flow of data are prevalent in this environment. This is one of the areas where institutional climate can heavily impact the response of the organization.

HIRING AND FIRING.   A second low-risk response by top management is to fire the current admissions director and look for a "superstar." Often people who have reasonably good skills are terminated, not because they are doing a poor job, but because they do not know what else to do. In these cases, people may be hired who are less familiar with or committed to the school and who, in the end, also are terminated.

PUBLICATIONS.   A very common response to enrollment difficulties is the creation of a new set of publications. Often these are more numerous and more expensive than earlier publications and are created with the hope that they are all that is needed—and, in fact, sometimes these new publications work well for a while. They may be effective if they are backed with research data so that the proper messages are given. The right timing will have an additional impact, and if all these elements work together, the results may be quite good.

Too soon, however, the results begin to decrease and another series of publications must be done. At this time, many people again will be asking questions about the future and the options that are available. Or the school will stop using the publications because they simply cannot afford them.

THE MARKETING APPROACH.   Marketing has been a part of the enrollment scene for about ten years. And the potential of this arena for solving enrollment problems has not been fully or sometimes even partially realized. Often the concept itself has caused as many internal problems as it might solve external problems. Marketing, too often, is only associated with advertising, new publications, or a high-powered sales force—all of which, again, may work for a while. But problems invariably return.

Much of the success of any approach depends on people's attitudes and beliefs toward it. In the case of marketing, its impact has been diminished. Educators have confused marketing with sales, advertising, hucksterism, and pressure. While this is certainly not true marketing, these perceptions have been held by too many people for the marketing concept to be totally successful for a long period of time.

RESEARCH.   Research also has been attempted by many schools. Too often, however, this research has been directed solely at the outside world. The questions asked frequently have been oriented toward image and awareness. While these questions are important, they have limited significance without corresponding research on the institution itself. The idea behind much of this research has been to change the market—not a wise strategy in business or in education.

In addition, much of this research has been done without determining how the data is to be used. This results in frustration as individuals try to use data that has little relevance to their needs.

LEVELS OF ACTION

The responses by schools to enrollment problems have been varied. In fact, the appropriate response will often not be market research, collection of data, or new programs. While all of these may be appropriate, it is making the right response at the right time that is critical: moving toward the capacity to manage enrollments rather than reacting to an enrollment crisis.

Analysis and determination of the status of enrollments relative to some ideal state is the key agenda for the enrollment manager. This means moving from the enrollment program as the sole determinant of enrollment success to the institutional response in terms of the appropriate strategy based on the consumer and the competition. It means movement from the era of admissions to the era of strategy.

THREE LEVELS

Institutional responses will have to go through three levels in order to reach a desired state of enrollment; that is, the needs of the students and the school are consistently and comfortably being met in a satisfactory way in terms of numbers, quality, and outcomes.

The responses to enrollment issues increasingly have had to involve more and more of the organization. The background needed by people doing this work and the attitudes and beliefs of people doing the work have had to change substantially. This scenario might best be represented in three levels of an institution's ability to deal with enrollment efforts:

Level 1: Doing the fundamentals well.

Level 2: Improving the work of the enrollment office and involving the school.

Level 3: Developing enrollment strategy. The whole school is involved and committed to enrollment success.

FUNDAMENTALS

The first step in problem solving in terms of improving enrollments is to examine the enrollment office in an effort to determine if the program is doing the fundamentals well:

- Is there an enrollment master plan?
- Is there a management information system? Do people managing the program know what is being done and not being done in terms of the enrollment program?
- Are the staff members familiar with their jobs and is the focus on communication with students?

A school that is not doing the fundamentals well will rarely benefit from research, product changes, extensive volunteer efforts, or the development of new publications. The first steps will involve management options and some very simple changes in publications and materials.

FUNDAMENTALS PLUS

In a school at this stage the enrollment program has the items of the first stage but needs to target them better. In this institution, enrollment strategy can come into play in the enrollment office. This can include:

- Targeting of publications.
- Developing territorial responsibilities for professional staff.
- Training people who have contact with students.
- Developing an extensive volunteer network for contacting students.
- Having the capacity to manage an enrollment database including both new and returning students.

Schools at this stage are not prepared to do extensive research but are approaching the stage where they might begin the process of collecting data and information.

STRATEGY

An institution at this stage is doing all of the fundamentals as well as can be expected. The management of enrollment cannot be improved greatly by better management techniques but must depend on a better overall strategy by the institution. This school is ready for a solid research program and can likely benefit from increased commitment, involvement, and dedication from people on campus. It also will need to look at the systematic development of its enrollment program.

In summary, this book is about the evolution of enrollment programs from the fundamentals through the fundamentals-plus stage to strategy. The approach that is presented represents a way of organizing theory, methodology, and applications to produce an enrollment program that can approach a diversity of populations: traditional/nontraditional, new/returning, graduate/undergraduate, and career oriented/generalist oriented—from beginning to end and back.

-2-
A MATRIX APPROACH TO ENROLLMENT ISSUES

Assessing and Dealing with Enrollment Issues Effectively

MATRIX APPROACHES AND INTERACTIONS

Matrix approaches offer the opportunity to isolate the critical variables that need to be addressed in dealing with problems and their relationships, and in identifying the actions needed to find and implement effective solutions. If combined with effective task force work, the matrix approach enables a school to create involvement, commitment, and effective change when dealing with an enrollment problem.

The use of matrixes is standard in many fields where complexity is an issue—in physics, mathematics, biology, and chemistry, they are widely used to help explain subjects that are multidimensional. Matrixes are helpful when there are relationships that cannot be explained unless they are visualized together. This approach also has been used effectively in business, where such concepts as the "Johari Window" have been used to explain the building of an effective group.

In the educational environment, the use of matrixes has been suggested as a management tool. When results are difficult to obtain in a program, the relationships of people that need to be coordinated often are at the center of the issue. In many cases, individuals from several offices need to interact to produce effective solutions. This has often lead to matrix management approaches that involve many parts of the organization.

Building a matrix of the factors involved in enrollment allows a school to manipulate the key variables one at a time or simultaneously to structure the best steps to an effective action. This means looking at the set of factors in horizontal and vertical dimensions to understand how they interrelate, and thus formulating a solution to enrollment problems that produces long-term, effective results.

RELATIONSHIPS IN THREE DIMENSIONS

A third dimension needs to be added to any potential enrollment matrix. Knowledge of the relationships among key variables and recognition of new factors or relationships are not sufficient. Knowing the right directions and acting on them are two different states. Attitudes and beliefs often get in the way of effective action. People see and hear what they want because of the filtering that results from their presuppositions and experiences.

Attitudes and beliefs are the culprits in many cases of unsuccessful enrollment programs. If those responsible for enrollment management have beliefs and attitudes that are different from what is needed for the appropriate response, conflicting data may not be seen clearly, or the "voices crying in the wilderness" may remain just voices. If the faculty and administration of the school still believe that the sun revolves around the earth, the efforts to create a better enrollment program will reflect this type of thinking. The institution itself will still be seen as the center of the educational universe, whereas the real focus should move toward students and influentials.

This situation is nowhere more clearly illustrated than in the case of a school that is doing well, but has hints of problems to come—decreases in inquiries, lower conversion ratios, and decreases in quality. Nevertheless, its faculty members do not understand why research is important, certainly not on themselves. It might be an acceptable strategy to study the outside world, they believe, but not the institution. This faculty thinks that it has all the right answers and that it is unreasonable to consider changes in the way it does business. These people believe that there is something wrong externally.

Attitudes and beliefs also can inhibit the operational area. If the director of admissions is fearful of rejection and does not like to be pushed, the idea of doing telephone calls will not be very appealing. Yet, the person doing telephone calls to potential students can expect to be rejected 80% of the time. This is a major difficulty for professionals, volunteers, and others involved in direct contact with students.

One of the greatest restraints, therefore, to doing the appropriate things to solve enrollment problems is a failure to understand attitudes and beliefs and their impact on the effort.

The task, then, is to recognize the relationships that are important, use this recognition to find the way through the "maze," and to realize how people may be their own worst enemies in accomplishing the required results. Enrollment managers need to know how to create the right ideas, gain acceptance for them, and implement them.

KEY VARIABLES AND ATTRIBUTES OF THE ENROLLMENT MATRIX

A system needs at least two dimensions to be called a matrix, but to management enrollment a third is added. The three dimensions include the key variables in enrollment management, critical attributes to address in relation to each variable, and attitudes and beliefs about the key variables and attributes. All three dimensions are graphically represented in the Enrollment Matrix, Figure 2.1.

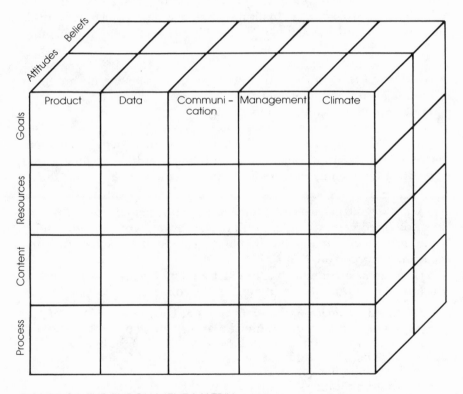

FIGURE 2.1. THE ENROLLMENT MATRIX.

To analyze the institution's enrollment issues in detail, each area should be examined individually and then studied as to how the variables, attributes, and beliefs interact.

THE FIVE KEY VARIABLES

The five key variables to address in terms of managing enrollment are (1) product, (2) data and information, (3) communication, (4) management, and (5) climate.

PRODUCT: what the institution offers to students. This represents the programs, curriculum, people, services, facilities, location, environment, cost, and character, all of which combine to make every institution unique. These affect the ability of the institution to meet student expectations.

DATA AND INFORMATION: used to understand the market and the school, to understand fit, to develop communication programs, and to deal with the allocation of resources. Institutional image data is included in this category. Data is the essential ingredient in producing enrollment strategy.

COMMUNICATION: efforts carried out with potential students and their influentials, combining elements of awareness, image, fit, messages, amount and type of contact, and quality.

MANAGEMENT: includes the leadership of enrollment activities and enrollment planning functions. Adequate training of the enrollment staff is included here along with sufficient management data.

CLIMATE: degree of ease with which tasks get done in the organization. How does an organization deal with the issues of doing the right things in the right way? What is the commitment of people to meet students' needs and expectations?

These areas are interactive, as illustrated by the following scenario, which is not far from the reality of today's college:

> Eastside University has been through at least two directors of admission and has now assumed that something other than the director is the problem. They have recently brought in a high-priced publications firm and have said, "We need to enroll better students who have more money."
>
> The publications firm replied, "Of course, you have difficulty doing this because your publications are terrible and the photographs are a big part of this. What we need to do is to create a better first publication and provide a couple of really interesting brochures for follow-up. And, of course, we should probably personalize all of the letters."
>
> A year later, the enrollment increased slightly, but the year after that the enrollment is back down and retention is down substantially. The students in their exit interviews are saying

that the school is not what they thought it was. They cannot find their faculty advisors and when they do, there is little help. No one seems to listen. And besides that, the heat is turned off in March and not turned on again until November—which makes it very difficult when your school is in Vermont.

This school had serious product problems, and after years of trying to motivate administrators to examine this issue, they had given up. The president's words were, "The people here are not creative. I have to do everything."

The director is blaming the product, the faculty is blaming the admissions office, and the students and parents are going elsewhere. This school has lost its chance for credibility for a long time to come.

PRODUCT AND CLIMATE.   No two issues should receive more attention from the enrollment perspective than product and climate.

The product the school offers to the potential student and influential (any person who can influence a student—parents, teachers, counselors, peers) is of critical importance to the enrollment process. Without this essential key—a product that clearly meets the perceived needs of potential students and the faculty—enrollment success is bound to be minimal. This is especially true if the school is in a very competitive market.

The product cannot only meet the needs of the marketplace. To take this strategy would create conditions that might lead to loss of commitment and lowered morale on the part of people, faculty and staff, who have the most to do with the product's success. Likewise, the product cannot meet solely the needs of the faculty. To ignore the marketplace will quickly lead to enrollment problems. This effect becomes more evident as an increasing number of schools begin to communicate well and compete aggressively.

The process of examining the product, or even debating the idea that the product should meet the needs of the external world, can be difficult to address if the institution does not value examination, discussion, risk-taking, and disagreements. If the climate of the institution is such that data and information cannot flow easily and be used without fear, nothing will be accomplished to encourage serving students' needs successfully and creatively as those needs change.

Climate is an issue that many schools are beginning to recognize as a part of their enrollment problems. This includes such specific areas as decision-making, basic communication, and problem solving. It also can include the flow of information through the system in general. If information does not flow well, very few issues can be addressed successfully. This is an area that is not perceived as critical until people have to react with care, speed, and success. Territoriality; fighting for funds; fear of upsetting the president, the board of directors, or others—all seriously reduce available options.

THE FOUR CRITICAL ATTRIBUTES

The four critical attributes to examine in relation to each variable are:

1. *Goals:* What are the guiding forces of the particular variable? To what will the resources, content, and process issues be addressed?
2. *Resources:* What resources will be needed to meet the goals of the program? These can be people, facilities, equipment, funds, hardware, or software.
3. *Content:* Are there right and wrong ways to do things in publications, training, advising, career counseling, financial aid?
4. *Process:* Are the ways in which people work together functional? How can these processes help or hurt us?

To illustrate how this might fit together, the goals for each of the critical variables can be examined.

PRODUCT.   The goals of the product variable are to have the best possible fit between the faculty, the needs of the institution, and the needs of society. It is important to emphasize the mutual nature of the fit issue. It cannot be a one-way street.

Too often the goals are strictly lodged in the faculty without much concern for the outside world. This is a typical closed system that cannot adjust easily. In research with many schools, it is almost universally true that people do not feel that colleges are easy to change or that taking risks is easy.

DATA.   The goals of the data area are to have sufficient data and information to understand the fit between the institution and the marketplace, to be able to create effective communication strategies, and to be able to use resources effectively in meeting enrollment goals.

Implied in the data and information area are issues of change. If the fit is not right, something may have to be done to change it. Change-related issues are what frequently makes the data and information area hard to approach.

COMMUNICATION.   The goals of the communication program are to have the ability to create sufficient inquiries and to be able to convert these from inquiries to enrolled students and eventually to graduates.[1] The school has control of the conversion ratios and can support these through an effective communication strategy.

---

[1]

MANAGEMENT.   The goals of the management area include setting enrollment goals. Few schools have real goals in terms of numbers, quality, or type of students. Without these, there is no driving energy for the program.

In addition, an effective enrollment master plan is required that guides strategy development and the conducting of actions. A management information system tells everyone how the program is going. This covers status of potential students and the communication effort.

Effective enrollment leadership—someone who is interested in and is able to energize people around enrollment issues—also is critical to the management function.

CLIMATE.   The goals of the climate area are covered with three C's. A school must have from the people associated with it:

- *Commitment* to the institution and its goals.
- *Confidence* in the ability to be successful.
- *Control* of the right things.

These allow the free flow of information that is badly needed to do the right things at the right time.

THE FINAL BARRIER: ATTITUDES AND BELIEFS

Where do the threats come from, outside or inside? Of course, they can come from both directions. But the hardest one to recognize and to deal with is the threat from within the institution in terms of prejudicial attitudes and beliefs. And this is the problem over which there is the most control. Consider the following statements:

- The students should come to us.
- I want students who can read.
- All we have to do is advertise.
- All we need to do is go to California for students (usually mentioned by a small school in Georgia).
- All students should take . . . [name of course(s)].
- There isn't a problem.
- What do you mean, I should know how students develop?
- I don't need to change for adult learners.

These represent a few of the beliefs that restrict listening and action in almost every enrollment area that needs attention. Being able to deal successfully with attitudes and beliefs such as these represents the secret weapon a school has in the competition for enrollments.

USING THE MATRIX TO SOLVE AN ENROLLMENT PROBLEM

The following is one example of how these factors are related and how efforts can fail if the total set of dimensions is not considered.

> Enrollment research had shown that two key elements were needed to attract applications to Smithfield in Alaska. The students wanted to know how much time they would have from the faculty and where they could go to get jobs from this school in the northern tundra country. The research also had shown that there was little positive feeling about the placement program and that faculty were, on the whole, not available to students.
>
> Given this information, the enrollment staff was reluctant to publish in the viewbook any information about placement, and the brochure that was going to discuss the faculty was put on hold. The president intervened and directed the public relations staff to discuss the placement of students at length, claiming that all students that wanted jobs could get jobs. She also directed that the faculty brochure be completed.
>
> Neither the director of admissions nor the director of public relations thought it was a good idea, but they went along, not wanting to risk the anger of the president. In fact, they had found that the president was unlikely to listen to anyone, and the faculty just tried to stay out of the way in any struggle of this type.
>
> The publications were completed and the faculty brochure was immediately relegated to the basement and never mailed. The viewbook had to be used, but the enrollment staff felt they could not support the placement issue. While this was not a problem in itself, the staff did wonder what else they might have to treat with caution. They could not ask because the faculty rarely liked to talk with the administrators, and the president kept the admissions people as isolated as possible from them.

Sound familiar? It may well be, for it represents issues that have been observed in similar forms at more than one school in recent years.

The next chapters examine each of the important areas of the Enrollment Matrix in detail, using examples and applying the concepts that need to be brought to bear on enrollment issues.

-3-
PRODUCT AND ENROLLMENT MANAGEMENT

Too often, enrollment professionals hear about a school that has hired its fourth or fifth director in a short period of time. In this situation, the morale of the enrollment office usually is at a low ebb and the new director has taken the job even though he or she is not prepared to undertake the real task. This is frequently the kind of situation in which an admissions counselor will accept a directorship when other, more experienced, people refuse the job. It also may be the case that overall morale is low at the school. People seem to be looking for any way out of the enrollment problems, and often are pointing a finger at the enrollment office. They are looking for the knight on a white horse to save the school.

Often, the school has very serious problems with its product and is hoping the next director will be able, in the words of the old saying, to pull the chestnuts out of the fire. Even though everyone is familiar with how the school is off target, the individual recently invited to accept the admissions job will take it on. It is the hope of the people at the school that they will not have to change. And it is surprising how long this pattern can continue.

In such cases, the school often needs to evaluate its product carefully and develop stronger appeals to the consumer. In many of these schools, the faculty does not want to do this and will oppose any suggestions that it be done. Often the heel-dragging comes from a faculty or administration member whose models of enrollment management and of the role of a college or university would be threatened if significant changes were needed. The attitude seems to be that it is easier to change the market than the people at the institution.

THE FOCUS OF THIS CHAPTER

This chapter cannot be prescriptive about programs and curriculum. There are so many potential hazards in dealing with the product area that any recommendations or suggestions would be applicable to some schools but not to others. In any case, programs and curricula are rarely the strategic problem unless it is too many programs or too complicated a curriculum. The available literature on curriculum as it relates to the product area is extensive and addressing this is not our objective. This literature usually has focused on faculty members and the outcomes that they would like to see. Too often, however, the literature has not focused on what faculty are or are not doing right from the point of view of the student.

The key strategic problems in the product area are likely to be associated with such areas as packaging, relationship management, or student services that are off target. The problem also may be that there is a faculty who wants *A* while the students want *B*.

The closest much of the literature comes to thinking about students' wants and needs are the considerations of cognitive outcomes such as the skills and knowledge that faculty members believe students should have. Somewhere, the student gets lost in this process. A great deal of the focus is on skills and knowledge rather than on a combination of the demands of the market and the expectations and offerings of the school. Under such circumstances the relationship between faculty member and student can get lost and yet it may be the most important part of the product area. When these factors can be integrated, both the student and the school are better off.

This chapter establishes some points of view that may motivate a school to find its best approach to product issues and to broaden its view of what a product is. If a school wants to address product from an enrollment management perspective, it must first ask how it should begin the task and what dimensions of the product should be addressed. With the information in this chapter, a school should be able to establish the product agenda for its enrollment task force and maximize the product of the school for its students and for itself.

PRODUCT GOALS

Begin with developing an overall goal. Developing goals for the product area depends heavily on concepts of the product and an interest in meeting the wants and needs of the marketplace. If the orientation is strictly internal, product goals will have one kind of perspective. If the orientation is outer-directed, considerations of the product will take another direction. It is generally most beneficial to adopt an orientation that considers both individuals at the school and those in the marketplace. It will become even more critical in the future to consider also the competition when dealing with product.

FIT

The better the product fits the faculty and the potential student, the easier it is both to attract and to retain the student. Fit is one of the key product concepts that will help a school construct its product most clearly to meet enrollment goals.

Fit is not a simple concept to apply. The school cannot, nor should it, change its product constantly to fit the tastes of the marketplace. The educational product is not a bar of soap nor should it be treated that way. A school that takes this approach is unlikely to remain credible for long with present students, potential students, or alumni. But the school often can do a better job of either creating a better fit or communicating to the marketplace how it can meet student needs.

With the proper use of data, the appropriate elements of fit can be determined. With a good climate, a school can gain a better fit on some key issues, and with the right communication effort, the school can let the public know where proper fit occurs. It is critical, however, that the product fit, in as far as possible, both the expectations of the faculty and the expectations of students.

MEETING WANTS AND NEEDS

The goals of the institution's product area can be focused on meeting the wants and needs of students. In this study, the section dealing with communication reviews in depth the process of working with students' wants and needs. Here, the idea of seriously considering this as a basis for structuring much of our product needs to be emphasized.

Potential students have expectations of the college or university they plan to attend. Related to this are some specific ideas about what is attractive in their ideal or first-choice institution. These relate both to fit and to wants and needs and likely will play a bigger part in the future in students' choices about their institutions.

In the 1985 National Study of High School Seniors conducted by The Ingersoll Group, students indicated that the school they were looking for would have to prepare them for careers (including graduate or professional school) and would do this through faculty who were concerned about students and who were available, up to date in their fields, and good teachers. This might be the start of a goal statement for a particular institution. To support this goal, the students expected good advising, excellent career counseling, placement, and good-quality programs.

The goal of the product area should be to maximize fit between faculty and students and work toward a better fit to the potential student population. This description represents a "want list" that many schools should if possible fit in order to meet enrollment goals. It is a group of desires that many schools could satisfy with some degree of change or emphasis in their product.

CONSIDERATION OF FIT IS CRITICAL TODAY

Why has the issue of fit become critical? All schools must be concerned about some dimensions of product. Some schools will have to concern themselves about these issues more than others. This is where the issue of fringe benefits comes into play for many schools. An institution does not have to worry as much about the details of product if it is a "fringe benefit" school or an "excluded" school.

The fringe benefit school is one that has intrinsic value. It is worth going to this school just to get the degree. At one of the Ivy League schools, for example, a student remarked during conversation that, because she was here, she could major in history. She felt that if she had gone to the small liberal arts college in her hometown, she would have had to major in business. She knew that with a degree from her current institution, she could always get a job.

Figure 3.1 represents the enrollment picture for a hypothetical school. It is suggested that there are three basic populations of students who would attend the school. The first is the group of students who will come to the school no matter what is done. This group automatically sees the school as their choice and the institution cannot keep them away. These are students, for example, who see the degree from a particular school as automatic entry into the marketplace. This also might be the student who must attend a certain school because a parent requires it. The fringe benefit here is simply avoiding conflict either with oneself or with others.

The second group of students is those who would not enroll no matter what the school does. These students have other points of view, and no matter what the institution does, it will not be able to make a difference to this group.

The third group is in the middle. These students can be influenced in one way or another and the product of the school is one of the factors that can do this job. The closer the product fits the students, the easier it is to influence them—and the school has to believe that to influence

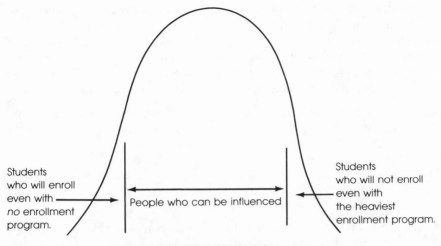

Students who will enroll even with *no* enrollment program.

People who can be influenced

Students who will not enroll even with the heaviest enrollment program.

FIGURE 3.1. SAMPLE ENROLLMENT DISTRIBUTION.

is acceptable. If the school is to accomplish the job of influencing, goal statements for the product should generally follow these directions: (1) they should reflect the belief that the institution's offering is a combination of factors that clearly demonstrate the capability of the institution to meet the wants and needs of the *selected* market; and (2) they should be based, to a large extent, on the fit of the school to the marketplace, to the degree that this is possible for the institution's faculty and staff. Of course, the wider the gap between the school and the student, the harder it is to meet enrollment goals and to influence students.

PRODUCT RESOURCES

A frequent source of contention within the institution trying to deal with enrollment is lack of resources. This usually means money or physical materials. "If only we had the money," goes the complaint, "we would be able to solve our enrollment problems." Or the thinking is this: "It is only a matter of advertising, finding more inquiries, and giving more scholarships."

This attitude may make people hesitant to act. Because of this type of thinking, the enrollment picture may deteriorate. The numbers continue to decline while there is less action by everyone. This can keep people from considering resource issues that are within their control or it may prevent people from looking seriously at their options. The re-source trap can be paralyzing.

In actuality, the resources that are needed are less likely to be phys-ical resources than other, more fundamental items. It includes many items besides the buildings, computers, and physical space that the schools generally view as assets. The resources needed now include:

- *People:* It is the *combination* of these people that will get the job done for the student:
  Faculty
  Staff
  Administration
  Present students
  Alumni
- *The service package:* These are the individuals whose relationship with the student and each other becomes critical to the success of the school.
- *Programs:* The actual majors or construction of courses the student pursues.
- *Curriculum:* The organization of the academic area around a theme or concept that creates enthusiasm.
- *Buildings:* With emphasis on any special facilities or benefits.
- *Services:* Include any or all of the following:
  Financial aid
  Career counseling and placement
  Advising
  Housing
  Personal counseling
  Athletics
- *Experiences:* Such as cooperative education, internships, independent study, and travel.
- *Location:* A selection of programs ideally suited to the location. Con-sideration of ways in which the location is especially helpful.
- *Environment:* The institution must be able to offer an environment that supports students. It ought to feel special to be a student at this institution.
- *The package:*

The required resources are much more complicated than they were a few years ago. In those times, the main resources were the buildings and grounds, the curriculum and programs. In the fight for resources, this became the primary area of recognition. If the school had more physical resources than a competitor, it was seen as doing well.

There are a number of problems with this resource approach. The main problem for many schools is that it is a losing battle to try to cope with the phenomenon of having more and better physical resources. The ground rules for evaluation and importance of resources may, indeed, be changing. This should be good news to those who have reached the limit of what they can do with their physical resources.

In enrollment-related research in recent years, the value of services and people has continued to climb. When asked what is attractive about an institution, the top factors always include faculty (see Table 4.2) or other people.

When asking about the ideal school, we find that services such as career counseling, placement, advising, and financial aid are highly rated. This is especially true for the process of converting inquiries to applications. Yet human resources and service often seem to be considerably undervalued by the institution itself. The future will likely focus more sharply on the people and services the school must offer.

THE PACKAGE

Theodore Levitt, author of *The Marketing Imagination* (New York, 1983), has raised an issue that could have impact on future ideas about resources. He has suggested that a package will be more important than will individual programs. Business programs, for example, will not be as important as the combination of business, core programs, services, and special environmental factors. These combine for the business area to create the opportunity, and the more these integrate, the easier it will be to meet enrollment goals. More will be said about the package in the content section.

PRODUCT CONTENT

As explained in Chapter 2, content implies that there is a right or wrong way to use the resource. Whether in the teaching of a course or the advising of a student, the institution likely has to be better at what it does.

Being better means knowing as much about the area that we are working with as possible. Educators should understand the critical issues involved, the way in which the activity fits the expectations of students, the skills and knowledge that are needed, and the attitudes that will produce the best results for the institution and the student. As the world changes more often and more quickly, it becomes harder to keep up. Staying up to date is expected by the institution in academic programs.

It may not be expected in such areas as advising, building rapport with students, teaching nontraditional students, or delivering the services that are critical to students' success. These will become the important areas of competition for the future.

The skills that are needed to be an effective faculty member, for example, are rapidly approaching the point where faculty need a better grasp on what is required, must know how they rate on a spectrum of critical skills, and understand how to develop the appropriate skills. Rarely are faculty members hired who are ready to do the whole job. There is much more to it than knowledge and skills in a particular area.

With students who are no longer comfortable with sitting in front of a lecturer, there will be demands to understand how to reach the student. This may require skills of persuasion, rapport-building, understanding, and motivating that far outweigh the expertness the faculty member derived from graduate school. While this has been true for many years, this may now be critical to the success or failure of many schools. Likewise, the student may no longer be content with advising that focuses solely on making certain the right courses are taken. Today's student wants advising with a focus on helping establish personal and career goals and strategies to meet them.

Attitudes, too, must be examined if institutions are to succeed. The presupposition that the school is teaching high school graduates who will be with them for four years and will then move into graduate school is rapidly fading. The number of part-time students has increased dramatically, along with the numbers of nontraditional students. Along with these phenomena, more students are working part- or full-time in order to afford college. Institutions have to deal with these populations in new ways if they are to succeed. The faculty members' expectations about work and time also may have to change.

The faculty and administration need an attitude of commitment to addressing several types of students in different ways. With this mixed group, it is important to develop a better sense for the approaches taken, rather than just increasing the overall level of activity. The key issue is that of doing things better and doing the right things.

REASONS FOR ATTENTION TO PRODUCT AND CONTENT AREAS

There are several reasons that the issue of product content is so important to enrollment work. These include the following:

- Changes in the mix of populations a school serves.
- Changes in the nature of the people a school serves.
- Changes in the needs of society, including students.

- Changes in the faculty as educators.
- Decreases in the relative amounts of dollar and other resources that the school has available to use in the educational venture.
- Any combination of these areas.

CHANGES IN THE MIX OF PEOPLE SERVED.   The trend for many schools has been toward an increase in age of students, increases in numbers of part-time students, increases in the numbers of females, and more work with people who leave and reenter schools to earn their degrees over a longer period of time. The trend toward part-time students and people who work while in school is very likely to continue. All of these factors can put a strain on the people in the organization—especially the faculty.

The nontraditional student may demand more flexibility about when and how a course is offered. The nontraditional student is unlikely to be one who will sit in a classroom for long periods of time listening to a lecture. This means that a faculty member may have to look at changes in teaching styles along with changes in the number of hours and time of classes.

The faculty member will notice a difference in having the nontraditional student in class. The nontraditional student is challenging and hardworking compared with traditional counterparts. This may or may not be exciting to the faculty member, depending on whether he or she is prepared for the challenge.

The student who is going to school part-time will not develop the same type of relationship with the school or the faculty members as the full-time student. If this relationship with the student is important to the faculty, it will be sorely missed. This aspect of the new student population may even cause the faculty member to lose some of the association with the school that may have been present before. If the connection is important to the faculty member, he or she may have to look for different ways to develop it. The school and the faculty member will need to compete harder for students' time and attention.

Likewise, the student who attends, leaves, and then returns may ask for considerations different from those of the traditional student. This student may need reorientation to the school, time to reestablish contact, and time to get back up to speed. Such a student will place new demands on the flexibility of teachers and administrators. The new motto of the institution must be: "Ask not what they can do for you, but ask what you can do to make them successful."

CHANGES IN THE PEOPLE SERVED.   As the mix of people has changed in recent years, so have the characteristics of those people, particularly the students the faculty at most schools would like to serve—the traditional student. These individuals have changed in terms of:

- Their feelings about themselves.
- The expected outcomes of the college experience.
- How they would like to have the college deliver the services.
- Their demand from the school in terms of services and activities.
- Their relationship with the school they are attending.
- Their preparation for the work that they will have to do in terms of skills, knowledge, and attitudes.

The student that we are dealing with today, particularly the traditional student, has several characteristics that set him or her apart from the same student a few years ago. These factors can be placed in categories of self-interest and wanting to make certain that the future is secure.

There is a trend for students to put less time into community and institutional services. This is accomplished by the desire of the student that the services of a school be directed, in as far as possible, precisely to his or her individual needs.

This student is less likely to sacrifice personal needs in any way for the needs of the institution, class, or group. The feeling is this: "If I can see a meaning in it, fine, but I will not do it just because someone else wants it done." There needs to be some application for what the student learns, and it has to make sense. This challenge has made some faculty members very uncomfortable.

Along with this attitude, the student of today is very much concerned with the direct applicability of the educational process to his or her future. The data collected by Alexander W. Astin and others has indicated that today's student wants a secure future with a good income. They see their parents and society as less likely to provide this for them, and thus it becomes a personal priority. They see the institution's role as providing preparation for a career through a strong major and with emphasis on in-depth preparation in that program.

While this latter emphasis may not please the faculty, it does represent the stated wants of students who will attend their institution. These are students who want a secure future and expect the college or university to contribute heavily to this outcome. These students expect automatic entry to the marketplace through attendance at a fringe benefit school or they expect the school that is trying to interest them to be able to demonstrate this skill.

READINESS FOR COLLEGE.   A common theme among educators seems to be the lack of readiness of the students of today for the work that is placed before them. The traditional student suffers from lack of adequate preparation in mathematics and English, and the nontraditional student may have been out of school long enough that the skills are either weak or the student is unsure of them, as the following comment shows:

> Did I have any fears? You have to be kidding. I had been out of school seven years. I wasn't certain that I would ever be able to pass a test again. I didn't want to fail, and the fear of this almost kept me from trying.

This nontraditional student was expressing a sentiment common among older students returning to school.

Along with fears existing among nontraditional students is the issue that traditional students seem less motivated to work hard on our terms. Faculty are more likely to have to look for ways to generate interest among these students. They can get excited, but only on their own terms.

Increasingly, students also expect that the institution will not waste their time—that it will go about the academic task effectively, quickly, and at a reasonable cost. When asked in focus groups about the characteristics of a good faculty member, students often include such items as coming to class on time, being prepared, and not wasting students' time. The direct implication of this type of statement is that faculty members often are not prepared in their work or effective at motivating students. Usually included with this is a favorable comment about the faculty who are excited about what they are doing. This excitement of the faculty member is the best strategy for motivating and keeping students.

CHANGES IN WHAT STUDENTS DEMAND IN TERMS OF SERVICES AND ACTIVITIES.   The services and activities that today's students demand have changed and will continue to change. The student of today expects more from the institution in terms of services. This includes such areas as career counseling, placement, advising, and, of course, financial aid. The student expects to use all of these services at one time or another in order to get the help needed to do well. In past years, these areas—except for financial aid—were considered as something of an "extra" for the student. Today, for some schools, they are essential ingredients of the product (see Table 4.1).

For many schools, these areas must be a critical part of the assistance the institution gives the student. These are schools that are not awarding automatic passports to the better jobs and outcomes. These are schools whose graduates are well prepared but have to compete harder, at first, in the marketplace. For other institutions, the name of the school is sufficient to unlock the doors to the future. In these schools, the services will likely not have to be as well developed.

In addition, some students may not expect much from a school in terms of social life and the arrangement of specific activities. This, again, is especially true of nontraditional students. These individuals have all the activities they can handle, in addition to school work, and they expect to get away from the school when the day's classes are done.

Another important change is the fact that increasing numbers of students who work or who are part-time put a different dimension on our expectations of them and on the need for the institution to develop an extensive program of activities. While some students will continue to seek this type of experience, the vast majority expect different things from the office of student affairs. Specific services and ongoing activities may replace the social event. The availability of a place to network may be more important than having a dance.

AREAS IN WHICH CONTENT IS CRITICAL

The broadest areas for consideration in terms of content are the programs that the school offers, its services, the people at the school, and the environment of the school. These are the arenas in which to consider whether the institution is doing things in the best possible way for students.

PROGRAMS.   The programs that a school offers are usually the first line of attention when considering a product issue. Here it is not a matter of the programs being present or not—this is a resource issue; rather, the question is whether the content of the program in terms of topics, approach, general goals, and strategies is appropriate.

In the areas of computers, for example, has the academic program kept up with the changing demands of the field? The changes from macro- to microcomputers? Changes in software and programming strategies? Ideas such as networking and optical disk technology can all be important considerations in terms of a program preparing a student adequately for the field. The developments in computers have been widespread over the last five years, and it is apparent in some schools that the changes in the programs have not kept up with the field itself. This may be particularly true of the smaller to midsized schools that are in a resource squeeze.

In the area of programs, there also may be a concern about how instruction is done. There is a tendency for students—and instructors, for that matter—not to favor lectures. One can see the eyes glaze over as soon as the individual doing the teaching begins to talk.

The student of today wants a more hands-on approach that produces the appropriate levels of involvement for the program. This includes internships, co-op arrangements, special projects, special topics, independent study, travel, and any other opportunities to deal effectively with producing student involvement. It will include discussion and case study work with more demands on faculty for preparation and creativity. A strong consideration, from this dimension, is the packaging of programs.

Of course, the need to investigate program content in terms of either subject matter or technique will involve questions about staff readiness— do they have the skills or attitudes necessary to approach courses and programs from this point of view?

SERVICES. For some time now, the services that a school has to offer have been developing more importance in terms of students' wants and needs. This includes such critical areas as advising, career counseling, placement, financial aid, housing, health care, food services, athletic services, and bookstores. The closer some of these items can come to what the student is already familiar with, the better the program will be. One school in recent years located their resources—bookstore, cafeteria, bank, health care—in a mall-type area that felt like any shopping center the student might find in his or her own hometown. The students at the school seemed very happy with the arrangements and felt that these services were exceptionally well done.

At the same time, the students at this school did not understand their financial aid packages, nor did they feel as if they were treated well in the financial aid office. It was apparent to the students that they did not come first. There was little rationale for packaging, and communication was poor. While doing well in many areas, the school had problems in financial aid that ultimately caused a problem in retention.

The content of running successful programs in each of the important areas needs to be examined carefully. And this requires that important decisions be made—the decision to construct a fitness center rather than a new gymnasium; the decision to reward good advising as well as good research; and the decision to train and develop advisors as if this were an important function and not a natural talent in every faculty member.

PEOPLE. Much of what has been said relates to *people*. People will also be an important part of any educational product. But in the future, institutions will need to pay much more attention to the way in which people interact. The people at the institution are the core of the relationship with the institution. It is people with whom the student develops the relationship—not buildings, programs, or other parts of the institution.

This is the key factor to be considered in the process area of the product. It is the critical issue of how people interact. This is the best way for one school to differentiate itself from another. Let's look at some specific examples of content areas and the types of uses involved.

EXPECTATIONS OF FACULTY.

A good example of content is the students' expectations of a faculty member. What constitutes a good faculty member continues to be a mystery to some faculty and to many administrators. This might have been very clear not too many years ago. Now, however, the question needs to be answered if the institution is to continue meeting student needs.

When asked about the characteristics of a good faculty member, students invariably will give a response that contains many of the following elements:

> A good faculty member is one who does not waste my time and is excited about the work that he/she is doing. This faculty member comes to class on time, is prepared, gives assignments, does follow-up on assignments, and is willing to give me time when I want it.

The faculty member that is least appreciated is the faculty member who talks down to students or makes it difficult for students to say that they do not understand. The faculty member who says, "Only during office hours" also loses rapport with students.

Note that there are several things missing from this definition of the good faculty member. Missing are the academic credentials, the school from which the faculty member graduated, the research conducted, and the prestige factors that may have drawn many faculty members into the business. The student wants someone who knows what he or she is doing. But that is almost an expected factor. The really important skills are things that faculty were not taught. Educators tend to hope skills come through basic human nature or from experiences in the educational process. Out of necessity, then, modeling has to be an effective teacher for faculty members. Those faculty members who will be effective and will generate the rumor that it is worth taking their courses have to be people who are clearly focused and excited about their jobs.

ADVISING. This is another area that has changed considerably as the attitudes and types of students change. The following example is a case in point:

> Susan has been asked to describe how advising works at her school. Her answer reflects the fact that she is very dissatisfied.
> Susan's advisor has not been in her office for two weeks. This, according to Susan, is not unusual. It happens every term. She has found one or two faculty members who are available to her if she has a problem. She can always go to them to discuss an issue, and her needs for advice and help are being taken care of—not through the structure of the system, but through the good will of a couple of faculty members. If these people were not there, Susan might be a casualty of the system.

This situation is not unusual. In part, it represents a content issue. The students increasingly want a certain type of assistance in advising—not every student, of course, but enough students to make this a critical issue. The student wants assistance in goal-setting and finding the right overall strategy to reach those goals. Too often, the faculty members are only ready to read from the catalog.

The student wants a type of advising that many faculty members have neither the skills nor the knowledge to deliver. The students of today want a great deal of assistance in setting personal goals. They want to set their own goals and look to the faculty for help with this task. The lack of skills and knowledge can lead to a situation in which the faculty member has an attitude that advising should be done a certain way, if at all. The faculty would rather deal with the fulfillment of graduation requirements than with meaning and direction. As the students are increasingly looking for meaning in their programs, faculty assistance will become more and more important.

Students generally would like an advising program in which they receive the time from someone to establish goals for their experience, talk long enough to clarify those goals, and then have help in developing strategies for making the goals a reality. This process can require more time than many faculty can give (considering other demands), and it requires skills and knowledge that may need to be developed, including these:

- Willingness to spend the time.
- Listening skills that allow the faculty member to hear what is being said.
- Questioning skills that allow the right information to surface.
- Knowledge of goal-setting and strategic pathways to reach those goals.
- Persistence in working with the student.
- An attitude that this is a worthwhile way to work with students.
- Knowledge of the growth of students of all ages. The question must be asked: what are the expectations that are reasonable for students at various stages of their growth?
- Knowledge of development cycles and the issues that people—including the advisor—may have to address at certain times.

The faculty member is a resource to help the student develop and pursue a pathway to success. Specific strategies and techniques must be applied to make certain that advising works.

Advising is a good example of an area where content has changed, in part because of changes in the nature of students. As the mix of students has become less prepared for college, more diverse in terms of ages, more career-oriented, and less prepared to handle the rigors of college, the need for personal care and attention has increased. This calls for sophisticated skills from the faculty advisor that often are unrelated to the skills developed in graduate school.

CAREER COUNSELING.   Career counseling and placement comprise an area that, in many smaller and midsized schools, is filled by people who may be unprepared for the task. This has been a position for faculty who are being retrenched, people who are tired of other positions, or those who are under stress because of reorganization at the school. This practice continues in spite of the great potential for the career counseling area to make a major contribution to the school and to the student. The area of career counseling has content considerations that can make a big difference in a product offering, as this example shows:

> The career counseling office was located in a building far from any of the main buildings on campus. The students had to take a long walk to get the assistance of the office in any concern relating to career or job. The director of career counseling and placement was swamped. This was a school with almost a thousand students—and one person was devoted to the task of assisting students with the career decision.
>
> Jane, the director, had many creative ideas. She wanted to start with the freshmen and try to follow students all the way through the college with assistance in making a decision about a career and ultimate placement in a job. But without computer resources and with a part-time clerical person, she got nowhere the first year and in the second had done little better. Every time she looked up, there was more to do; students were upset because they could not get the assistance they needed.

This situation occurred in a school on the East Coast. It is not much different, however, from that found in many other schools. It could have been much better, but Jane could not articulate her needs well, and the administration could not view career counseling and placement as anything other than a basic service.

THE POTENTIALS FOR CAREER COUNSELING.   There are many ways to view the career counseling area as a valuable resource for school and student. First, the career counseling area can serve as a link between the people at the school and the business community. This office can initiate and maintain the connections that are critical for fostering a career-oriented academic program.

This connection can be used to create internships, part-time lecturers for the school, placement, and career resources. The business community also can serve as a user of the services. The person in the job must be able to deal effectively with a great diversity of people, from a student to a president of a business. This person also must have a role with parents of present and prospective students.

The career counseling and placement office can serve the faculty of the school as a resource. This person can orient the faculty to career-related issues and to the feelings, skills, and attitudes that are most productive as the student moves through an academic program.

The faculty can and must be prepared to serve as career counselors in their classrooms and in informal conversations with students. The faculty member can use the services of the career office to create the best blend of major or field-related knowledge tied to the world of work. Students increasingly look to the faculty for general advice about directions in their careers and career/life situations.

The office can play the traditional functions of helping students with decisions and developing specific skills needed for successfully landing and succeeding in the first job after graduation. This includes testing, use of computer-oriented programs that assist students, workshops, individual counseling, and bringing interviewers to campus.

The services of this office can continue after graduation with newsletters to students on job advice and low-cost career services to graduates.

This is only scratching the surface of an area that can make a dramatic difference from school to school. But this change will not happen if others, like Jane, have to function as second-rate citizens in an environment that is not in tune with the needs of the student attending the school.

ANOTHER VIEW OF PRODUCT: ORGANIZING KEY VIEWS

A basis for work with product content that has been very productive revolves around four main points. Each of these represents rather recent considerations of product issues and avoids the aspects of curriculum and specific program strategies:

1. A four-point view of the product that the college or university needs to offer.
2. Change from unit view to systems view of what the product is.
3. The likelihood of there being a best way to do things—a best way extending beyond a particular major or program.
4. The system approach to product changes.

THE FOUR POINTS OF PRODUCT

In *The Marketing Imagination*, introduced earlier in this chapter, Levitt develops an idea that is very helpful for examining the content of the

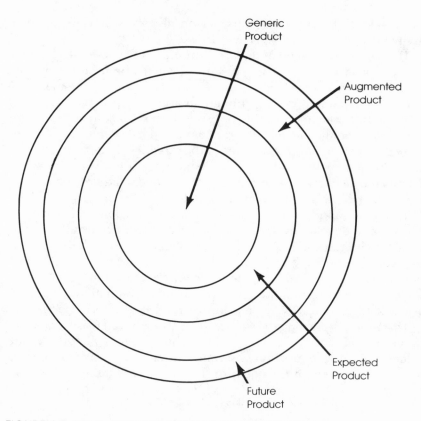

FIGURE 3.2. FOUR CRITICAL ASPECTS OF A PRODUCT.*
*Source: Levitt, Theodore, *The Marketing Imagination* (New York: The Free Press, 1983).

product area. The view, which is similar to some views of Philip Kotler of Northwestern University, represents his analysis of what it takes to obtain users for services offered. Because an educational institution is a service, much of what Levitt suggests is applicable to enrollment management. According to Levitt, there are four critical aspects of the product (see Figure 3.2). These include the generic product, the expected product, the augmented product, and the potential product.

In this model, the *generic product* is the potential consumer's immediate views of the college experience. It can be viewed as an education or it can be seen as the emotional expectations of the individual. This piece of the product can be represented by the theme of the college and often may be an initial differentiating factor.

The generic product, may, however, pose problems. It can include images that arise when using terms such as rural, small, large, public, or Catholic. These universal views of types of schools will often develop internal images and stereotypes that develop barriers to the student considering college. The stereotypes develop perceptions that take the school out of the picture or create a situation wherein it starts with several negatives against it. These views differentiate the institution, whether the school wants it that way or not. (Differentiation is a key issue. The problem for most schools is to differentiate themselves adequately from the competition.)

Finding a way to deal effectively with problems of the generic product may be a key enrollment management issue. The general images need to be turned into opportunities by the school; developing a theme that presents a clearer view and making certain that any negative stereotypes represented are corrected through the communication program.

The *expected product* is the part of the product that students and influentials require of the school. The school must be able to meet their expectations. This includes such items as good faculty programs, career preparation, advising, and services. This is what much of the research of a school is directed toward. Once the institution knows what students expect, it is important that it possess as many of these characteristics as feasible.

But expectations are not the only thing that is appropriate for meeting enrollment goals. All schools attempt to convince the public that they can do these things. It is not sufficient just to meet expectations. A college or university will have to go far beyond this to compete successfully, and sometimes new expectations can appear when least expected. If students, for example, enrolled at a school hoping to be able to brag about the winning football team, and it loses . . . expectations are not met. This can lead to increases in attrition and in reduced enrollment of new students.

Checking on the meeting of expectations may represent a reason for having an excellent advising program. The contact between faculty member and student can be an opportunity to "check in" in terms of meeting expectations. If the advising system works well, the school has an early warning system for expectation matching.

The *augmented product* is often the most active area for enhanced enrollment management. In this area, the school develops options that the consumer did not expect. Here, the institution offers possibilities that enable it to demonstrate that it can not only meet expectations but can exceed them. New and unknown points of view are raised that will cause the student and influential to say, "That makes a lot of sense." Examples of augmented product include:

- An excellent career program with many internships in very good companies.

- A mall on campus that provides better services and opportunities to socialize.
- A better-than-average athletic center that has opportunities for fitness.
- Faculty members who are excited about their teaching and courses.
- Alumni who will help students find and be successful in their first jobs.

The research that is done by the college should contribute to the development of these three key ingredients. Dealing effectively with generic product issues and having augmented product possibilities can contribute to the success of the enrollment effort. This is especially true if the school is already perceived as being able to meet student expectations.

The *potential product* contains the new things that the school will develop in the future. This is the area that will attract new students and cause present students to remain with the institution. In this area, the institution may talk of new programs, new markets, or other new opportunities that exist. Without adequate energy devoted to this area, the college or university will leave itself open to possible trouble in the future. Potential product can include:

- Developing special programs for the nontraditional learner.
- Adding a new area to the school's programs.
- Developing special programs for alumni.
- Providing new services that increase retention.

THE SYSTEM VIEW

The next general product concept suggested by Levitt and others is that certain institutions will have to deal with a whole system of opportunities rather than with the traditional unit of major or program. In this concept, the institution is packaging a group of options that together are bigger than the sum of parts. The people, programs, services, environment, and locations are combined to represent the opportunity. An example of this concept is the small college that cannot offer all of the majors a bigger school would offer. The smaller school—or the larger institution, in many cases—would no longer focus on the major. Rather, the school would focus on a collection of opportunities that serve the students' needs.

The package at such an institution might include a restricted number of majors, experiential options, a core program of arts and science opportunities, services that are directed at new skill and attitude development, excellent advising, and financial planning. In the system concept, the various areas are directly related to each other and integrated.

One is not felt to be more, or less, important than the others. In addition, aspects such as experiential options, skill development, or core are developed on an equivalent basis to the major.

DOING THINGS RIGHT

The institution will have to deal with the fact that there are right and wrong ways to do everything. This is certainly a standard point of view for the academic majors. The faculty will carefully develop the best way to offer the major. This is what they were trained to do in graduate school, and accreditation agencies and associations are very careful to see that this happens. The assumption is often made that the right people bring the right majors.

However, in the areas of advising, career counseling, placement, experiential options, co-ops, and internships, this is rarely the case. In each of these areas, the things that are done may often not relate to any base concept or model in terms of how the service or function should be delivered and how it will benefit the student in meeting his or her goals. This may also be true of the people at the institution. The student has expectations of faculty and staff, and there are adequate ways to meet these expectations, but too often the student will come up short. Meeting students' expectations is a part of the expected product area— doing it well is an augmented product. This gratification may be something most students have not expected, or it may not have been their experience in high school or their previous college or university.

THE SYSTEM APPROACH TO PRODUCT CHANGE

If the institution has, on examination, found that change is needed, it is likely to be a major issue. Success will not be possible unless the change is done systematically. It has to be carefully considered in terms of attitudes about units and systems, climate issues, funding, and transitional programs.

UNIT TO SYSTEM.   The change to a systems approach can be difficult. The faculty and staff now have to consider a complex set of issues outside of their major area of interest or skill. More integration is needed and people need to work toward a common goal.

For example, the college or university may want a certain set of majors. In these cases, the unit is the major, and some thinking has to be devoted to the quality of the major. If the system is to include, however, advising, experiential options, career planning, skill building, and a liberal arts core, the package will have to include all of these elements.

Planning will have to include how the experiential options will contribute in a major way to the results of the major. Combining the experiential option with the core concept can be a real opportunity, for example, for the institution. Helping students develop the right attitudes about their program and future will be part of the package. This is one of the reasons that we have recommended that a task force be developed that can move forward on major recommendations. This group can begin to deal with system issues early in the process. The following example describes a college that used these tactics to make an asset of what had previously been a disadvantage:

> Johnstown College was located in a very remote area of the state. It was at least a two-hour drive to the nearest city or airport, and the size of the city hardly supported a great many activities for students or faculty members. Morale was low on campus and enrollment was moving lower and lower each year.
>
> With twenty majors, most in very popular areas, and already offered at many schools around the state, there did not seem to be much of a reason for students to need to enroll. The school was too isolated and too small to be very appealing.
>
> The faculty, after an audit of the enrollment program and some preliminary studies (a very limited budget prevented the school from looking for much more data than they had), decided to take drastic action.
>
> The school reduced the majors to ten and decided to develop programs that focused on the recreation and leisure-time area:
>
> - *Business*, with a primary focus on retail and restaurant management in camping and park areas.
> - *Computer systems*, focused on the unique needs of resort hotel management.
> - *Communications programs*, developed for service people in wilderness locations, along with public relations and promotional issues.
> - *Internships*, required of all students, usually focused on the career area the student was headed for.
> - A *wilderness experience*, building confidence and self-reliance as required for a successful effort.
>
> With these pieces in place, plus enhanced advising, placement, and career counseling, the school was now ready to compete with a specific focus and energy. This competition could now occur in many locations outside the state where there were students looking for specific opportunities in creating both a career and a lifestyle.

CLIMATE ISSUES. As the institution thinks about changes, it needs to recognize the impact on the climate of the organization. This is especially true in product change. It is critical that communication, decision-making, participation, roles, and trust be high (see Chapter 8). The change may displace some faculty, staff, and students. It also will make new demands on everyone in the system. Yet the change will develop better opportunities for others. In both cases, doing it will be important. In the following example, drastic changes were managed through careful planning:

> Wilmont College had seen its enrollment decrease substantially over the last five years. They now needed to make some important decisions about major programs. The decision was made to drop from twenty-three majors to six. This would obviously be difficult for most of the faculty.
>
> Those who were fortunate enough to be a part of the surviving five would have to cope with the loss of many close friends and associates. Those who were leaving would now have to find new associations. For some of the faculty, it had been more than twenty years since they had looked around. In the feelings of the "haves" and the "have nots" there was the potential for great animosity.
>
> The task force had been working on these issues for some time. The decision was not a complete surprise, and some groundwork had been laid. The task force had built a good common ground for communication, and people were used to talking with each other. The changes went along in a very positive way.

FUNDING.   In addition to climate issues, the administration at Wilmont College had found some funding for helping some faculty to change schools and for others to change jobs. Funding was a key issue in Wilmont's changes. Significant changes require significant support. Having the funding issue under control will help the change to go well.

The funding plan should be developed before the project starts. This includes seeking funds to support various transitions as the institution moves through the process. The funding can include money for such items as training of faculty and staff, development of new services, resources, the dislocation of staff and faculty who cannot stay, and the development of the environment of the institution to support the enrollment effort.

This funding can come from many sources, but it is likely that the funding will have to come, at first, from local sources, including the people at the institution. Getting local support will be very impressive to people who may need to contribute major funding. Alumni, local friends, and faculty should be asked to support the effort in whatever way they can. This support will include emotional as well as financial commitment to the institutional community.

TRANSITION STATES.   Another key to the product changes that are needed for many schools is the concept of transition states. The use of present state and desired state analysis is an important tool in deciding what needs to be done.

Breaking the change into smaller units will make the movement from present to desired state much easier to accomplish. A major change, for example, might be divided into three or four steps taken over a period of one to two years. The actions needed to accomplish the goals and the funding efforts can be easier if seen in this light. The institution can deal with the issue of two or three transition states rather than single changes. Progress becomes easier to achieve, and the whole experience is more positive. This process is generalized in Table 3.1.

PROCESS AND PRODUCT

How can process influence enrollment results? Developing the idea of process among staff and fostering a good environment can make a difference when the key issue is to influence. The process area will clearly relate to people and the role of people in the enrollment and retention of students.

PROCESS DEFINITIONS

There are a great many definitions of the term *process* in behavioral literature and just as many, or more, perceptions of what process is. In enrollment terms, process may be taken to mean the interaction among people at the school. This interaction can be of faculty to student, student to student, faculty to administrator, administrator to board, or student to staff. It is the sum of these relationships that gives the school its tone in terms of how it feels to be at that institution. Some examples of inefficient process follow.

- The student who has to spend a great deal of time trying to find his or her advisor.
- The student whose advising cards are signed after they are left on the door, who in fact never sees the advisor.
- The nontraditional student who cannot get the attention of admissions or registration personnel because his or her needs are not typical.
- The bursar who will not assist the student who is having some financial problems.
- The faculty members who will not recommend another faculty member's course nor talk to that faculty member about it, but go on making recommendations that may hurt the student and the other faculty.

TABLE 3.1. General Transition State Diagram

Present State	1	2	3	4	5	Desired State
The present state and the desired state are defined from the research. This could be done in many dimensions, including product and climate.	A task force is now defined in detail, along with the options available and the appropriate first step in the follow-up stages.	Funding is now available to support various aspects of the program. This can include training for change for moving people on to another school.	Changes in programs are in place and the first phase of work is beginning. Faculty and staff training and development begin. Initial preparation of the marketing efforts now occurs.	Marketing begins. People who have had to leave are gone and the remaining staff deals with building a new climate.	First class enters for new product. Evaluation process is in place and the staff and faculty are ready.	The desired state is defined from the research. This becomes the present state when the process is completed and the whole sequence can start over.

- The president who does not interact with students.
- The dean of students who will not mix with all of the students—whose favorites get special treatment.
- The telephone operator who will not answer the telephone pleasantly or promptly.
- The security person who sees himself or herself as needing to enforce the rules of the kingdom.
- The maintenance people who give students grief about even the smallest item that needs to be fixed.

If enough of these issues occur on a campus, they can add up to a situation in which the student feels as if it is not worth the effort. In some cases, the student may end up feeling that he or she is there only to pay the bill.

PROCESS AND TYPE OF SCHOOL

As with many issues relating to enrollment management, the area of process may have more or less importance depending on the nature of the school.

The "fringe benefit school" may not have to worry about process. It really does not matter how well the student is treated—the student who values the degree will remain with the school and complete the program. This is the case in many professional schools that offer the student high incomes through the services of the school. The student, once graduated, may not value the school at all.

For other schools, probably the majority of the schools in the country, the process area is quite important. Its actual importance will depend a great deal on how much value the student places on items such as programs, majors, services, or facilities. It also will depend on how much the student wants from the school in terms of involvement, association, or the need to belong.

For the resident student who has no place to go after classes and is making the school his or her home, it can be very important as a way to keep the student. It can even compensate for weaknesses in other areas:

> The buildings were run down, and, because the lawn had grown over the asphalt, one could hardly find the parking places. Maintenance was not good as judged by the condition of the floors in the dorms and the general appearance of the buildings. Windows had not been washed in some time. The trash had not been picked up, and the overall feeling was one of depression—at least in terms of the physical plant.
>
> The students, however, were a bright and happy lot. Looking at the institution's data, the consultants noted that the rate

of attrition was very low. It appeared that the student once there, stayed on.

This was not a prestigious school. It was very small, was a second or third choice on the part of almost every student, had very late applications, and was unknown to the people in the community.

Why were these students staying at the school? This was a group who said it was hard to leave. The people here were attentive to student needs, available, and concerned, and the faculty were perceived as up to date and interested in what students were doing. This was a group of people who the students thought were really giving them something. They were providing a good example of how people should get along. Student satisfaction levels were high, primarily because they were satisfied with the people who were on the campus.

This shows how important a good climate can be. It can make a solid school much better, and it can make an average school superior, in many ways, to other opportunities available to students.

WORKING WITH THE PROCESS AREA

As with any area of enrollment concern, the best way to know how to work with it is to understand the component parts. For the process area, this is difficult because the concepts that go into consideration of process are often intuitive and not easily subject to analysis. These issues also are likely to be areas that people feel are already personal strengths for them—and they get sensitive when issues regarding process are raised. This can include such items as communication, listening, and reacting to criticism.

Moreover, the issues of process are additive. That is, the total is more than the sum of the parts. There is a great deal of synergy that occurs. It is possible, however, by comparing relationship management with process, to come up with some concepts that can help to structure a better process for people at a school. This can be done, in part, by thinking of process as we would think of a good personal relationship— what are the elements of developing a good relationship if this is to be a key area of success for student enrollment and retention?

GOOD RELATIONSHIPS: THE BASIC ELEMENTS

The first point of comparison is time. If faculty members are going to have a good relationship with students, they must be willing to spend time with the students. It must be time when they both want it, and it must be time that is perceived as willingly and carefully given. If the student perceives that no one wants to give time, or that the time given is used for the benefit of the faculty or staff member and not the student, the relationship will suffer. Quality time represents the key ingredient—availability. This always rates high on attractive characteristics of schools when students are surveyed. The more available the people at the school, the better the students seem to like the institution.

Likewise, rapport is important. The faculty must be able to establish and maintain rapport with students. In some instances, this must be done very quickly and then maintained over a significant length of time. Rapport can start with a good feeling of immediate comfort. This comes from the faculty members who seem to fit naturally with the student. It needs to be maintained, however, with trust, consistency of actions, predictability, and concern—all of these felt by the student or others as characteristics of the relationship. These items help the student trust the faculty member. They need to exist among all members of the college community. For those faculty and staff members who seem *not* to have this natural capacity for association, there is the need to work harder at it.

Meeting expectations is another aspect of any relationship. This means that the student needs to perceive that the faculty and staff of the institution are meeting his or her expectations on many dimensions. This will not be just classroom expectations, but expectations, wants, and needs that may reflect the students' personal needs as well as academic needs. In the following case, sensitivity to a student's needs led not just to a better career, but to the realization of a dream:

> The advising session was going well. This was a demonstration of how to work with a student, and a senior student was being interviewed.
>
> After a few minutes, the question was asked of the student what she was going to do when she graduated. She responded that she would go into business in the biggest city in the state. When asked if there was anything else she had wanted to do, she said, "Yes, I would have liked to look at law but never did."
>
> She said that she had never thought she could accomplish that goal, had never been encouraged to try it, and had never been asked about it by her advisor. When asked if she would like to try an internship in the spring in a law office, her face brightened, and she said, "Is that possible?"

It was, she did, and she went to law school—a clear case of what can be accomplished with a better grasp of student expectations.

PROBLEM SOLVING, COMMITMENT, AND MUTUALITY

In a relationship, problem solving is very important. There always will be problems, and the people who are willing to make the effort to solve problems will create good rapport and develop the type of process that is critical to the school and to the student.

Commitment is another dimension of good process. The student wants to feel that people at the school—and this may mean just one or two people—are committed to their work, to the school, and to the student. This means that the student must feel the concern and real effort on the part of the people of the school to see that he or she is successful. This can come out in many small or large ways. But it is an intuitive feeling that will cause a student to find it difficult to leave for the wrong reasons.

A final key ingredient of the process area of product is mutuality. The student feels that he or she is an important part of the school. In response, the student must be given the assurance that this is not an institution that is there only to meet the needs of the faculty. It is a school that meets the needs of the students and others who are part of the institutional climate. The student is primary.

In the process area, relationship management actually becomes realized. The school needs to help every person on campus examine interactions and set goals to improve them. This becomes a very personal and individual commitment to the success of the enrollment effort. It includes not just faculty and student relationships, but development, on a day-to-day basis, of better relationships with people overall.

DEFINING THE DESIRED STATE FOR PROCESS

This is a very complicated area to try to improve. In many ways, it is like trying to teach an old dog new tricks. Many administrators and faculty have tried to change themselves and others, but their experiences have been disappointing.

This is no reason to think that we cannot accomplish change if the process of an individual, a department, or an office is poor. It may be absolutely essential, in some cases, that the changes occur. If it is needed, the best approach is to define the desired state for product process and develop a wide understanding of and commitment to this desired state. This cannot happen for everyone, nor can it happen quickly, but it can happen over time if it is important enough to key people at the school. The process of the school that the student experiences will, overwhelmingly, be one that contains most of the following characteristics.

The institution must provide the best classroom experience possible. This will depend on more than the knowledge and skills that the faculty brought from their graduate programs. Being good in the classroom requires that the faculty be able to match styles, the subject, and the things that they want to accomplish with the wants, needs, and expectations of the students they serve.

Next, faculty members need to help students develop the relationship that allows them to become involved and interested in what the faculty are doing. It makes sense, then, to ask students before any course begins what their expectations are. The faculty and staff continually will find themselves dealing with students who have different expectations than the faculty in general. This means that the faculty may not know what the student sees as potential barriers. The only way they can find out is by asking, as was done in the following case:

> The notes were prepared, overheads ready, and Tom was conducting his first lecture. Fresh out of graduate school, he had spent a great deal of time making certain that the first lecture would be perfect. He dazzled the class with formulas, used his best examples, put all his energy into the effort, and was exhausted when the lecture was done.
>
> When the lecture was over, he expected an enthusiastic response from the students, but it was not there. They left silently. One student came up and said, "You know, you can continue to teach this way, but it's not going to be helpful to us."
>
> Out went the overheads and notes and up came a meeting with the class on expectations—the most productive decision Tom made that year.

In or out of the classroom, the faculty must take the time to develop rapport with students, so that the student and the faculty member get to know each other. Time also must be expended until the student understands the faculty or staff member and develops confidence, understanding, and trust in that person.

In addition, the faculty and administrators must be willing to spend time with the college, spend time on campus, and participate in events and classroom work—they ought to be excited about the school and about doing what they do best.

Unfortunately, there are many schools at which the opposite is true. The faculty members are worried, tired, and uninterested in working with the recent high school graduate, and they project this message to students. The desired state should be one of excitement and energy.

The following are comments that appeared in the *New York Times* on Sunday, April 13, 1986, reflecting the importance of process. This came from an editorial by Virginia L. Lester, former president of Mary Baldwin College:

> I'd hire people who I thought were more sensitive. I'd work for better student registration procedures and computer rooms. And better timing can surely be developed in apportioning work on semester breaks and school holidays. Towns don't usually think about the universities in their midst; they take them for

granted. We should change that, or at least learn to take up the slack better so that housing is available, meals are accessible, and our students feel safe.

"Also, I'm more in tune now with student evaluations of faculty, and I would find a way to get students to judge teachers honestly without feeling threatened. And I feel more strongly than ever that great scholars don't necessarily make great teachers. I'd discourage any publish-or-perish program in favor of getting teachers who can set a class on fire day after day.

"Adjustments to a new environment are unavoidable and unpredictable. There's no question in my mind that the larger the number and the more unpredictable these changes are, the more anxiety they produce—and consequently, the more significant is their impact on an individual's learning curve. One job for educators is to predict these upheavals, not add to them."

–4–
INFORMATION AND ENROLLMENT
Goals and Resources

Colleges and universities promote in their classes the importance of information and its impact on the success of all types of institutions and programs. Many theorists now view information in terms of economics and suggest that, in the future, data and information will become as valuable as money in the success of organizations.[1] The actual use of data in educational institutions, however, is varied. Colleges and universities are often very proficient at collecting it, but sometimes not very good at using it. They are often not very good at converting enrollment data into enrollment strategy.

Much information is available to institutions to assess financial positions and to monitor and control the way money is used in higher education. The penalties for not having adequate accounting and budgeting systems are very high. This does not mean that all institutions use money well. It does mean that financial data is generally accessible. Yet, use and availability of information in other critical areas are sparse at many institutions. This may prove to be one of the biggest threats to the success of colleges and universities in their enrollment futures. The inability to collect and apply data might prove to be a bigger barrier to enrollment success than changing demographics or the economy.

Many institutions have data-gathering programs that are used to accumulate information about students such as residence, sex, high school attended, areas of interest, and ACT and SAT scores. This is very basic *attribute* data that can be found in the information data banks of most colleges and universities. How much of this data is really used on

---

[1]Data in this section, if not otherwise referenced, is from the National Student Database, created and maintained by The Ingersoll Group, Inc.

a daily, weekly, or monthly basis to keep programs on target is another question. It is possible that the very institutions that stress the value of research are not able to practice what they teach.

In short, it is often the case that a great deal of data is available but goes unused. In fact, a speaker in a convocation at a school in Pennsylvania suggested that the availability of information is increasing dramatically while our ability to use the information is decreasing proportionately. This situation is often due to a lack of clarity of goals in enrollment programs.

THE GOALS OF THE RESEARCH AND DATA COLLECTION FUNCTIONS

Difficulties in the use of information often start with the fact that key people do not want to hear the answers to the questions that are being asked or that the answers have no meaning in terms of their problems.

"Let's do some market research," is a statement made at many institutions. When presidents, academic deans, or directors of research are asked what they want to do with the data and why, the answers often are very obscure. Many institutions do not have a good idea of why they are collecting the data that they have been encouraged to get involved with; it just seems like the thing to do.

CHANGE AND FOCUS

One of the basic reasons for this phenomenon is that data and information frequently relate to two general themes that can be threatening, especially if they impact a whole institution—*themes of change* and *themes of focus*.

Individuals frequently are resistant to change. They find change difficult even when confronted with overwhelming data that indicates they are moving in the wrong direction. This may be especially true if it is a direction they have felt good about. In addition, people can become resistant when someone attempts to point them in a specific direction. Both change and focus cause barriers to go up, resulting in blocks to actions or to hearing and seeing solutions. It may be difficult to hear or see the very information that may help a school to deal successfully with a threatening situation.

THE REASONS FOR COLLECTING DATA

If the reasons for collecting data are understood, and the school knows how this would help it to be successful, it might be easier to deal with the changes needed. A way of achieving this, to use a biological metaphor, is to look at data as food for development and growth.

Organizations, in many respects, may be viewed as organisms. An organism has a choice to live or to die; this theme was developed in a book by George T. Lockland in the early 1960s called *Grow Or Die*. He states that living systems must grow or die; there is no standing still.

Organizations have the same choices, and the food that contributes to its growth and success is information. Just as in the organism, the data and information that are absorbed by the organization must be somehow digested and sorted into things to keep and things to eliminate, and then the items that are kept must either be used or stored until they are ready for use. Once the items are used, just as in the biological organism, feedback tells the organization whether or not it has made the right choice; positive feedback from the environment will tell the organization, "Yes, you were correct," and the cycle begins again.

Many of the problems of educational organizations in dealing with enrollment come from the fact that they are cut off from the food that would nourish them, or they do not have a way of separating good from bad. In the latter case, everything is kept or the good is thrown out with the bad. In addition, there may be very little feedback to understand how this collective organism—the college—really functions.

The implications of this model for institutions may be found in the following questions: (1) "Why take in data?" (2) "What's worth keeping?" (3) "How is feedback interpreted?"

THE SIX ESSENTIAL COMPONENTS OF DATA COLLECTION: THE DEVELOPMENT OF STRATEGY

There are six reasons to collect data and information within an educational organization.

The *first* is to understand the "fit" between the organization and the environment, and with this information be able to develop product strategies that work. The *second* is to develop communication strategies with the outside and to communicate more effectively within the school. The *third* is to understand the problems the institution may face in its enrollment program and develop program strategies with this information. *Fourth* is to develop an overall enrollment strategy that will meet the goals of the institution. *Fifth* is to allocate resources to the effective management of the enrollment program. *Sixth* is to understand the issues of change and successful ways of effecting change to improve enrollment results.

Consider one or two general observations in terms of these goals for an information program. Gathering data and information makes very little sense if there is not some reason to do it. The goals of the information program and the use of data must be established before data is collected. It is useless to collect information if it is not going to be used. It wastes energy that could be directed into other activities.

A second general observation is that the research may often require the institution to consider the possibility of change. After all, to study fit implies that something will be done if the organization does not fit the environment. If a communication strategy is developed, the underlying assumption is that attitudes can be changed in regard to the organization through better communication. The idea at work is that the student can be influenced.

Even the development of enrollment strategy will cause changes in attitudes and opinions about what people will or will not do to meet enrollment goals. The resource allocations clearly imply to many people that there is the potential for winners and losers in the outcome of the research effort. Seen as a whole, the issue of change is fundamental in designing the recruitment program and in collecting and using data effectively.

FIT

Fit is one of the primary factors in the enrollment management effort. The closer the fit between the student or influential and the institution, the easier it is to meet enrollment goals. If the fit between the institution and potential student is poor, it may be very costly in terms of dollars, energy, and time if the school is to meet its goals.

Figure 4.1 represents a hypothetical relationship between the school and its potential students. Points A to G could represent any of the following arenas:

- The expectations of the student and the institution; what he or she wants the institution to deliver.
- The student's concept of the ideal school.
- The characteristics that the student or influential would find attractive about the institution.

Points A, B, C, and D represent what the institution believes it has to offer. These features are what the student is supposed to receive during four years of college in exchange for a payment of up to $50,000. There is, in this example, a great degree of distance between the wants, needs, and expectations of the student (B, E, F, D, G) and what the institution has to offer (A, B, C, D). The institution apparently does not have F and G, and the student or influential does not want A or C. To make matters

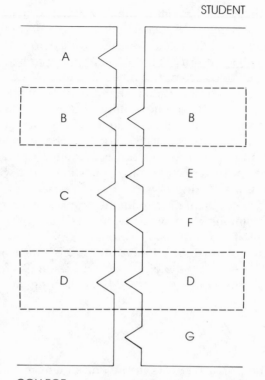

STUDENT

COLLEGE

FIGURE 4.1. HYPOTHETICAL RELATIONSHIP BETWEEN SCHOOL AND POTENTIAL STUDENTS.*

*A, B, C, and D (left side) represent items the school has to offer, while B, E, F, D, and G (right side) represent what the student wants. In this case, the school has a good match at B and D, and a poor match at E, F, G, and C.

worse, if items B and D are trivial—things the institution can offer but which are unimportant to the potential student—the institution has little to use in a competitive situation or in cases where there is a need to influence students.

CHANGE: TWO OPTIONS

The options available to a school in this situation are to change the institution or to change the student. In the first option, the institution may decide to offer E, F, and G or to strengthen A if it is perceived by the student to be an important expectation. Or, it could be that the institution has capacities in these areas that are not perceived by the student and his or her influentials. In such a case, the institution may want to undertake the task of making the features more visible. An institution that is willing to consider this type of change is more likely to be successful in the marketplace and might be considered a learner-centered institution.

Changing the student in terms of what he or she expects can be a very difficult task, but this is the second option in dealing with the situation and can occur in two ways. The first is to help the student understand what is available. If the college has the desired features but lack of fit occurs because the student or influential does not know this, creating awareness will help both the student and the school.

The second way is to create a desire for option A or C. In this case, the institution will use the communication program to create an expectation where it did not exist—a very tough job, especially if there is little value perceived in these features and if there is a great deal of market competition.

The data that is collected may require that the institution think in these terms. If the university has available only two features and those features are perceived by students as trivial, the school may be in for a rude awakening. In any case, the institution should understand its options. If it is not willing to consider that some change must be made in the student and some change in the organization as well, there may be a serious problem. A low importance may be placed on data and information because the institution does not want to react to the data. It already has made assumptions about its role in the problem.

CASE STUDY

A few years ago, the president of a medium-sized college in the Midwest was asked how her school should be described. She answered very quickly, "It's right there in the catalog. We are a small liberal arts college for women located in Wobegon, Minnesota." At that time, there was very little interest in a small school (especially when a high school was likely to be bigger than most colleges); only a moderate interest in liberal arts schools (25 percent); and even less interest in a women's college. To compound the issue, almost no one can find Wobegon, Minnesota. The points of contact between the student and the college were very few indeed.

Options that were discussed were very helpful. During the research, the faculty of the school were rated very highly. They were said to be responsive, good teachers, available, and highly interested in students' success. The faculty, present students, and administration all agreed on these issues. At the same time, the potential students said that these

TABLE 4.1. Summary of Characteristics of the Ideal College*

Lost Inquiries		Present Students		Faculty/Administration	
Good reputation	4.68	Good reputation	4.75	Good reputation	4.85
Good career counseling	4.65	Good financial aid	4.59	Good placement services	4.75
Good placement services	4.64	Good placement services	4.55	Good financial aid	4.62
Good financial aid	4.60	Good career counseling	4.48	Responsive	4.58
Good housing	4.60	Responsive	4.44	Good housing	4.50
Extensive opportunities for social		Personal	4.39	Good career counseling	4.45
life	4.38	Socially involved	4.30	Diverse leadership opportunities	4.44
Socially involved	4.37	Good housing	4.24	Socially involved	4.31
Career oriented	4.36	Extensive opportunities for social		Personal	4.30
Responsive	4.33	life	4.10	Extensive opportunities for social	
Personal	4.21	Career-oriented	4.10	life	4.26
Diverse leadership opportunities	4.06	Diverse leadership opportunities	4.06	Prestigious	4.25
		Diverse student backgrounds	4.01	Academically rigorous	4.23
		Academically rigorous	4.00	High admission standards	4.20
				Demanding faculty	4.18

*A semantic differential approach was used here to understand how the students viewed selective aspects of the institution. The higher the value, the more desirable the characteristic. In this case, there were twenty-eight variables. The average is represented. Students could respond on a range of 1–5. This data is from the national studies in 1985 and 1986 conducted by The Ingersoll Group, Inc.

were highly desirable characteristics for the school to have (see Table 4.1). In this case, after making the potential student and his or her influentials more aware of the faculty, the applications and enrollment increased. The connection was made.

CHARACTERISTICS OF THE IDEAL COLLEGE

Table 4.2 represents the issues for a midsize school in the East. The students generally wanted services from their school such as good placement and financial aid and desired that the school they were selecting have a good reputation. Reputation in this case was an interesting factor. What it essentially meant was that the potential student wanted his or her peer group to respect the decision to attend the school. (This information came from the focus group studies). In fact, it took considerable courage for high school students to say that they were going to this particular institution.

There is very little chance for any college to impact peers, especially a small to medium-size college with low visibility. In this case, it was also clear that the school was not perceived as having a strong placement or financial aid program. Even the present students or faculty would not say either of these areas was especially good.

Because there were few points of overlap, the school opted to look at the placement and financial aid program and to develop strength in these areas. This turned out to be a very wise choice because it did not need to involve the faculty in a significant way. Faculty members had indicated they did not want to take risks or to be change oriented. They did not want to be heavily involved in the enrollment program.

DATA AND THE COMMUNICATION STRATEGY

A well structured communication program is heavily dependent upon the messages that are delivered and the overall concept used to present the school. Because people have a limited capacity to absorb messages, an institution will be far better off if it can highlight the important messages and not overlook the relevant details. Likewise, if it is difficult for the school to be visible—if it is not a well-known educational institution—the student's interest will rise faster if there is a unifying concept to the communication program. This would give the student something to think about when he or she is not in contact with the school. The concept would continue to reinforce the efforts of the institution.

Both the specific messages and overall concept should come from information collected from students. These would be messages that relate directly to what the student expects from the institution or to the student's perception of the ideal school.

TABLE 4.2. Summary of Attractiveness of Characteristics of the Ideal College*

Lost Inquiries		Present Students		Faculty/Administration	
Excellent teachers.	85%	Excellent teachers.	88%	Financial aid.	91%
Excellent job placement.	79%	Concerned faculty.	82%	Concerned faculty.	86%
Financial aid.	77%	Financial aid.	78%	Excellent teachers.	85%
Concerned faculty.	76%	Accessible faculty.	74%	Accessible faculty.	77%
Accessible, caring staff.	75%	Accessible, caring staff.	73%	Excellent job placement.	66%
Excellent career planning.	71%	Excellent job placement.	72%	Personal counseling.	29%
Accessible faculty.	66%	Excellent career planning.	64%	Liberal arts curriculum.	29%
Practical learning opportunities.	63%	Leadership opportunities.	25%	Innovative curriculum.	27%
Academic advising.	61%	Strong minority/international student dimension.	23%	Leadership opportunities.	22%
Leadership opportunities.	29%	College for women.	21%	Excellent athletic facilities & sports program.	18%
Strong minority/international student dimension.	26%	Religious affiliation.	19%	Strong minority/international student dimension.	16%
Excellent athletic facilities & sports program.	22%	Excellent athletic facilities & sports program.	15%	Religious affiliation.	11%
Religious affiliation.	18%	Hard to get into.	8%	College for women.	11%
Hard to get into.	9%	Students from high social/economic standing	3%	Hard to get into.	6%
College for women.	4%			Students from high social/economic standing	2%
Students from high social/economic standing	4%				

*This data is a small selection from a study done to understand students' expectations of the college. The questions used a scale of 1–5, with 5 being very attractive and 1 being very unattractive. The percentages of very attractive responses are represented. This data is from the national studies conducted in 1985 and 1986 by The Ingersoll Group, Inc.

THE RIGHT MESSAGES AND THEME.   The messages that need to be delivered are those that have meaning to the student. It really doesn't matter what the school feels compelled to say. If the institution delivers a long lecture on quality and the advantages of liberal arts education, and the student wants to hear about faculty and career programs, the school probably will not be heard. Likewise, the academic dean, president, or faculty of the school are unlikely to be the best people to test the concepts. The publications staff can almost be assured that what appeals to the president and dean will not appeal to the students.

In the case of the hypothetical college, if the student wants B, E, F, and G and the school wants to talk about A and C, the school will miss the boat and so will the student because the college has B but is not communicating about it.

Basic to this way of thinking is the view that people can be influenced. A great deal of research indicates that this is very likely true. This is an important issue since, if this assumption is not accepted, the collection of data will be an exercise in futility. It was clear, in the case of Wobegon, that messages needed to be delivered that were true. The students wanted to hear about the faculty and the school could clearly talk about them. This college could very likely influence students who were open to considering different types of schools. A double effect was obtained with the withdrawal of the wrong messages—liberal arts, single-sex, and small—and the initial communication about the faculty. There would have been minimal impact on the student if the school had continued the three messages that the student did not want to hear and only later talked about the faculty. It was clear in the case of this school that they were willing to consider the three critical issues:

- There is such a thing as the right message.
- People can be influenced.
- Data should be used in developing a communication program.

ENROLLMENT PROGRAM STRATEGIES

Data can be used in an enrollment program for three essential reasons:

- Identification of problems and opportunities—of which situations are not what they should be and which situations, if they existed, would provide a boost to the program.
- Strategy development to impact enrollment efforts.
- Resource allocation.

CHANGE AGAIN.   Here, again, the issues of change must be faced. Examples include:

- The enrollment staff that must change from roles as application processors to active communicators with the outside world.

- The program that finds that its conversion ratios in its home state have fallen, requiring a change in travel schedules—no more winter travel to Florida.
- The academic dean who finds that a request for word processing and computer support will eat into the funds for outfitting the computer laboratory.

Data in this area may indicate changes that are required, but may involve issues about which people would rather not think. In areas oriented toward enrollment programs, a large amount of data is likely to be available for use. Yet, it is not unusual to find that the data is not applied. Actions are taken on intuition and hunches and not on a combination of data and experiences.

CASE STUDY

In a certain medium-sized state university, the enrollment function is divided into admissions and recruitment. The recruitment staff is the first contact with the student while the admissions staff processes the applications. The recruiter who visits schools through college nights, college fairs, and high school visits depends on the admissions office for inquiry data. Unfortunately, inquiries generally come to the admissions office and may not be entered into the computer on a timely basis.

As a result, the recruiters generally have to visit schools without this data. This means they see students who have contacted the university, and yet the counselors are not aware that they should have information about the student. The student expects to be recognized but is not, and leaves the event feeling less enthusiastic about the school. A school that can treat students more personally, therefore, will have a better opportunity to develop the relationships.

The reason for the problem at this university is the belief on the part of the admissions office that loss of the inquiry function will mean a loss of status and dollars that go with the program.

The second reason for resistance to solving the problem is the fact that the transfer of the inquiry function to recruitment would mean the loss of computer terminals and a good deal of data-handling capability.

INFORMATION TO ASSIST WITH CHANGE

The final goal is information related to bringing about successful change. Change usually will be a factor if the college is going to influence people to enroll. Change will likely be needed internally and externally. People will be challenged in their beliefs and this may cause difficulties in the collection of data and its applications in programs.

ATTITUDES AND BELIEFS

Attitudes and beliefs are the most influential factors in this phenomenon. They will serve as barriers to actions or as a stimulus to move ahead. However, if the attitudes and beliefs are clearly understood, strategies can be devised to change them or to avoid them. An example is a group of faculty who do not agree that the school's internal environment is critical to enrollment success. Rather than fighting the battle of changing how the school feels, other activities might be undertaken that would match the school more closely with the enrolled student.

The exposure of people to their own attitudes and beliefs can also help them to have insights into the results of their opinions. Often when people see or hear their opinions, they recognize the potentially destructive nature of their beliefs. Having data on attitudes and beliefs and knowing how to use it can be very helpful. This can happen more quickly and with more positive results if a task force is working on the enrollment problems.

GOALS INFORMATION

The following is a suggested set of goals to guide thinking in the area of information. If the school can not accept these goals, one would have to wonder about the ability of the institution to succeed in the long term. The college will collect data and information in order to:

- understand the "fit" between the institution and the potential student and influential; to use this to understand options in maximizing this fit; to produce a product strategy to impact enrollment.
- develop effective communication strategies with the potential student and influential.
- develop an effective enrollment program and enrollment strategy; to use this data to allocate resources.
- understand how to bring about change in the organization. To produce a change strategy within the organization.

-5-
INFORMATION AND ENROLLMENT
Content and Process Issues

There is a right way and a wrong way to do enrollment research: this is the key concern in dealing with content of any issue.[1] This chapter does not deal with detailed issues of statistics and surveys, as these are rarely where the basic problems exist. Even if the assumption is made that surveys are constructed correctly, that sampling has been done well, that the right statistical formulas have been applied, there are still many ways for research to miss the mark—to not have impact on the enrollment process, the meeting of students' needs, and, ultimately, on final enrollment figures.

Research efforts need to be considered from several strategic directions: (1) why the research is done; (2) its validity; (3) from whom to collect data; (4) how to collect data; (5) how to analyze and present the data; (6) what issues have an impact on success of the research effort even before implementing a survey; (7) the extent of involvement in the design and content of the research by those who will use the resulting information.

THE RESEARCH RATIONALE

The first step in a successful research effort is to make certain the goals of research are well understood. This point is worth mentioning again since many research projects stray because these goals are not firmly in

---

[1]Data presented in this section is primarily from research studies conducted for colleges and universities by The Ingersoll Group, Inc. These were conducted as annual research studies for a national high school student database.

mind. Research and data collection are conducted to improve enrollment programs by:

- better understanding of fit issues and how to bring the faculty, administration, and students together. Here managers are dealing with what people want, what a school has to offer, and what a school is willing to give. This is the development of the *product strategy*.
- being able to develop an effective *communication strategy*, the use of data to target the right people with the right messages, and developing the right relationship with students.
- allocating resources to the enrollment program in the most effective manner—where to send PR people, where to mail, how to cover particular territories, and how to develop overall management strategy.
- using program data—a history of results. It is important to identify opportunities for improvement in how the enrollment program is conducted.

The key issue is the importance of data—converted to usable information—in developing strategy (discussed in detail in Chapter 10). As competition has increased and students have decreased, the importance of strategy has increased.

THE COLLECTION OF DATA AND INFORMATION: WHAT DATA SHOULD BE COLLECTED

The areas of importance to enrollment management will define, to a large extent, the questions, issues, agendas, and formats for collecting data. The data collection needs to examine specific characteristics of each of the key variables. If any of these is ignored, the problems of strategy development and use of data will be compounded. The following models may be used to assess the key attributes of each of the variables important to enrollment management.

PRODUCT DATA.   In the area of the *product*, expectations, the generic image, people, programs, and character of a school need to be examined. There are specific characteristics such as the involvement and availability of faculty, perceptions of career counseling and placement, the quality of advising, faculty time with students, and location/type characteristics (such as single-sex, religious, public/private) that can heavily impact enrollment results. Research questions need to be organized to explore specific areas directly.

Of the many issues to explore one of the key elements to examine is the service package. The service package contains such items as how telephones are answered, how problems are solved, what parking arrangements are made for visitors, what arrangements are made for meeting the desires of students looking at the college. Calling the school and determining how the telephone is answered then becomes a part of the research effort.

COMMUNICATION.   In the area of communication, information about the image, awareness, and fit of the school to the marketplace need to be available. In addition, there must be awareness of the quality, type, and amount of communication. Research should address expectations, ideals, and attractiveness as perceived by students and influentials. The student will make a number of decisions requiring communication, among which the key decisions will be to:

- inquire
- apply
- complete an application
- confirm
- enroll
- remain to graduate[2]

CLIMATE DATA.   Climate variables also need to be studied. These include the following: Information flow; impact of political systems; cultural characteristics; beliefs; norms; amount of trust. Understanding these issues will go far in making certain people will work together effectively to deal with enrollment issues. Variables affecting climate can be grouped as follows:

Information
- Flow
- Availability
- Use

Political System
- Winners
- Losers

Culture
- Beliefs
- Norms
- Trust

This model is developed more completely in Chapter 8.

---

[2]This sequence is developed further in Chapter 6, pages 000 to 000.

PROGRAM/MANAGEMENT DATA.   In the enrollment program, managers need to know:

- Inquiries by number and by source.
- Conversion ratios of inquiries into applications and enrollments.
- Contact figures by staff members.
- Staff activities.
- Publications used.
- General contacts.
- Geographic distribution of students.
- Budget.

These represent some of the critical data elements for each part of the enrollment matrix depicted in Chapter 2. They are the elements that help to identify the ways in which the institution needs to communicate, the changes that may be needed in the product, the climate issues that may hinder communication, and the ways in which the resources and content of the admissions program may need to be adjusted.

THE COLLECTION OF DATA AND INFORMATION: WHOM TO STUDY

There are many populations that can be studied in enrollment research. If an institution were to study them all, it would be impossible for the enormous amount of data to have any significant impact. The project would be far too costly in terms of dollars and energy. The overflow of information could create serious problems for those trying to analyze it and use it in terms of strategy development.

Costs can be very high in terms of real dollars, but research also is expensive in time, energy, and frustration. For example, to do a study including present and potential students, faculty, administration, alumni, parents, and counselors at a large institution easily could run $150,000 and take up to two years to conduct. These costs include staff time, mailing, printing, postage, coding, computer time, analysis, and report preparation.

Even in limited studies, the cost can be high. In a recent proposal to a group of eighteen schools for research covering only potential and present students, faculty, and administration, the total cost for the study and the follow-up to impact enrollment was more than $200,000. And even if the money were spent, the amount of data gathered might be so large that it could not be used. An average single report may go to more than three hundred pages of data. When analysis, recommendations, and follow-up work are added, the report may reach five hundred pages and can leave the school with more than four thousand pages if studies were done of eight separate divisions. To coordinate this data in such a way that it can have impact can take so much time that the information may be outdated by the time it is used.

THE INSIDE WORLD.   In making the decision about whom to study, enrollment managers should not overlook the population of the school itself. In order to assess "fit," the faculty, administration, and present students must be examined along with the potential students. Too often, an institution wants to study the people outside without looking at the inside world. Without this internal data, there is little chance to understand how:

- the institution performs in meeting the expectations of potential and present students.
- the institution fits the characteristics of the college described by present students and potential students.
- the institution performs in terms of the features that potential students find attractive.

Without this knowledge, the marketplace can control the institution. There are few options in terms of making the right decisions; the marketplace makes the decisions. This type of approach is taken in cases where the school plans on changing the outside world and not changing itself—rarely a successful strategy.

CRITICAL GROUPS.   The critical groups to examine in research are the faculty; administration to the level of dean, director, or department chair; present students; and potential users. For community colleges especially, it is important to study all staff because secretaries and security staff have a great deal of contact with students prior to the faculty. For graduate programs, both faculty and peers are important.

The faculty should be included in the research with sufficient classification to be able to differentiate the data by: (1) part-time/full-time; (2) faculty rank; (3) years at the school; (4) departments; (5) campuses, if multiple campuses exist.

The present students should be sampled, unless the school is very small and all students can be surveyed. The attribute questions appropriate for present students and other groups are found below. In analyzing present student data, most critical data often relate to part-time/full-time, resident/commuter, male/female, and age. The data collected will depend, to a large extent, on the market segments the institution wishes to capture.

POTENTIAL USERS.   Potential users include anyone the institution feels could be consumers of the product. Because this can include a variety of groups, the desired enrollment state of the organization must be clearly present in mind before one answers this question.

The institution that is concentrating on traditional students should study either lost inquiries (students who inquired but did not enroll) or high school seniors. It may be better, at times, to study lost inquiries because they are already in the system—names do not have to be purchased—and they will know something about the institution. It is frustrating to do a high school senior study only to find that students are not aware of the school and, therefore, can give little insight about the institution's image. In many cases, the awareness level of the school may be such that the students can say very little about that school.

Potential users can include many groups, such as:

- College juniors or seniors, for professional schools in areas such as law or medicine.
- Career changers; people who are currently employed but want to consider a new occupation.
- Nontraditional students, for schools planning institutional growth in that market—either in degree programs or in terms of continuing education.
- Area businesses, if the faculty and programs at a school are to be directed to this group.

TABLE 5.1. Selected Attribute Questions for Various Groups Studied

Present Students	Faculty	Nontraditional	Prospective Students
Freshman, sophomore, junior, senior	Rank	Level	Going to college
Resident/commuter	Department	Major	Cost of the college
Major (undecided)	Length of service	Ideal size	Major
Ideal size	Full-time/part-time	Satisfaction	Career objective
Ideal distance from home	Satisfaction	Age	Are you junior, senior, college student
Satisfaction		Marital status	Distance of ideal institution
Receiving aid		Children	Commuter/resident
Income		Income	Ideal size
Sex		Where to have program	Awareness
ACT/SAT		Race	Visited
Highest degree		When to have program	Impression of visit
Race		Distance from school	Income
Age			Sex
Your distance from home			Grade point average
			SAT/ACT
			Highest degree
			Race
			Age
			Zip code

For these populations, there are various types of attribute questions. These are summarized in Table 5.1. There must be sufficient attitude and belief questions to examine how various groups view the institution. For example, messages may need to reflect how expectations of the school vary depending on the age of the student. The questions usually have to be very specific for the school.

Obtaining names of potential students sometimes can be a problem. There are, however, vendors who are able to provide accurate lists of names for almost any population. They can supply high school seniors and juniors, college students, businesses, and nontraditional students. They usually will be able to supply those lists with various types of segmentation (see Chapter 10 page 000). If you are going to study your inquiry pool, you will not have to deal with the issue of mailing lists or costs in this area. The following firms have been helpful:

Harte-Hanks Direct Mailing
400 Quivas Street
Denver, CO 80204
    (303) 534-2097

Alvin B. Zeller, Inc.
475 Park Ave. South
New York, NY 10016
    Toll Free (800) 223-0814

Metromail Corporation
P.O. Box 81637
Lincoln, NE 68501
    (402) 475-4591

COLLECTING DATA AND INFORMATION

Two concepts impact the methods for collecting data and information: (1) validity and associated issues around confidence in the data; and (2) how the data will be applied. The following is an example of a school collecting too little data to have impact.

> The business program at Gulf Coast College was down 24 percent in applications. The school wanted to study high school seniors to determine its image. There was obviously something wrong and if they could understand it, this problem could be fixed. The survey instrument they had designed was very short and gathered little real information other than how aware the students were of the school and, possibly, the academic program. The instrument identified little about the students' ex-

pectations, what was attractive about a school, or how the school or program was viewed by those who were supposed to use it.

In fact, the only thing the school found was that awareness was very low. So few people knew Gulf Coast that the institution could have gained a great deal of ground simply by developing a good awareness program. This would have represented a real opportunity if they only knew what students wanted and expected. Since they did not know, they gained nothing but frustration.

The staff had done the best they could, but had not thoroughly thought out the use of the data. They also had not dealt with issues of validity in their information beyond the assumption that they would use an old statistics book for data analysis.

In order to use the data for communication, they would have had to understand what potential students wanted from the school. Once this was determined, they needed to know whether the school could meet these expectations. They needed to understand fit, but in the end they did not have sufficient information from anyone's point of view.

Ensuring validity is important in research and is a very tricky business at best. Even with good survey design, research efforts can fall apart when the first student decides not to respond to a survey or a focus group session. To make the research more meaningful, sociologists and behavioral researchers have adopted a process called convergent validity to develop confidence in data. This process avoids some of the pitfalls of rigidly applying statistical data to the point of getting no information.

The convergence concept is based on the idea that finding similar answers through dissimilar pathways can confirm the stage when the researcher has arrived at an acceptable answer. In enrollment research, the use of focus groups, surveys, and secondary sources to test key variables will provide better reliability.

Surveys can give clear answers about feelings in regard to attributes of a school. They can demonstrate, for example, that potential students want quality, advising, services, or responsive faculty. The surveys also can reveal how aware people are of the school and what the institution's image might be. The survey approach to data collection can give numbers that help form basic ideas and that allow for comparisons of various types of issues.

Surveys do have limited capacity, however, to tell the school about the meaning of terms. If focus groups are used as part of the research process, the institution can look at the general issues in a second way and begin to define what various terms mean.

A survey may reveal that financial aid is important, for example. In a focus group, there also may be high energy on the issue of financial aid. Students will also discuss their feelings about cost. The focus group can tell us students' feelings about loans, work, grants, and, in some ways, how to structure the aid program. In a particular focus group on this topic, when asked how they planned to fund their education, the students generally gave the following responses:

- "Financial aid."
- "Summer work."
- "Work study."
- "Take part-time jobs."
- "Borrow."

When asked why they were willing to borrow or to take jobs, they answered:

- "You have to take a chance."
- "It seems like the rest of your life is based on what you do right now."
- In the sixties, everybody was fighting the war. Now everybody is going to college—it's what everyone does. You have to do it."

In another focus group were students who identified the three things that were important to them in selecting an institution. One of the key items was work. This did not mean work-study, but meant the capacity to hold down a thirty-to-forty-hour-per-week job. This put a specific dimension on the issue of work.

The focus group not only confirms the issue but adds dimensions to how students are willing to cope with the cost if they feel the educational experience is valuable. Addressing this issue from another direction, data from "The American Freshman: National Norms for Fall, 1984," published by the American Council on Education and the University of California at Los Angeles, again confirms the importance of aid. In this survey, 66 percent of the respondents had some or much concern about financing college and the number seeking work from part-time employment increased by 4 percent between 1983 norms and 1984 norms. This data, however, does not address the *dimensions* of work or the type of work needed.

If this is backed up by data from the content analysis of newspapers and magazines in which students and their parents discuss the impact of aid, the conclusion about financial aid clearly can be accepted. The issues have converged. The school knows how important the aid issue is and has a great deal of information about how to deal with the problem. While other issues may not be as critical to approach from this perspective, the process of convergence always is valuable.

ANALYSIS, PRESENTATION, AND USE OF DATA.   If the research program has been conducted carefully, there is a set of data available for analysis. The results of this analysis will be used by a wide variety of people to enhance the school's ability to meet its enrollment goals through the strategy developed. It will not do much good if it can be understood only by the research director, or if it is available only to those who co-ordinated the project.

FURTHER THOUGHTS ON VALIDITY.   Validity may be a constant issue as research information flows through a school and the research moves toward application. There will always be individuals within a school who will question methodology and the data itself and thus decrease the like-lihood that the data will be used. This can be minimized by paying at-tention to the following, *most of them prior to the conducting of the research:*

- Use, as far as possible, good sampling rationale.[3] The selection of lists and the selection of students and other groups on campus must be done carefully. In as far as possible, the whole universe (all possible individuals) should be used, and this can often be done with faculty.

- Make every attempt to get the return of surveys. Unfortunately, this will be *far from possible* in many cases. The harder you try, the better your results will be, within reason.

- Return can be enhanced by using more than one mailing, by using return cards, by putting special messages on the front of the survey, and by making telephone calls to faculty.

- Date all surveys as they are returned. By comparing the results of early returns with late returns, one can get an idea if nonresponse bias exists and for what factors.

- Test all instruments, materials, and procedures prior to their use. In this process of testing, observe where there may be problems of ac-ceptance or credibility in terms of questions or in the process of col-lecting data.

- Make certain that all materials and procedures are reviewed. This must be done with those people in the school who need to be involved in acceptance of the end result. They should have an opportunity for input.

- Use several sources of collecting data so that the process of conver-gence can be used to assess reliability.

[3]Present student surveys usually must be administered in classes. Other methods of administration have been almost universally unsuccessful. Determine the distribution of students needed and then select classes in which the survey can be distributed. This process will require the close cooperation of the faculty and the registrar.

TABLE 5.2. Expectations of High School Seniors

Expectations	Very Important
Prepare for graduate school	49.37
Prepare for a career	89.44
Prepare to communicate	60.33
Appreciation of music	14.99
Identify personal goals	68.28
Identify problems	68.30
Prepare to be an expert	71.07
Provide experiences	61.90
Judge ideas critically	60.40
Personal advising program	53.08
Develop leadership	45.64
Train to make more money	48.42
Provide awareness	31.53
Offer depth of knowledge	73.73
Academic advising program	38.99
High-quality academics	69.34
Train for probable career changes	54.09
Intercollegiate athletics	20.80
Adequate housing program	41.07
Intramural athletics	21.02
Fraternity/sorority system	16.52
Extracurricular involvement	33.65
Become broadly educated	72.62
Christian context	26.24
Sense of confidence	59.06
Hands-on education	63.02

DATA FROM SURVEYS AND FOCUS GROUPS: EXAMPLES

Table 5.2 represents the results of a national survey of high school seniors conducted in the fall of 1984 by the Ingersoll Group. In this question, students were asked about their expectations of college. The percentage who said the particular area was very important is represented. What do these students expect of their ideal college? This issue becomes critical for the product and communication area since, at a minimum, the institution must be able to meet expectations.

In Table 5.2, the respondents indicated that they expect:

- To be prepared for a career (89%).
- To be prepared to be experts in their field (71%).
- To acquire depth of knowledge in a major discipline (74%).
- To be broadly educated (73%).

These students expect career-oriented outcomes and career preparation. Being an expert in a field and acquiring depth of knowledge clearly indicate specific targets for gaining career skills.

TABLE 5.3. Objectives Considered Essential or
Very Important*

Achieving in a performing art	11.8%
Becoming an authority in his or her field	72.5%
Obtaining recognition from colleagues	55.2%
Influencing the political structure	13.9%
Influencing social values	30.7%
Raising a family	66.1%
Having administrative responsibility	40.6%
Being very successful financially	69.3%
Helping others who are in difficulty	61.7%
Making a contribution to scientific theory	14.5%
Writing original works	11.2%
Creating artistic works	12.0%
Being successful in his or her own business	49.6%
Helping clean up environment	21.2%
Developing a philosophy of life	44.1%
Participating in community action	22.1%
Promoting racial understanding	30.3%
Keeping up with political affairs	35.1%

*Source: Cooperative Institutional Research Program, American Council on Education, *The American Freshman* (Los Angeles: University of California, 1986).

   Results of ACE/UCLA studies confirm the points listed above (see Table 5.3). Although this data represents college freshmen, the information may reflect the attitudes they had as seniors in high school.
   In this study, the following were key objectives for these students:

- Becoming an authority in the field.
- Being successful in his/her own business.
- Being successful financially.

   These two studies come to the same conclusion. Preparation for careers is important, and certain specific characteristics of the school are critical. This does not tell the researchers about the characteristics of the school, but it does reflect student expectations (see the chapter on product for the role of expectations). The ACE/UCLA data also deals with the issue of success, but this may need to be further clarified from focus group or content studies.

FOCUS GROUPS.   The question of career outcomes seems to be confirmed by the surveys. Focus group data can now be brought to the question of expectations. This should help to focus the subject of expectations and perhaps help define the terms. When asked what they were seeking, some student responses were:

1. "Classes I am going to learn something from and not just slip through."

2. "Not to learn things I am never going to use in a career. If I have to learn that material, I would rather do it in high school."

3. "Education and atmosphere—atmosphere is the kind of people you are associating with. This develops the right attitudes for careers."

4. "The school should have a good reputation—as seen in the quality of the education and the rate of people going out of college and getting a job right away."

5. "The school has a lot of clout and when you come out of a program like that, employers know that the program is good."

6. "The school has a good reputation and has put out a lot of good engineers."

These six pieces of information clearly indicate that the student is attracted by a school who, in effect, can make the following statement: "We prepare students for careers as evidenced by the number of people who graduate from our school and go on to good jobs. You will learn about your area in some depth by associating with students and faculty who are clearly motivated to achieve."[4]

Of course, this does not say much about the school itself or how the potential student would want the school to perform these functions. Another set of basic questions in terms of research then would identify what is attractive about the school that does this task. It also is important to understand the characteristics of the ideal school.

A VIEW OF WHAT IS ATTRACTIVE.   Table 5.4 represents responses to the question of how attractive each of the following characteristics is in the "ideal" school. In this case, the percentages represent those who very strongly agree that the particular feature is attractive.

The attractive characteristics of a school that prepares students for a career are:

- Faculty concerned with helping students reach their maximum potential.
- An up-to-date faculty.
- An adequate library.
- Financial aid.
- A job placement program.
- An accessible and caring staff.

[4]This is only one question from several that were on the survey. All of the questions need to be reviewed before any final conclusions may be drawn.

Focus group responses to this issue include the following comments about what is attractive:

- "Good teachers—so that you feel you are going to get something out of class."
- "Good teachers care about you. They are very interested in their work."
- "I want quality people. This is seen in how they act toward each other . . . their friendships, values, goals."
- "It's important to hear other people talking about the school, and to talk with somebody who has been through it."
- "I want to know what the people are like so I know what to expect."
- "I want faculty members who are excited about their work."

These excerpts clearly indicate that students would respond to messages about people—people who are responsive, caring, will spend time, and know what they are doing. These students want to know as much as possible about the faculty.

It is important to consider what is essential to these students about

TABLE 5.4. Characteristics Rated Highest in the Ideal College

Attractive Features	Strongly Agree
Concerned faculty members	81.31
Affordable financial aid	75.30
Active social life	55.70
Concerned with students' values	47.65
Practical learning opportunities	56.10
Liberal arts curriculum	26.37
Accessible faculty members	60.70
Academic advising	62.73
Personal advising	54.16
Student life program	57.28
Job placement program	72.71
Athletic facilities	30.19
Up-to-date faculty	85.62
Career planning program	72.70
Excellent housing	27.99
Excellent teachers	86.65
Fraternities/sororities	19.10
Accessible, caring staff	72.82
Adequate library	79.01
International dimension	47.05
Basic skills courses	49.13
Hard to get into	10.02
Leadership program	33.12
Technical curriculum	25.17

these attractive features. The degrees or academic backgrounds of the faculty, for example, are not as important as their ability to interact well with students and to create energy and excitement about their programs. Students seem to assume that faculty are knowledgeable, but students generally want more. They want to get involved with the faculty.

SEGMENTATION.   Enrollment managers need, more and more, to be able to segment their markets. Schools are not dealing with a homogeneous potential student population, but with a group that is getting progressively more diverse. Handling this situation can best be accomplished by carefully considering the messages to deliver and the type of attributes involved. These can be clarified by looking at attractive features for various market segments.

The appropriate messages in the communication strategy can vary, depending on the segment of the population being recruited. Messages also can vary in terms of actual content or emphasis. Suppose the institution wants to recruit "A-grade" students, as does everyone in the country. Some attitudes and beliefs of these students are represented below in Table 5.5.

TABLE 5.5. Student Expectations Grouped by Academic Standing*

	A	A−	B+	B	B−	C+	C
Concerned faculty	85.81	81.49	84.57	78.49	78.68	76.98	80.11
Affordable financial aid	78.99	76.07	78.92	70.57	76.64	73.02	62.01
Active social life	55.07	55.84	56.85	55.06	56.57	52.80	50.01
Concerned with values	49.28	32.71	47.70	46.44	50.36	49.60	54.01
Practical learning opportunities	49.28	52.68	58.58	56.77	61.40	53.60	55.10
Liberal arts curriculum	28.26	28.27	26.45	24.24	29.52	15.32	16.33
Accessible faculty members	74.64	64.76	62.76	56.02	57.88	48.01	38.78
Academic advising	63.77	62.61	65.12	61.51	63.74	60.80	57.14
Personal advising	54.35	50.75	55.29	54.14	57.51	56.01	50.01
Active student life	56.20	56.17	60.67	54.14	57.66	53.60	52.01
Job placement program	63.77	69.23	77.51	71.70	74.09	76.01	80.01
Athletic facilities	28.99	28.11	31.17	30.19	31.02	31.20	26.53
Up-to-date faculty	89.13	86.20	87.55	82.71	89.78	76.61	84.01
Career-planning program	67.39	68.59	76.95	69.85	77.66	69.60	82.01
Excellent housing	66.67	61.91	63.94	53.01	57.14	46.80	50.01
Excellent teachers	92.75	89.32	86.11	85.23	86.81	82.40	84.01
Sororities/fraternities	8.03	16.70	19.81	22.35	17.88	26.61	14.01
Accessible, caring staff	79.41	69.87	75.14	71.10	74.45	68.80	68.01
Adequate library	82.49	80.47	80.67	79.70	79.20	72.01	58.01
International dimension	42.03	44.52	48.70	44.91	52.01	49.19	40.01
Basic skills courses	36.50	42.01	53.35	50.75	51.09	57.60	52.01
Hard to get into	18.84	14.66	9.57	5.70	5.24	4.07	2.01
Leadership program	40.58	32.90	33.46	31.66	35.21	27.42	30.01
Technical curriculum	28.26	21.21	26.09	24.62	27.99	23.58	32.01

*From The 1984 National Student Database. Percentages of respondents who said "very attractive" are represented.

Observe the differences between the "A" student and the "C" student. The "A" students wants (1) more concerned and accessible faculty, (2) excellent teachers, (3) up-to-date faculty, and (4) an adequate library. Schools that are going to try to attract the "A" student will have to have superior products. The faculty and academic program emphasis must clearly be related to meeting students' goals.

The same messages generally can be used to attract interest from both the "A" and the "C+" student, but the institution must be able to demonstrate extreme competence if it is going to enroll and retain the "A" student. It must be able to demonstrate, without doubt, its ability to *deliver* if it plans to compete successfully in this arena.

FIT. Once segmentation is addressed, messages are available to work with. At this point, the key issue to face is whether the institution can deliver the product. Does the institution fit the identified wants?

If the institution does fit, it is in good shape. Publications and other promotional strategies can be prepared and the enrollment issue becomes one of communicating the right messages. If it doesn't fit, the institution must now deal with the issue of change after the development of an appropriate product strategy. A basic question at this point is whether people in the organization want to fit the market. If the proper groundwork has been done, it is very likely that the requirements for change are clear.

In Table 5.6 inquiries, present students, and faculty are represented in terms of expectations. This chart represents about one-third of the items that are actually present on the survey. There are some general agreements about student and faculty expectations:

- The school should provide high quality.
- The school should help achieve personal goals.
- The school should provide an athletic program.

There are also some areas of disagreement in regard to:

- Preparing the student for a career.
- Teaching students to judge ideas critically and express ideas effectively.
- Teaching students to identify problems, evaluate evidence, and pursue solutions.
- Preparing the student to be an expert.

There are areas of dissonance between students and faculty. The areas of disagreement exist in some areas that are very important to the student. In these areas, messages are critical in terms of delivering the right information about fit. If the faculty members give signals that they

TABLE 5.6. Rank Order of Common Expectations of a College or University on Ratings of Very Important*

Expectations	Lost Inquiries	Present Students	Faculty/ Administration
Number of Repondents	381	752	140
Provide the highest academic quality of which its faculty and students are capable.	89%	88%	91%
Prepare me to move into a career when I graduate.	88%	87%	56%
Help me acquire depth of knowledge in my major academic discipline.	83%	87%	77%
Help me to become a broadly educated person.	76%	78%	86%
Prepare me to communicate effectively both in oral and written form.	71%	75%	96%
Help me to identify personal goals and to develop means of achieving them.	68%	67%	74%
Teach me to judge ideas critically and express ideas effectively.	60%	69%	95%
Teach students to identify problems, evaluate evidence, and pursue solutions to them.	64%	64%	89%
Provide me with an athletic program that features intercollegiate athletics.	15%	9%	11%
Prepare me to be an expert in a particular field.	64%	47%	6%

*Source: A study conducted in 1985 by The Ingersoll Group, Inc., for a midsized university on the East Coast.

do not value preparation for a career or preparing people to be experts, students will feel short-changed—if they were recruited with that particular message. There will need to be some changes of beliefs on the part of the faculty and administration if these messages are to be used.

Other areas of dissonance are not so difficult to address because they can be related to career preparation. For example, teaching people to identify problems, to judge ideas, and to identify goals can be discussed as career-related factors. A strategy will need to be developed to produce the desired fit. (Fit is also an issue that relates heavily to strategy, and it is covered in Chapter 3.)

DO WE HAVE TO CHANGE? HOW MUCH?

In the area of strategy development, data should be used not simply to understand but should lead to identifying changes that may need to occur in the institution. This is precisely why most data becomes suspect, foreign, forgotten. The project was acceptable until the research became available. People were involved, accomplished tasks together—but now it is time to part company. "No thank you, I don't care to change" may be the overall response.

This topic as it applies to colleges and universities is a complex one and demands an extended discussion. This is discussed in Chapter 9. But it also requires comment in this section on research.

Change involves aspects of climate and fit as important parts of the approach—fit because a critical question becomes who fits when, and climate because it determines how easy it will be to accomplish change and the process for changing.

Fit is, for a college or university, a two-way street. The college must fit the image of the faculty and the students—both present and future. To some extent, the fit will have to satisfy past students. Striking the balance will not be easy and some schools will have to choose one way or the other in terms of satisfying particular publics. It does little good to try to change faculty who do not want to change, because this may cause them to lose commitment to the mission of the school. In some cases, the institution may have no choice—in other situations, there is always room for compromise. In some schools with particularly difficult enrollment problems the emphasis may need to lean more toward prospective students. In others with less severe enrollment challenges, the balance may be more toward the faculty.

How easy the change will be depends on the organization's climate. When a great deal of cooperation is required and major decisions need to be made, the climate becomes critical. A poor climate can doom the effort before it starts. This issue is covered in detail in Chapter 8. If people are committed to the students and the institution, change may be easier to obtain, for example, and the process is likely to be positive.

CLUSTERING OF DATA

A final way to consider the data in application to messages is clustering. This concept allows the researchers to consider what messages might fall together because they tend to reinforce each other. By using clustering, the school can avoid problems by recognizing that the overall impact might be negative if the wrong messages are combined in a publication.

To study the relationships of data elements, principle component analysis is a powerful tool. This technique is a way of clustering large amounts of data to understand relationships. In the case of the National Student Database developed by The Ingersoll Group, if there are 1,934 people and twenty-six variables in a question, this process would be used in looking at the relationships among the variables.

When using principle component analysis in a study, the researcher is trying to determine which messages may associate. Component analysis can help to find messages that may interact either positively or negatively. To run the analysis, a 2×2 matrix is developed with north/south and east/west poles. An examination of the distribution helps the analyst to label these poles and find the distribution of the variables in the matrix.

For example, the researcher might find one pole to be high quality, the other low—or the north pole might be conservative and the south pole liberal. In any case, in developing these charts, better message combinations can frequently be constructed. Charts may help to create the right message combinations. To cite another example, an association might be made between high-quality work and hard, demanding faculty. If this were true and students were concerned about the demands of faculty, messages could be delivered that might soften this issue and express the relationship between quality and demands in a positive way.[5]

IMPLEMENTATION OF COMPONENT ANALYSIS

Figures 5.1, 5.2, and 5.3 show principle component analysis on the basic attitude and belief questions. In Figure 5.1, the quality factors seem to separate into the four corners of the graph. On one end of the x-axis are the words *rigorous, competitive,* and *demanding faculty,* which might represent internal quality factors, while on the other end are *pressure, prestigious,* and *standards,* which could be labeled as external quality features. The y-axis divides into quality-related factors on one end and campus and housing on the other.

When this information comes to be used, it would appear that the word "prestigious" might be associated with pressure and standards, while demanding faculty would be associated with rigor and competitiveness. Messages including pressure might be negative, which would mean, in this case, that the developer of copy would have to be very careful in using the words "pressure" and "standards" because of their implications. Likewise, it may be true that developing a feeling of reputation may not be associated necessarily with faculty, campus, or prestige, but may be inherent in other factors at the institution.

In Figure 5.3, some elements may separate into conservative and liberal elements with *routine, prestige, specialized,* and *standards* being located on the conservative side. These may be terms that can be used together to develop a conservative image. If the institution creates the impression of being liberal, it should recognize that it is implying that the school is not prestigious.

[5]The following studies in the area of statistical analysis have been found useful: L. Lebart, A. Marineau, and K. Warwick, *Multivariate Descriptive Statistical Analysis* New York: John Wiley & Sons; "Statistical Significants in Psychological Research," *Psychological Bulletin,* 70 (1968): 151–159; and "Causal Modeling Applied to Psychonomic Systems," *Simulation, Behavior Research, Methods and Instrumentation* 12 (1980): 193.

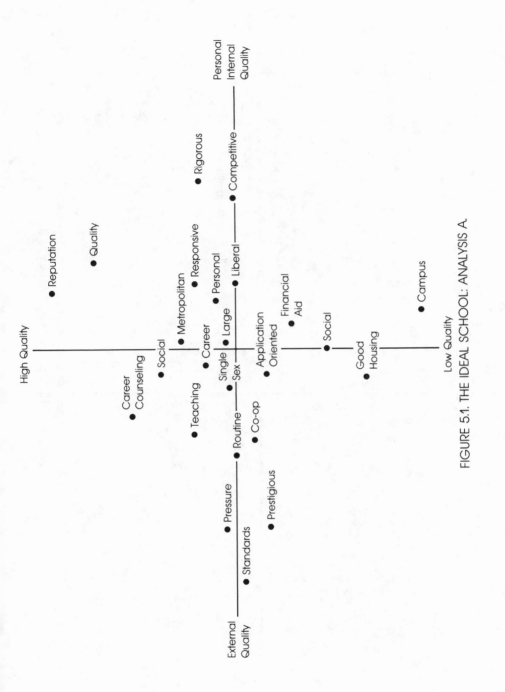

FIGURE 5.1. THE IDEAL SCHOOL: ANALYSIS A.

FIGURE 5.2. THE IDEAL SCHOOL: ANALYSIS B.

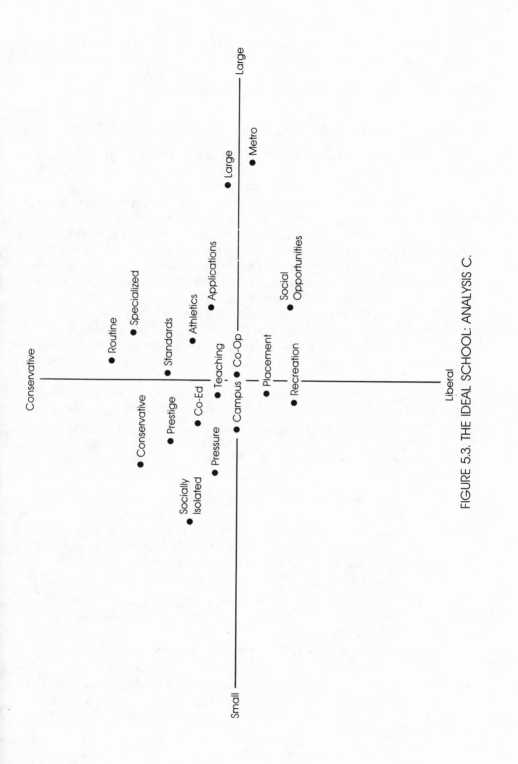

FIGURE 5.3. THE IDEAL SCHOOL: ANALYSIS C.

The terms *socially isolated* and *prestigious* seem to associate with the small school, and *metro, social life,* and *athletics* on the side of the large school. The larger school would not have to work hard to convince students that they have good opportunities for student involvement.

THE PROCESS OF RESEARCH AND DATA COLLECTION

The key process issue is that of introducing enrollment-related research into a college or university. This can have as much impact on the results as validity issues on the actual number.

The application of the matrix is a holistic venture, with potential for widespread impact on the institution. There are usually early issues of doubt, change, or questioning why resources are being used in this process. These resources, it should be pointed out, are not just dollars but energy, time, and commitment. This concern may not be uniform by type of school. The doubts and the concerns about research are sometimes stronger at schools that are doing well.

A case must be made before discussing research that there is a need to manage enrollment more effectively—either there are clear threats to enrollment stability or there are potential threats. A school with no pressure to consider new ways of doing things is unlikely to get excited about research. People at the school, in any case, will need to understand how the research work will benefit them. How will this information translate into points of view that will make the faculty more effective and the graduates more successful? How will research and data help faculty members obtain the type of students they are looking for?

There are several things that will help in getting a good start on research:

- Explain carefully why this work is being done and how it will benefit the school.
- Explain exactly what is going to be done and the channels by which people can register their feelings about it. Here, cover the types of studies contemplated and deal with issues of convergence.
- Explain how the data is expected to be used. Deal with the areas of fit, communication, and resource use.
- Carefully develop the ways that decisions will be made and how people can impact them.
- Identify when the data will be available. How will people get to see it? How will it be interpreted to people on campus?
- Have the commitment of the president and the academic dean. Make certain these people understand the importance of the project and are available for interaction with faculty and staff.

This process to accomplish the selling of the research effort might include meetings (group and individual), memos, newsletters, and telephone calls. The more contact there is in setting up the research, the better the results will be.

COMMUNICATION AND ENROLLMENT MANAGEMENT

The results of an enrollment program, once the right product is present, depend to a large extent on good communication with the marketplace. And communication is, at best, a very difficult task. Consider the problems that can be encountered just between two people, or among family members. When the outcome of any process depends on good communication, positive results often can be hard to achieve.

Think, then, how difficult it can be to control the communication with the marketplace—to manage communication with up to fifty thousand inquiries. Communication in the family versus communication with thousands of people: this is the challenge institutions face in using effective communication in enrollment efforts.

To a large extent, the problem is compounded by the fact that competing colleges also have likely concluded that communication is important. This means that potential students can receive much more information than they can handle. In addition, potential students have many more options from colleges, universities, and other organizations than in the past. In the future, for example, the armed services may be a stronger competitive force. The institution needs to make certain that it clearly understands the options available so that its offers are clearly understood and can be acted on.

There are three scenarios that are not uncommon when a president develops a communication strategy. They will be referred to as the Robert Redford Scenario; the Real McCoys; and Madison Avenue Returns.

The Robert Redford Scenario. The president has decided the image is all there is and is looking for a "Robert Redford" to run the admissions program. The director, professional staff, and clerical people all will be carbon copies of the near-perfect person in terms of looks, dress, and demeanor. Without a director of admissions for six months, the president finally puts the pastor of The Little Church by the Road in charge because he looks the part—at least of an older Robert Redford. This is all there is to communication and the meeting of enrollment goals in the mind of this president.

The Real McCoys. "Gee, ain't it nice to have you all here." Whatever you want we can provide. We cannot provide parking spaces, but we can provide about everything else.

The staff, two men and two women, have been hired for their down-home friendly charm. The director is always available. The office has cake and cookies always on hand.

Madison Avenue Returns. Slick—that's the strategy here. Everything is bigger and better than life. This office is out to "sell you," and you know that as you nurse your hand, which still aches from the first time it was grasped by the director.

All of these scenes exist somewhere and have been found to have one thing in common: a simplistic solution to a complex problem. Usually when these scenarios exist, the school has ended up relying very heavily on the communication program as its only enrollment effort.

RELATIONSHIP MANAGEMENT

The parallels to family communication can be taken even further, and they provide one way of examining the nature of challenges in this important area. The subject is closely related to the issue of what the students purchase when they enroll at a school. Are they purchasing a particular program? Not likely, although interest frequently cannot be generated without the program. If not the academic program, what is it? Levitt, in *The Marketing Imagination,* has indicated that students are purchasing a relationship with the school. They purchase their relationship with your counselors and the vision of what their college experience should be.

Like the metaphor of family communication, which reflects building and maintaining relationships, the institution is dealing with relationship management when it examines student decision-making about college. This may be true for all kinds of programs, even those in the graduate area. In the graduate area, it is usually assumed that the programs are the main drawing card for a school. However, even in this area, the faculty members in the graduate departments can have an influence on the potential student.

Two scenarios are frequently found in this part of the communication process:

In considering his school, Tom pictured himself associating with future lawyers—the cocktail parties, weekends at the beach, socializing with the right people, and fraternity parties. This association was weighing heavily on his mind as the representatives of a small college tried to sell him on the idea that their school had an excellent prelaw program.

Tom already was convinced that there were good prelaw opportunities on most of the campuses he had considered, so now there were other issues. Besides, Tom wasn't certain he wanted all that goes along with a really strenuous prelaw program. Long hours of work, the library on weekends, the pressure of grades. He would rather avoid those and move on to other things. The ivy league was the only place in which he could truly picture himself with the right people.

Joan was feeling lonely as she considered her choice of a college. She did not want to be isolated and, therefore, felt she should be at a small school where she could rub elbows with everyone on campus, especially the faculty and her friends from town. She wanted security and people around her and felt most comfortable at Lawrence College nearby.

She will be staying close to home and will probably remain there until she can feel more comfortable being alone. If one of her friends were to go elsewhere, she might consider it in the future, but not now.

Tom will be using his vision to develop a relationship with a school where he can meet the right people. Joan will do the same with a smaller and more select group of individuals.

WANTS AND NEEDS, TIME AND ENERGY

If students are purchasing a relationship, what are the implications? There are several areas to consider, including the wants and needs of the student and the time and energy that must be expended by the institution.

As the educators consider relationships, they will realize that many of the most satisfying have developed because of the fulfillment of wants or needs. Individuals form relationships with things or people that have meaning to them. In the case of college selection, the wants and needs of the student are paramount. Much of the failure to communicate well is due to a focus on the *college's* expectations and not those of the student. In applying research data to the communication programs, the institution is trying to identify the wants and needs of the potential student. These would then be used to try to change the student or influential into what the school wants. The wants and needs of the school have taken precedence over those of the student. The relationship, in this case, has become one-sided.

In dealing with relationship management, the school will also have to apply more time and energy toward potential students and their influentials. It takes contact to begin a relationship, to keep a relationship intact, and to build it. When the school loses contact, it can be certain that it will lose interest in the people they are dealing with and it is likely the student will lose interest in the school.

It definitely takes a contact to begin things, as the following example demonstrates:

> It was the last call of the night and Robin, the newest admissions counselor on the staff, was discouraged. So far, no one was interested in her school and this call was proving to be no different.
>
> "Have you received the materials?"
>
> "Yes."
>
> "Do you have any questions?"
>
> "No . . . actually, I haven't read it. It is at the bottom of the basket somewhere."
>
> The thought "How bad can it get?" passed through Robin's head as she groped for her next move.
>
> "In what subjects are you interested?"
>
> "Music, but I am not certain yet. I sort of like science and I have selected Tate for next year."
>
> Robin's confidence was disappearing rapidly, but she persisted. Because her school had a good music program and the science faculty was outstanding, Robin had some things that the student might want.
>
> Robin went through several questions before asking the student if he would read her materials and talk with her next week over the telephone. The student said he would, and a time was set for the next week.
>
> In the end, the student enrolled at Robin's school. A combination of contact and wants and needs had turned the tide. The admissions counselor had created enough interest to keep the process going.

Once that relationship is established, it is unlikely to move to the application, confirmation, or enrollment stage without continued attention. If the attention stops, it is unlikely that the relationship will build further. As the student moves from the uncommitted to the committed stage, the relationship will need to become stronger and stronger.

PROBLEMS. If the relationship is established, the representative of the institution will have to be prepared to solve problems. After all, if the individual cannot depend on friends, who can be depended on in a time of need?

If the school has a relationship started with a student—particularly a student that it would really like to enroll—admissions people will want to develop the capacity to listen to and hear problems and deal with them. This allows the relationship to be built one step further. The students are often confused or simply unaware of options. They can be truly impressed with the person who will help them understand critical issues. A large percentage of the inquiry base are likely to have problems and not talk about them. If they do talk, the school's chances of enrolling them increase significantly.

It may also be difficult to get people to listen if they have problems. This is another very good reason to do problem solving. The potential student will put up the filters and, no matter how much the college representatives try to pursuade, the student will not hear the words until the filters are removed. Thus, bringing together the issues of relationship management and communication is the task as communication becomes a part of the enrollment matrix.

CONVERSIONS: THE GOAL OF THE COMMUNICATION PROGRAM

The institution's communication goal is to establish and maintain a relationship with a sufficient number of students to meet enrollment objectives. This is largely done through the development of the ability to establish and maintain conversion ratios.

This lament is one that is repeated at many schools: "We are having terrible trouble meeting enrollment goals. This has been going on for five years now. We have tried everything that we can to bring in the applications, but there are just not enough students out there."

Enrollment problems are rarely the results of getting an insufficient number of enrolled students. Neither are they application problems. These benchmarks are certainly very visible, but they are only two of several with which we have to be concerned. The two most critical items are the graduates of a school and the initial inquiry. The most critical points occur at the very beginning and the end of the process.

THE FLOW OF PEOPLE

The enrollment process starts with inquiries and ends when the student graduates as a satisfied and productive alumnus. The ability to create the right enrollments and graduates from this pool is a most critical task and represents the ultimate goal of the communication area.

In Table 6.1, various steps on the way to graduation are represented.

TABLE 6.1. Model System

Status	Conversion Rate*	Comments
Unaware and uninterested		Through research, this figure can be established. Figures may go as high as 54 percent.
Aware and not interested		In the same case, 7 percent were very aware and 39 percent somewhat aware of sample schools. In this case, a goal might be to increase the number of aware students by 5 percent and the number of very aware students by 3 percent.
Inquiry (interested)		This step is the one at which a school can have high impact on overall results.
Applicant	10%	Follow-up here can pay high benefits. This is especially true of the less selective school.
Complete applicant	90%	Spending the time to get students' completed applications is critical.
Acceptance	70%	The acceptance rate is set by your school.
Confirm	55%	Telephone calls and contacts by the faculty and present students can be helpful.
Enroll	90%	This has been a vulnerable area in recent years. Losses can be very high at this point.
Graduate	60%	Concentrate here each year. There can be better retention at all levels but the specific actions needed will vary with the level of the student.

* In the conversion rates above, the percentage indicates conversion from the previous step. Ten percent of the inquiries become applicants in the example above.

Conversion ratios based on actual experience need to be established and decisions made to improve them if the institution is not satisfied.

RESOURCES

To accomplish the conversions, certain resources are available. The following is a list of these resources to consider for an enrollment program.

As the list is reviewed, consider the ways in which these might be used to meet enrollment goals.

Resource Outline
  Publications
    Viewbook
    Brochures
      Departmentals
      Parents
      People
        Alumni
        Faculty
        Students
      Financial Aid
      Student Life
      Careers
      College
    Direct Mail
    Catalog
  Events
    On-Campus
      Special Programs
      Major Days
      Campus Visit
      Services
    Off-Campus
      High School Visit
      College Fair
      College Night
      Home Visit
      Alumni Visit
  People
    Professional Staff
    Volunteers
      Alumni
      Faculty
      Students
  Media-Related Activities
    Movies
    Slideshows
    Videotape
    Television
    Radio

Posters
   General
   Departmental
   Scholarship
   Events
   Services
Business Cards
Stationery
Envelopes
Forms
   Application
   Housing
   Medical
Computers
   Hardware
   Software
   Printers
Theme
Messages
Design

The discussion of content that follows argues the importance of *type* of communication in terms of a successful communication effort. The essential items that must fit in terms of a successful enrollment program are the computer, the use of letters, and the viewbook. They need to be present and they need to fit.

The computer is important for the sorting of the database in a way that will allow the office to send personal letters to the people receiving the materials. Frequently, this is not possible, as the office has not been able to get the time or energy of the computer center staff to get the programming done to connect computer, database, and word processor. Without these elements, a viewbook or letter will lose its impact because of the loss of personalization. This is clearly true if the school is a very small institution.

Letters constitute a major impact to the success of the viewbook. The letters, if personalized, let the student know that the school cares enough to make the attempt at personalization. The letter also develops the main theme of the communication and can introduce the viewbook.

The viewbook itself can be greatly enhanced if the letter provides the introduction to its content and if it contains a theme and messages that are easy to follow and that clearly meet the wants and needs of the readers. The letters should move along the same direction as the viewbook in terms of theme and content.

The scenario that too often unfolds is that of an office that struggles to get the letters out barely in time, if at all. In addition, the letters may be very formal and not relate to the content of the viewbook or the theme of the enrollment program. In the viewbook itself, there can often be a very positive theme that is not supported or even referred to in subsequent copy. The result of all this is a lack of communication that hurts general enrollment efforts.

CONTENT: WHAT TO USE AND HOW TO USE IT

Each of the items in the previous list is useful in some programs and not in others. Each can be very useful if applied in the right way, with the correct content, at the proper time, and with the right people. This leads to the content issues that must be considered for each resource. The content and use of the following resources is critical:

- The attitudes of people who have direct contact with students. If there is a great deal of contact by counselors with poor attitudes, the results will be unsatisfactory.
- The structure of a viewbook including the messages, the photographs, and the design. It is not adequate merely to publish a viewbook. It needs to be done as carefully and with as high a quality as possible to accomplish the task.
- The timing in which these resources are applied or used. Sending information to the potential student several weeks after receiving the inquiry will hardly do the job.

This can be a complex process with many variables to consider. The complexity of the process makes the whole communication area difficult because similar schools using basically the same materials will have very different results. One school will do very well and the other school, which adapts a similar process, will not be able to accomplish the same outcome. To achieve the right results, a school must use its particular resources to manage relationships effectively with potential students.

THE COMMUNICATION FORMULA

The following communication formula is a practical way of organizing the most essential components of this process so that their interrelationship can become apparent:

$$E = (K_1, K_2, K_3)(X_1, X_2, X_3, X_4)(D)(\text{TIME FACTORS}),$$

where:

K_1 = *awareness of the institution.* How many people would say that they knew the school if asked? How many would know the school very well, somewhat, or not at all?

K_2 = *the image of the institution.* In this case, asking the people who said they knew the school what they knew. How do these people view the institution?

K_3 = *the fit of the institution.* How well does the institution fit the perceived wants and needs of the marketplace?

X_1 = *the amount of communication.* How many times does the school communicate with each individual in the database? Is it assumed that one contact will be sufficient to meet objectives?

X_2 = *messages.* What are the messages that are delivered? Is the school telling people what they want to hear or only what the school wants to tell them?

X_3 = *the type of communication* (personal or print). Today schools must communicate in a more personal way as opposed to printed materials.

X_4 = *quality.* How good are the materials that are sent to the student? This includes the quality of both the printed and the personal contact.

D = *a disturbance term.* Here is put everything over which there is little control. This includes demographics, economic factors, employment, and so forth. This section usually contains unknowns that can have a significant impact on the enrollment program if they are not accounted for.

Time factors = The way in which communication occurs over time— what messages are communicated at what stages and how quickly the school is able to respond.

THE K FACTORS (AWARENESS, IMAGE, FIT)

AWARENESS (K_1).   Awareness reflects the number of people who will say that they know a school when asked. It is much easier to meet enrollment goals if people are highly aware of the school. But for most schools, awareness will be very much lower than expected.

   In Table 6.2, for example, only 6 percent of the people who re-

TABLE 6.2. Awareness*

Status	Percentage
Very familiar	5.55
Familiar; I know about them	12.82
Somewhat familiar; I have heard about them	36.22
Not familiar	45.23

* Awareness data collected by survey. Represents a school in a metropolitan area of the west.

sponded were able to say that they were very familiar with the school. Another 13 percent said that they knew the school.

This data indicates that it would take a great deal of effort to meet the enrollment goals of this institution. The communication strategy would have to address the fact that only 18 percent of the public knows enough about the school to say even that they are interested if they hear the name. The bulk of the people the admissions staff will deal with have never heard about the school.

IMAGE (K_2).   Image can be viewed as the way the student defines the institution if asked about his or her school. In a recent study, a school was defined by the students in various ways:

- A "loser."
- A nice little school that you can attend if you do not have any other options.
- Easy and not very challenging.

Rather than being viewed as a first-rate challenge, the school is seen as one with very little value. These are not the kind of descriptions that would make it easy to meet enrollment goals. These are the words that will circulate in the marketplace, and word of mouth can be very effective in keeping students from any school.

Some aspects of image can be harder to interpret. Table 6.3 represents how a school was described by a population of students who were asked about its image.

In this case, the school is seen as:

- Having a strong religious affiliation.
- Being personal.
- Being responsive.

The school will need to consider these points of view as it selects the messages it should use. The current image may be very different from the image of the kind of school to which students would apply. This institution would likely do very well with these messages after the application is submitted.

TABLE 6.3. Image of College

Item	View of the School
Metropolitan	2.68
Career oriented	3.72
Inexpensive	3.08
Strong religious affiliation	4.10
Diverse academic program	2.51
Attractive campus	4.05
High admission standards	3.58
Small	3.37
Innovative	2.56
Active	2.41
Good social life	3.52
Personal	4.11
Demanding faculty	3.73
Competitive environment	3.62
Academically rigorous	3.55
High quality	3.98
Liberal	2.24
Responsive	4.01
Good financial aid	3.88
Liberal arts oriented	3.35

A second issue here is the treatment of the image of having a strong religious affiliation. Through focus groups, this concept would be clarified and discussed. The outcome of the focus groups would contribute to how this area is treated.

FIT (K_3).   The key question to be asked for the school described in Table 6.3 is whether this is the type of image that fits the marketplace. If the image and fit are not close, the management effort to meet enrollment goals needs to be intense. If the gap can be closed, and this is usually possible, the enrollment results can be more economically and comfortably achieved.

In the image descriptions of this school, it was clear that some of the words used were emotion-laden in a potentially negative way. Management decisions would have to be made about the way to treat this information. A frontal attack may be called for in which the school develops specific strategies to move "strong religious affiliation" into a positive appeal. The school may also need to segment its inquiry pool to find the people for whom this would be a positive benefit.

THE IMAGE/FIT RATIO.   In order to determine what the potential image and fit issues are, data needs to be compared for the school with ratings for the ideal college. In Table 6.4, pay particular attention to the ratio of the school to the ideal school. The higher this ratio is, the better the

TABLE 6.4. Fit Data

Item	View of Ideal	View of the School	Ratio School/Ideal
Metropolitan	3.50	2.68	.77
Career oriented	4.67	3.72	.80
Inexpensive	4.00	3.08	.77
Strong religious affiliation	2.10	4.10	1.95
Diverse academic program	3.80	2.51	.66
Attractive campus	4.00	4.05	1.01
High admission standards	3.20	3.58	.85
Small	2.10	3.37	1.60
Innovative	3.50	2.56	.73
Active	3.75	2.41	.64
Good social life	4.13	3.52	.85
Personal	4.50	4.11	.91
Demanding faculty	4.23	3.73	.88
Competitive environment	3.55	3.62	1.02
Academically rigorous	3.98	3.55	.89
High quality	3.99	3.98	1.00
Liberal	2.20	2.24	1.02
Responsive	4.23	4.01	.95
Good financial aid	3.88	3.88	1.00
Liberal arts oriented	2.20	3.35	1.52

school is relative to the ideal. In the case of the particular school analyzed, the school is higher than the ideal in terms of:

- Religious affiliation.
- Small size.
- Liberal arts orientation.

The school is lower than the ideal in terms of:

- Metropolitan location.
- Career orientation.
- Diversity of academic program.
- Activities.

Yet the school seems to be on target in terms of:

- Financial aid.
- Being liberal.
- Quality.
- Being competitive.
- Attractive campus.

The basic image of this school is not poor because it is on target with the ideal for some important characteristics. It is of concern here to be so far from the ideal in terms of an important area like career preparation. This difference will likely cause the school some difficulties in terms of producing inquiries.

If a school with a good image and fit is not doing well, there are actions that can be taken. Perhaps this situation exists because of low awareness. In some ways, this situation can be positive because the school has an opportunity to create the image it wants through its communication program.

Likewise, if a school has an unfocused image, there are actions that can be taken. The actions that can be taken are embedded in the X factors of the communication formula and in timing. As a result, the school is in control most of the time. If it is known that the school has an image that is not positive, or that awareness levels are not high or they are confusing, awareness can be raised and image built. *The school is in control.* If the institution has some very positive characteristics, it can help people to understand reality.

THE X FACTORS (AMOUNT, MESSAGES, TYPE, QUALITY)

These actions that need to be taken must be taken as a system because one action alone may do nothing more than eat up the budget.

> "I know that we have very few people who know about us, but we have sent out a great many mailings this year and things are even worse."

> "The image we have is poor, but we have sent out a lot of mail telling students how personal things are here. I can't understand how they could still not be enrolling."

> "Look at this picture of the administration building with the sun going down behind it. How could anyone not want to go to a school like that?"

In every case these people thought they had their problems solved only to discover the following fall that they still had difficulties. They were lacking at least one of the essential ingredients for a successful active communication result, which are represented by the X factors in the formula: amount of communication, messages, type of communication, and quality. If all of these work together, success will be likely and communication goals will be met.

AMOUNT OF COMMUNICATION (X_1). The fact is that much more is required. The amount of communication required with potential students will increase in the future faster than anyone could have expected. The institution should not expect that one or two mailings will be sufficient to energize the student to take actions, especially when those actions are likely to be very costly and demanding. It is unlikely to happen this way in the future. With competition increasing and the sophistication and expectations of the marketplace, each school will have to work much harder.

THE NEED TO INFLUENCE.   Schools are (or should be) in the business of influencing people. The difficulty of doing this is complicated in several ways but may be clarified in a diagram such as shown in Figure 6.1 (presented in simplified form in Chapter 3).

The students who potentially could be interested in going to a college or university are represented in this diagram. This reflects the distribution of the total population.

Segment *A* represents the group of students who would come to the school no matter what was done. To keep these students from the school, it would have to put up barriers, lock the doors, and, even then, many of them would still find their way to enroll. An admissions staff is not needed in order to recruit these people. The only thing the institution really has to worry about is that it might offend some of these people in some way, and they would not then follow through. A school that deals only with these students is an order-taking institution.

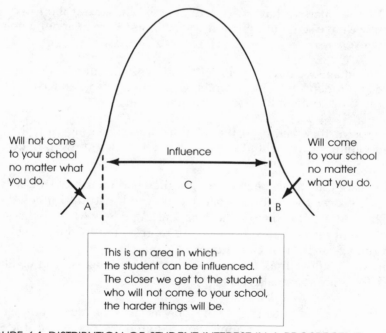

Will not come to your school no matter what you do.

Influence

Will come to your school no matter what you do.

C

A

B

This is an area in which the student can be influenced. The closer we get to the student who will not come to your school, the harder things will be.

FIGURE 6.1. DISTRIBUTION OF STUDENT INTEREST IN A PROSPECTIVE COLLEGE.

On the other hand, in segment *B* are those students who would not come to the institution for any reason. If they were captured and brought to the school, they would escape. They do not want to be at the institution, and if they enrolled, they would not stay.

The problem facing many schools is that the group who would never come is getting larger while the students who would attend a school no matter what happened is decreasing. The school needs to look very carefully at how to replace the latter group. An important factor to consider is that many admissions staffs are working with the people who would come anyway. After all, there are fewer hassles and fewer opportunities for rejection this way. This makes the enrollment job very comfortable with much reinforcement for the counselor. These schools need to shift their attention to the middle.

The people that a school really has to work with are those in the middle, who can be influenced (*C*). These are the students that should take up time and energy and who will require increased contact as the school moves closer to the people who will not come. The closer to the right-hand group, the harder the school has to work. The amount of contact to produce interest, knowledge, and commitment to your school is greater than usually recognized (see Table 6.5).

As an institution approaches closer to the right-hand area of Figure 6.1, more communication needs to be added. One midwestern university, it was found, was using fifteen contacts between the point of confirmation and enrollment. This was still not producing the kinds of enrollment needed—primarily because fit was so poor and messages were off target.

MESSAGES (X_2). It does not do much good to communicate a great deal if the wrong things are being said. If the amount of communication is increased, it may build awareness in the marketplace—but about the wrong topics.

> Metro University had published a recruitment prospectus for the past year that featured a picture of the administration build-

TABLE 6.5. Contact Frequency Required for Enrollment Productivity

Amount of Communication	Applications 4–5 times	Confirmations 3 times	Enrollments Multiple
Suggested strategy	Viewbook Application Brochure (faculty, career, visit) Telephone Personal	Letters Telephone Student life Parents Visit	Control of mailings from other offices. Need to maintain telephone contact to find people who are having severe dissonance.

ing on the cover. Inside, it talked extensively about how good it was to attend school in the city—the places you could go, how easy it was to get downtown, and the safety of the city.

These seemed like the messages that ought to be delivered, because the president of Metro was convinced that students were not coming to the school because they thought it was unsafe, hard to get into, and not much fun.

In order to deal with his current problems, he decided to send the viewbook to 20,000 people in the city followed by a brochure about the safety record of Metro versus its suburban competition. The brochure would show that it was safe here, and the president's belief was that he would saturate the market with this publication.

However, in actual conversation with students, it was found that they had had little fear of going to the school until the brochures came out. They then began to wonder why the administration was so concerned about safety. There must be some problem, they thought, that was not being addressed.

Not only had the administration failed to influence prospective students positively, but it had created a new problem. In this case, the wrong decision had been the messages on safety and on difficulty in getting downtown. The image being created about the school was negative and did not stress strengths that potential students and influentials would have found important.

There are several issues to consider in this type of situation:

- What are the sources of the messages? How do we find out what the messages should be?
- Messages need to be delivered in small numbers.
- Messages can be targeted and general.
- Messages may vary over time.

THE ROLE OF DATA IN DETERMINING MESSAGES.   As presented in Chapter 4, data is important in determining what the messages should be. Prospective students need to hear about things that they want and not simply what the institution wants to say. Data will help to sort out proper messages—especially data about what is expected, what is attractive. This becomes especially critical if the school is trying to work with the student who needs to be influenced. And the closer the school may be to the student who will *not* come, the harder the institution will have to work at designing the messages and making certain they register and make sense.

EXPECTATIONS.   One of the key concerns in developing messages is expectations of potential students. These are what the student expects the

TABLE 6.6. Data on Expectations*

Items	Percentage Very Important
Prepare me for a career.	89%
Make me a broadly educated person.	73%
Prepare me to be an expert.	71%
Provide depth of knowledge in a major.	74%
Provide high-quality academics.	68%
Help me identify personal goals.	68%
Help me learn how to identify problems.	68%

* From a marketing survey of a midsized college. Conforms very well to other data of this type.

school to be able to do. They represent what the student and his/her parents are willing to spend money, time, and energy for.

In the Table 6.6, it can be seen that the expectations of students are very high for career-related factors such as preparation for a career, preparation to be an expert, and in-depth preparation in a major field. In addition, the students in this survey seem to be looking for quality academic programs and for a school that will help them learn how to set goals and to gain good problem-solving skills.

With this information, the school has some idea about the topics that it should be talking about in publications and personal contacts. While the school does not know exactly *how* the student expects the institution to fulfill expectations, *what* students want is known. These particular messages are very helpful in producing applications.

In the case of Metro, even if they were concerned with students' feelings about the school's safety, they would have been better off, at first, making a case that they could meet their expectations on careers than trying to prove how safe it was. The messages developed have to show the student and his/her influentials clearly that the school can meet their expectations in these areas.

ATTRACTIVENESS.   The information about expectations does not tell much about how to *develop* the messages. It still needs to be determined what these students would find attractive about a school that could meet these expectations. How would they characterize the ideal school?

In Table 6.7, people generally, and specifically faculty members, are indicated as very important in the enrollment picture. These students have said that concerned and expert faculty members are important. They also have said that services related to careers and a good library are important. Messages should be delivered early in the enrollment process on these particular issues.

TABLE 6.7. Data on Attractiveness*

Items	Percentage Very Attractive
Excellent teachers	87%
Up-to-date faculty	86%
Concerned faculty	81%
Adequate library	79%
Financial aid	75%
Job placement	73%
Career planning	73%

* From a marketing survey for a small school in the Midwest.

THE ROLE OF FOCUS GROUPS.   To this point, survey data has been discussed in trying to identify effective messages. While this is important, there are some limitations. Suppose that concerned faculty are important. What else needs to be known? It still needs to be determined exactly how students define "concerned faculty." What are the characteristics of faculty that should be emphasized to develop the relationship between the potential student and the faculty member? In focus group interviews, there is a chance to find out what these items are. Students can be asked what the characteristics of a concerned or effective faculty member are and they will give their definitions. When asked about this issue, the students in one focus group said the following about good faculty members:

- They come to class on time and are prepared.
- They do not waste students' time.
- They are excited about and like what they are doing.

Now the messages that should be used begin to come alive. Faculty are important to students as determined by the survey; warmth and life can be breathed into the description of the faculty through the focus group data. In many cases, the actual words used by the students can form the copy that ends up in publications. If the messages are developed using actual people, the whole publication begins to come alive.

The Message Matrix shown in Table 6.8 can help in building a message strategy. In the matrix, the question can be asked how each message can be developed to appeal to the different ways people construct their internal "maps" about a subject. In general, it is known that there are three types of people in this regard:

- Those who need to see things before they make sense.
- Those who hear things and only then does the idea or concept become firmly established.

- Those who understand only when they feel or experience things, people called kinesthetics. These people will not understand until they have actually come in contact with the thing in some way.

The disadvantage of publications is that it is not known what the person who reads them is going to be like. The publications have to be prepared to appeal to all three channels of understanding. Part of this challenge can be met through a careful consideration of the copy and design for the major messages and a complete test procedure in place to get people's reactions to anything that will be used.

TIME.   The issue is that once the messages are known, the fact needs to be considered that people want to know some things early in the enrollment process and other things later in the process. Once the school has convinced the student of message A, the student and influential will want to know about B. It is important to adjust messages to the status of students in the enrollment process. Here the key variable is time.

In Figure 6.2, the interest level of students is viewed over time. This chart represents several factors, including an increase in personal contact over time, the fact that an institution will have to communicate more than once when communicating with a student, and the fact that messages need to vary.

Early in the process, generally prior to the application, messages need to be sent that are cognitive in nature. These messages should relate strongly to the expectations listed in the Message Matrix. They will include such items as educational outcomes, career preparation, quality, faculty, and, of course, academic programs; if the institution does not have the program it rarely will be able to interest a student.

In the period after application and prior to enrollment, the messages shift to affective ones. The student is now interested in how it would feel to be on campus. The messages need to relate to environment, faculty concern and availability, other students, and, in general, how the college "feels." Students have said during meetings of on-campus focus groups that the characteristics of their fellow students play an important part in the decision-making process. The messages may have to shift among these general categories, but, as a matter of general rule, the emphasis must be more toward the affective as the student moves through the enrollment process.

Of course, once the student has enrolled, the institution needs to deliver on the promises made. It is this delivery that continues to keep the relationship strong. For many schools, there may need to be marketing once the student has enrolled. This would be especially true of public institutions where the interest of the student may be low when he or she enrolls. The interest of these students needs to be built

TABLE 6.8. Message Matrix

Expectation	Ideal/Attractive	Seeing	Feeling	Hearing
Career preparation	Concerned, available, up-to-date faculty Career services Placement services	Print that develops the key faculty members. What do that indicates they are available to students? What the faculty are doing that indicates they are up-to-date in their fields. Pictures of faculty members with equipment or other items that indicate involvement and/or expertness. Discussion of services and pictures of people that provide the services. Pictures and words about people who have used the services.	Pictures should help the student develop the feelings of working with the faculty. Getting the student on campus is critical. Through time on campus the actual experience of being with the faculty can come through. This is especially important after the student has applied.	Telephone calls from faculty members at the right stage can go far toward demonstrating how involved, concerned, and expert the faculty is. On-campus events are also important. They can demonstrate the faculty and administration in all of the roles that will be important to students. Contacts by alumni will help in this regard as will contacts by current students.

Become an expert

Copy about graduates. What the student will know after finishing the program at the school.

Copy about internships and other experiences.

A copy strategy that pictures the student in specific positions, in which the student will be able to visualize him/herself.

Having potential students visit the places where they might work or do their internships.

Talking to alumni or others who are using the skills that will be acquired.

Visiting the campus to talk with students and faculty.

Visiting the alumni.

Quality

Quality should be communicated in everything that is prepared.

Photos and copy should be very well done. Use good printers and see that letters and materials sent have no mistakes and are printed well.

Good-quality paper stocks.

Very high standards in terms of dress and behavior on the road.

Making certain that the campus and the admissions office are well maintained and attractive.

Making certain the telephones are answered well.

Training all people who use telephones in good telephone technique.

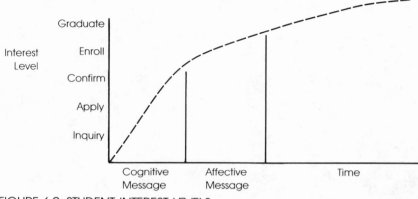

FIGURE 6.2. STUDENT INTEREST LEVELS.

throughout the first year to a higher level in order to have adequate retention.

TYPE (X_3).   In the recent past, the predominant way to communicate with potential students has been with printed materials. This has been due to the fact that admissions offices were primarily processing centers dealing with the paperwork of enrollment. The primary personal contact was limited to answering questions or providing information as requested. This did not require a great deal of effort or personal contact with students.

Today, people have become a critical factor in enrollment.[1] As competition and, therefore, communication becomes more difficult, the use of people needs to increase. This is represented in Figure 6.3.

The personal contact process communicates the unique qualities of the organization to the public. The more people are used in the communication effort, the better the results will be, especially if they are well trained. Efforts to have personal contact will be rewarded with better understanding as students are reached through all the communication channels. It is the people on the enrollment staff who can reach the students in a direct way and target messages directly to the wants and needs of the potential student. It is the people at the institution who really make a program unique.

Personal contact may start with the professional admissions staff, but it soon will have to include the following:

- Alumni volunteers who are organized as contact teams to work with students and their influentials. This group will do telephone calls,

[1]This is a return to the past when the president of the institution would personally be selling the school in the community.

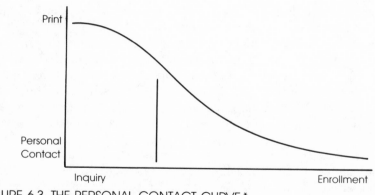

FIGURE 6.3. THE PERSONAL CONTACT CURVE.*

visits, host receptions, and they will be available to potential students in their areas.

- Faculty members who can talk with accepted students by telephone or meet with them on campus. The faculty can be influential in dealing with accepted or confirmed students.
- Present students whose contact with potentials can go far to impact peer influence on the decision-making process. The present student is perhaps the most credible of the people available.
- Parent-to-parent calls and contacts that can help the parents of potential students understand the school and what it has to offer.
- Campus visits, on-campus events, home visits, special programs on- and off-campus, and any other event or contact that allows you to present your school in a more effective way.

QUALITY (K_4).   The quality of what is done in the area of communication will have to be much better each year for most schools. The potential student receives so much material from so many sources that to compete, a particular institution will have to stand out. The potential student is now accustomed to reading materials that are well designed and professionally photographed and that have impact. The quality will have to improve, not only for printed materials, but for personal contacts.

The quality issue includes some items already discussed. For example, determining the right messages to send is a way of dealing with quality. Increasing the amount of communication will, to a certain extent, address issues of quality. Being careful of what is said also involves the quality of personal communication with potential students and their influentials. Better training of the enrollment staff relates to quality. But it also includes some new items of concern.

An issue in terms of quality is photography. Much of the message for a school is carried by the pictures put into a publication. The words are important, but they may not be as important as the pictures that in essence allow students to see, hear, and feel the school on their very individual terms. Even though this area is important, the quality of photographs in most college and university publications continues to be very poor.

It will help the cause considerably if the school is able to engage professionals who can create the kind of photographs or artistic renderings that will do the job. Good freelance photographers can be obtained by contacting most design houses or by asking for help from organizations such as CASE (Council for the Advancement and Support of Education).

When a photographer is scheduled, planning time should be allowed to make the shots work. A typical sequence for a photographer might be three days, with one of the days devoted to planning.

A second help in using a photographer is to have a good game plan with a "shoot" schedule that makes it possible to have photographs that fit a unique message, themes, and overall communication strategy.

Another key item to consider in the communication program is consistency. It is not unusual for a school to produce a very attractive prospectus and then devote little consideration to the follow-up materials. The school will use photocopied forms, badly constructed letters, old-fashioned stationery, and poor design in the support pieces and then conclude that the viewbook or prospectus did not work. The same attention that is lavished on a high-quality viewbook needs to be given to *all* the materials.

In addition, personal contacts must be as carefully constructed as possible. If print materials are done well, it is important to be certain that the people making these contacts represent the school equally well. This includes personal appearance and the quality of the way people representing the campus work with students. If the materials used in communication are very attractive and the messages are clear, then to have staff members that do not dress or communicate well will confuse potential students. The skills and attitudes of staff who deal with students also need to be developed as carefully as possible.

Another area to examine in terms of the quality of contact is campus events. The events need to be well structured with specific purposes. The care and feeding of the student are essential, with the event matching the messages that were developed and conveyed in other materials. The student will come to the campus if the school is able to conduct events that have benefits.

DISTURBANCE (D)

WHAT CAN BE CONTROLLED?   The disturbance term in the communication formula represents all of the outside forces that may cause problems. These can include demographics, economy, employment opportunities, attitudes and beliefs, and location issues.

These are external items that cannot easily be controlled. The institution can be aware of them and take them into consideration in planning, but there is no way to affect them. As one president put it: "Our problems are the demographics and the economy. This is making it very difficult to recruit students. It's making it necessary to give away a great deal of financial aid and accept a lower quality of academic performance." This president was stating her problem in a way that has become a familiar rhetoric to enrollment managers. Yet, some schools are doing well in the same environment. The institution needs to be aware of the things that it can control, and it must manage them well. But it also needs to be conscious of the disturbance factors—and then put them aside. These can influence thinking like a poison and lead a school to give up long before it should. Work hard on the key content issue and this will be a giant step toward success.

PROCESS ISSUES IN COMMUNICATION.   There are two major process issues that heavily impact abilities to communicate effectively. The first of these is the process of working with students. Too often these efforts are not done well; most schools could benefit from more attention to this area. This does not include the hard sell, but it does include the ability to promote the school through helping the student understand it on his or her own terms. The second is the issue of getting tasks accomplished, which relates to responsibilities for the communication program. If too many people try to get into the act in a detailed way, the program may fail.

MAXIMIZING PERSONAL CONTACT—THE FOUR-BOX MODEL

There are special opportunities that are available because of the school's ability to use personal contact with students. Through personal contact, a school, through its contact staff, can have the positive impression sought with the communications effort. The direct steps to these results can be represented in a chart:

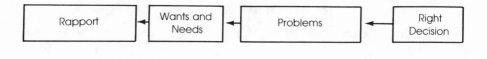

With the personal contact sequence represented here, a school can be assured that it is doing the best job possible to help students with the right decision. This means the right decision in terms of the institution that is best for them. If the job has been done well, it is likely that the student at least understands the institution and can relate this understanding to the decision-making process. The three steps to a positive result are building rapport, meeting wants and needs, and solving problems.

RAPPORT.   Rapport is the existence of trust and confidence in the college and its representatives. If rapport has been developed with the student and influentials, the student will be willing to spend time with the school, listen to, and seriously consider the options that are open.

Let's talk about Joan:

The school had 125 applications for an admissions position and decided to interview everyone. This was done because the staff clearly recognized the importance of *rapport* in their efforts.

The position would send the lucky candidate from Chicago to New Jersey for six weeks, would pay $10,000, and would require extensive amounts of time on the road, beside the six-week trip to Newark.

In she came. She drove a Lincoln, wore a fur coat, two diamonds, good hairdo—a class act. She had two kids, fifteen and sixteen, a well-to-do husband, and had not worked in sixteen years. Had we looked at the résumé and history, we probably would not have looked twice.

As she walked through the office, it was like the pied piper. Everyone wanted to talk about personal issues and at some length. People opened up immediately. She had the gift of rapport.

She was offered the job, took it, and produced a 30-percent increase in applicants and a 20-percent increase in enrollments the first year. There were better candidates on paper, *but not in terms of results.*

Having rapport is critical because, as can be seen in the model, without it there is no reason for the students to share their wants and needs, nor is there a reason for them to expose their problems. Without this sharing, the school will lose much of its ability to have a real impact on students. Without knowledge of these factors, the school cannot be accurately matched to students. It may take a great deal of time, but school representatives are wise not to move ahead until rapport has been achieved.

The important things to do to create and maintain rapport are:

• Initially, talk about things that are of interest to both the school and the student. Find topics that are interesting to the student being interviewed.

- Use an open and inviting posture in work with the student.
- Know something about the student before the process starts.
- Ask questions that will encourage interaction. Use open-ended questions to get the student involved.
- Listen carefully.
- Demonstrate patience in what is being said and in the time that is spent with contacts.
- Be enthusiastic about work with potential students.

When contact staff is hired, these skills are important to keep in mind. Often, the staff may be hired on the basis of their ability to produce rapport easily.

WANTS AND NEEDS.   Wants and needs are the driving forces behind what is important to the student. These are the forces that need to be understood and responded to. The driving forces behind most of our decisions in life are wants and needs. This becomes especially important when there are large investments to be made in terms of time, energy, and money; for students the issue often is not money but the psychic cost of making a decision to attend a school.

The advantage of the personal contact part of a program is that what people want can be determined. The institution can then respond with the right information about the school. Instead of simply telling the student what is important, the school can also talk about what is important to the student and the student's influentials.

PROBLEMS.   Problems can effectively block all the best efforts to communicate with students. If the students think that a given college is too small, too expensive, or too far away, it will have trouble getting their attention to help them understand the ways the school may be attractive to them. A barrier goes up that makes it impossible for them to hear the good messages (see Figure 6.4).

The student comes to an interview or contact and brings along potential problems; these can be seen as barriers. There are several ways to move students from point A, where they are uninterested, to point B, where they are interested. One is to lower the barrier so far that the student faces no challenge at all. While this is possible for some items—cost, for example—it is not possible for others such as size, location, or type of school.

Even if it were possible, the question has to be asked whether it is really desirable. If a student can avoid a barrier because it is removed,

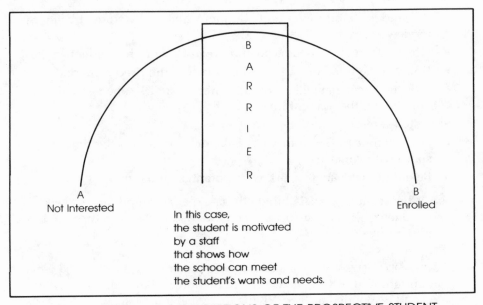

FIGURE 6.4. PROBLEMATIC PERCEPTIONS OF THE PROSPECTIVE STUDENT.

it becomes very easy for that student to move in the other direction as well. There is little real motivation to make a commitment. In this case, the student may leave the selected school for another option that comes closer to meeting wants and needs.

A better way to deal with barriers is to excite the potential student about the school to the point of evoking true interest in its programs and opportunities. This can be done if the institution works with the student's wants and needs. The school will be able to speak the words the student wants to hear, or it will be able to describe the school so the student can truly hear and feel the way the school may fit his or her needs.

MAKING AN IMPACT IN PERSONAL CONTACT

Knowing the theory is one thing, but applying it can be difficult; however, in this case, it can be easy if the enrollment people follow a certain process. This process will increase the quality of personal contacts substantially; the process, outlined in Figure 6.5, refers to the use of time in working with contacts. The essential elements of the model are rapport generation, questioning, summarizing, responding, asking for a decision, and planning the next contact.

CREATING RAPPORT.   There is no point in moving very far into the process of working with a student until rapport has been established. This can

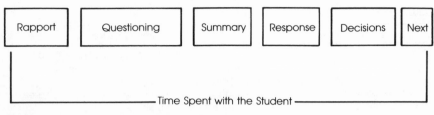

FIGURE 6.5. PERSONAL CONTACT PROCESS.*

*As can be noted in this diagram, most of the time used in the first contact is spent with questioning.

take more or less time depending on the personalities of content people and the student. If this is a student the school really wants to enroll, time should be spent at this stage to make certain the student is ready to work with the enrollment staff. A valued characteristic of a counselor is the ability to establish rapport quickly and to recognize when it is accomplished.

It is helpful for the staff to remember that they will have considerable time in the future to talk with the student. The staff controls this time and can make up for lost time later if they have created the needed rapport. This attitude is especially critical if students have been prioritized and the current student is one the school particularly wants to enroll.

QUESTIONS.   It should be noted that the greatest amount of time spent with the student is occupied with questioning. This certainly is true of the first contact—and every recontact. It is wise to make certain that the enrollment staff understand what they are dealing with, and this can only be done if time is spent asking. This may also be a place to return to periodically as more information is needed to do the job properly.

One skill that is important for enrollment staff is the ability to ask open-ended questions that get the student involved. These are questions that cannot be answered with a yes or no. Such questions are shown in Table 6.9 to be an inventive way of rephrasing ordinary, yes/no questions. During these initial contacts with a prospective student, it is important to be able to ask clarifying questions to be certain the issues involved are really understood.

Listening is also a skill that many claim they possess, but few are really able to do. The ability to listen at all levels actively and creatively is the only way enrollment staff can get the information needed to do the best possible enrollment job. This is also a critical skill to seek when hiring new people.

SUMMARIZING.   This is the point at which the enrollment people take the time to summarize what was heard and to test our impressions. It

TABLE 6.9. Question Matrix

Closed Question	Open Question
Are you interested in my college?	Can you share with me a couple of things that interested you about my college?
In response to a "no" in terms of having received materials:	
I will have some mailed to you.	Can you tell me a couple of things you are
Do you want to receive materials?	looking for in a college?
	What are some things that will be important about the school that you pick?
	What will you be looking for in a major?
In response to the statement, "I am looking for a small school":	
You start telling about your size.	Can you tell me what is important about size?
	Can you tell me a couple of other things that are important to you?
In response to a question about test scores or to the question, "Can I be admitted?":	
You tell them what the cutoffs are.	You indicate that you want to discuss this with
You ask them about their grades.	the student, but need to know more about him or her before proceeding.

is very easy in normal day-to-day activities to have misunderstandings. In work with students, it is even more likely. It is helpful to let the student know that the school is interested enough to try to be certain that the issues are heard properly and that responses are accurate.

If the student did not understand, the contact person can then go back. The student can always be seen in a high school, college night, college fair, or home visit, or the contact person may make a telephone call. But having accurate information is so critical as to make the process invalid if the summary step is omitted.

RESPONDING.   If the summary correctly captures the student's wants, needs, and problems, a response is in order. The response can be targeted precisely to the things that were discovered.

If the student wants a small school, for example, the interviewer knows what that means and can share the school in the student's terms. The school can be discussed on this point. The summary should contain mostly the information that is most important to the student.

In addition, the contact person will likely have information that must be communicated. These may be issues that deal with admissions requirements, costs, and special opportunities.

DECISIONS.   To determine what to do next is now the main agenda. A critical issue here is whether or not the student is motivated. This can be determined by asking the student to make a decision—a minor decision and not a major one.

Too often the staff will force students into major decisions before they are ready. It may take some time to determine if students will apply, deposit, or enroll. To ask these questions is to push too hard. Ask for these types of decisions if you think that these students are ready, but otherwise keep it on a minor level. If they are not ready, the school might lose them by moving too quickly. Ask for a minor decision such as:

- Can I contact you again? Or, would a call next week be good for you?
- Ask for the campus visit.
- Ask what a couple of things are that the student would like to know.

PRIORITIES.   Each of these types of questions will help determine if there is enough interest to warrant follow-up and what that follow-up should be. Because the school may be working with many students, the need to prioritize in terms of contacts can be critical.

Priorities can be developed regarding many issues, including geography, quality, programs, time of inquiry. Often the development of priorities may depend on the goals established for the enrollment program.

NEXT TIME.   One contact will rarely do the job. This is unrealistic today, unless the school is dealing with the student who would come to the school no matter what was done.

Follow-up contacts need to be carefully planned and carried out. The persistence shown will pay big dividends in the end for both the college and the potential student.

DEALING WITH TOO MANY COOKS.   Creating a communication strategy can be one of the most difficult processes in the whole enrollment area. It is here that everyone gets involved because they feel they have special talents to contribute:

- The president is an expert on copy.
- The president is an expert in public relations, and thinks this activity represents all there is to communication.
- Each faculty member is an expert on strategy.
- Everyone is an expert on design.
- One of the faculty members takes pictures as a hobby and feels fully qualified to do the photos.
- The president has final say on everything.

It is wise to agree beforehand on who has responsibility for what before starting the development of a communication strategy.

Behavior	General Strategy	First Draft Copy	Design Concept	Final Copy	Final Design	Mechanicals
To be kept informed						
Veto power						
To provide information						
To discuss						
To review						
To do the work						

FIGURE 6.6. THE RESPONSIBILITY MATRIX.

The responsibility matrix (Figure 6.6) may be helpful in developing agreements in terms of the tasks involved in developing the enrollment effort.

In general, only one person should have the veto power over the materials. In general, this should be the office that will need to use the publications, materials, or other items. Too often, this is given over to people who do not have to be accountable for the result of the program.

While many people may need to be informed or review material, it is generally wise to know who will be involved before starting the project. This will give the enrollment office a good idea of how long it may take for materials to be prepared and made available.

When seeking approval of materials, it is important that the school keep in mind who the person is that must finally approve the material— the student. The material to be used should be completely tested before final approval is given. Have a student panel review the copy and react to the design. Use pre-prepared questions and surveys to avoid the situation in which the student becomes analyzer rather than reactor. If the reactions of the students are negative to any part of the presentation, look at how this reaction can help improve the part in question. This can help make the material more effective and can help you in selling the material to the people who need to "buy into" your campus.

–7–
MANAGEMENT OF THE ENROLLMENT PROCESS

This section is devoted to the management of enrollment programs. Without adequate attention to the management area, the process of enrollment management will come, sooner or later, to a halt. In this area, the fundamentals must be done well before anything can happen in terms of strategy. Institutions are rapidly moving to the point where the institutional planning process must be largely enrollment driven. Thus, enrollment management is directly linked to the overall financial success of the institution. However, if the administration does not recognize this truth, the enrollment program may be blamed for falling enrollment, as in the following example:

> Sandra was the director of admissions at the University. She had been in the position for fifteen years and the last three had been miserable. The enrollment results had been going down from year to year, and in the last year, the enrollment had dropped 15 percent. Ten percent was due to a reduction in new students and 5 percent was due to an increase in attrition.
>
> Pressure from the faculty was intense. They had considered and implemented three new programs—one in business, one in computers, and one in music.
>
> The publications staff was not producing anything new, and Sandra had tried to get them to publicize the efforts of the faculty, but their agenda was set. They simply were not co-operating.
>
> In addition, the financial aid director had just resigned to take a better position at the regional office of the school association. There was no financial aid officer, and there were very few people to select from as fall approached.
>
> The president had become unavailable this year and was relaying the message that Sandra had better meet expectations. This was to be the last year of decreases in enrollment.
>
> Without a plan and with what looked like little cooperation, Sandra had her letter of resignation in hand as she left her office.
>
> Sandra had considerable talent to do her job. Unfortunately, the job had changed and she had been given little opportunity

119

to change with it. She would do her changing elsewhere. Sandra's problem related largely to her management ability and the lack of recognition by others that the enrollment issue requires institution-wide commitment.

While a great many management fundamentals should be mastered by the enrollment professional, this chapter will not rehash basic management theory. Instead, it will focus on those aspects of management and leadership that are critical to the conduct of a successful enrollment program. If management fundamentals are done well, attention to these issues will carry the program to success.

While some of this may be familiar, the application of these ideas to enrollment will be directed to the needs of managing the process. It is the *collection* of actions that is important as management impact on enrollment is examined. How the management area interacts with other areas of the matrix will also be discussed.

KEY AGENDAS

There are several key issues to consider in terms of managing enrollment efforts:

- *The scope of responsibilities.* The enrollment manager will need to deal with issues of retention and new students, a broader range of types of students, and key areas of the matrix including the product and the management of institutional climate.
- *The number of people involved in the management process.* As with many areas of management, there will be fewer middle managers. The use of data will allow the key manager to understand what is going on and to interact with office staff members directly.
- *A manager's use of time.* Less time will be used in detail work and more time in direct contact with people doing the job. The enrollment manager is carrying out his or her own process of relationship management to motivate a wide diversity of people to accomplish the institution's enrollment goals. This is particularly critical given the low salaries and low initial motivation of people beginning in the field.
- *Involvement of people in the enrollment process.* Success requires that a large number of people be involved in the process. This must be a diversity of people ranging from faculty to students. The need is to create commitment from the entire institutional community to work in the enrollment area.

- *Leadership versus management.* Enrollment management requires leadership—this means a person supplying the energy and direction to be certain that the right things get done. The leader will need to have a vision that drives enrollment results.
- *Ownership issues.* Each individual in the program needs to develop ownership and responsibility for the results. The results are not the property of one person.
- *The enrollment master plan and its creation and use.* The enrollment master plan needs to focus the energy of people on the job. It needs to be a process and tool that can be used to evaluate where people are and keep them focused on doing the right tasks at the right time. This is not the kind of plan that can sit on a shelf and gather dust.

SCOPE OF THE MANAGEMENT PROCESS

The management of the enrollment effort, to a large extent, is an issue of the scope of attention that is given by the manager. The manager is no longer concerned only about the admissions office, but also about management of all resources directed at enrollment programs. The enrollment manager needs to consider all aspects of the program from product to climate.

All of the signs seem to indicate that the management of today's enrollment programs needs to be examined in a critical way. Answers are needed in order to be certain that the best approach is being used to meet the enrollment goals of colleges and universities. Often the programs are *perceived* not to be managed, and in some cases, the programs literally are *not* managed. In too many schools today, the faculty and others at the school are not confident that the programs are being managed properly.

GOALS: FOCUSING ENERGY FOR ENROLLMENT

The goal of enrollment management is to focus the energies of the institution on meeting enrollment goals. Like a magnifying glass, which focuses energies of sunlight on an object and can set it on fire, so the management program should be able to focus energies and ignite the institution for meeting enrollment goals. This is the essential reason for the existence of the management part of the matrix. The tools to focus energy will vary, but it has become more and more apparent that schools that are able to focus the energy of the institution successfully on this area are those that do well.

RESOURCES

Generally, resources used in the management area are related to people—their characteristics and what is used to help them do well. These people can include the admissions staff at all levels and the many volunteers who work in the program. The volunteers can include alumni, faculty, present students, and others who may at times bring extra energy to the enrollment effort.

The people involved in the program need to be considered carefully from the perspective of attitudes and beliefs, knowledge, and skills. And the order in which these are listed is indicative of their order of importance in finding the right people for the enrollment program.

The hardest characteristics to develop in people, if these characteristics are not already there, are the right attitudes and beliefs. These have to come with the person—or it may not be worth the cost in energy and time to develop them. Negative attitudes and unrealistic beliefs can be disastrous:

> The staff members had just finished a set of interviews with the new director and it was clear that part of the problem was that most did not want to be in the work they were doing.
>
> John, a veteran counselor, was certain that he knew how to take care of everything that was a problem with the school. The faculty were not available, they did not know what they were teaching, and the student life was terrible. Yet John was now trying, for another year, to do the job of "selling the school." He just could not be credible anymore, and the students he worked with and their parents could sense this.
>
> Sally, on the other hand, never really wanted to be in admissions yet, with no training or background, was certain that she could do the job with very little effort or practice. She had turned into a nightmare for the director, who was afraid to lose her because he needed staff members.
>
> Tom, a graduate of the school, could say nothing good about the liberal arts. His experience with the arts and his view of them in making the student successful were very limited. He could not talk about the liberal arts with real excitement and felt, to some extent, that they were a waste of time.
>
> In general, the staff did not like the school, the director, the job, or in some cases, the people with whom they were working—students and parents.

If this sounds farfetched, it is not. Unfortunately, these kinds of situations do exist, and they are part of the fundamental problem for many schools trying to meet enrollment goals. In many cases, schools are dealing with attitudes that are difficult to change. The solution is to look initially for any or all of the following attitudes in the individuals interviewed for the enrollment job:

- Hard work is good. I am willing to work more than an eight-to-five job.
- Working with people, *really working with people,* is an important part of the enrollment process.
- It is acceptable to influence people in their enrollment decisions.
- The telephone is a productive enrollment tool.
- Learning should continue throughout life. I probably have a lot to learn about my work and I want to pursue that learning.
- I do not mind being evaluated.
- I like the type of school for which I am working.

The time to look at attitudes is when people are hired. Creating your list of desired attitudes and being certain, as far as the school can, that the person hired has them will be a very important first step to the development of a strong enrollment effort.

The same items can be reviewed for volunteers that work in a program. These individuals can have great influence on enrollment. They must, however, know what they are doing in order to meet expectations. Volunteers also must have the right attitude, and it is even more difficult to develop it in them than in the professional staff. The school must be certain that volunteers like the school, want to work with young people, and see their volunteer time as a major benefit to the student, themselves, and the school.

THE MANAGEMENT INFORMATION SYSTEM

Management information is a key resource for your program, and is used to make certain that the program is on target. The management information system (MIS) is built on the plan that the enrollment staff has prepared. It contains all elements that will allow the program manager, staff, and the other institutional managers to understand the probability of reaching the targeted enrollment goals.

Management information systems reports should be reviewed on a weekly, monthly, and semiyearly basis to construct strategies and actions that will keep the program on target. These will be covered in more detail in the section on content.

KNOWLEDGE AND SKILLS

Every profession has a body of knowledge and a set of skills that must be mastered by new professionals who wish to excel in their work. Physicians, lawyers, psychologists, businesspersons—all are educated in specialized fields. All undergo extensive training before beginning successful practice.

The same is true for admissions professionals, but with a significant difference. Few people enter college intending to prepare for a career in college admissions. Those rare students who aspire to jobs as admissions counselors quickly discover that no institutions offer undergraduate majors in college admissions. No prescribed curriculum is available to prepare students for careers in this area.

Consequently, admissions counselors are an unusually heterogeneous group. Some majored in history, English, art, or music, while others studied math, business, chemistry, or psychology. Nearly every field of study is represented by those working as admissions officers in colleges or universities. As a result, admissions counselors bring a unique mixture of knowledge and skills to their jobs.

It is the pluralistic nature of the admissions profession that requires new counselors to study the specialized body of knowledge and develop the particular skills that relate to college and university admissions. Unfortunately, this body of knowledge has not been organized or clearly articulated. Frequently, the necessary knowledge and skills have been open to interpretation. New admissions counselors have been free to apply their individual perspectives, based on their respective educational and vocational backgrounds, to their work.

Yet, regardless of educational background, every admissions professional must have some basic abilities. The areas of knowledge that are needed by an effective admissions counselor include the following:

- Self-knowledge.
- Knowledge of the institution.
- Knowledge of the market in general and of an assigned territory in particular.
- Knowledge of the prospective students.
- Knowledge of procedures used in the admissions and financial aid offices.
- Knowledge of the competition. (Against which schools is the institution competing? How does each institution market itself to students?)

The following skills are needed as well:

- Planning.
- Questioning.

- Listening.
- Problem-solving.
- Matching benefits to needs.
- Time management.

SUPPORTING THE STAFF

Giving support and recognition to people who are doing the enrollment job is very critical. These are individuals whose efforts are constantly scrutinized and evaluated. It is pretty clear when the job has not been done. Some days are bad, and some are good, but to keep the best people performing well, the school needs to look carefully at how the staff are supported.

To help these people do well, several items must be in place, including the enrollment master plan, the management information system, and the talent development program. These are essential ingredients for focusing the energy of the people in the program on results.

In addition, the time that everyone spends with the enrollment effort must be acknowledged. Notes, letters, lunches, telephone calls—all can be used to acknowledge the importance of these people and keep the energy flowing.

THE TALENT DEVELOPMENT PROGRAM

The final ingredient, in terms of human resources, is the talent development program. This is the program that helps develop the skills and knowledge of staff members. This is essential because of the complexity of the work and the lack of serious background of many who are intimately involved in the program.

People going into admissions work generally have not been prepared for this specific job. This was fine as long as the job was relatively unsophisticated. However, now the enrollment professional is required to have a wide array of skills, from research to counseling to preparing effective design and copy. These skills are not luxuries; they are essential to effectively impacting the enrollment effort.

In order for the enrollment program to have ultimate success, there must be a master plan. The plan is likely the single most important element in developing enrollment results. The plan itself is important, but the process of creating the plan and the way the plan is organized is critical to getting the commitment, involvement, and ownership to provide for a successful enrollment program. This is a way to maximize the development of talent as the program unfolds.

CONTENT ISSUES

Just as there are right and wrong ways to deal with communication and data issues, there are varying ways to deal with the management of enrollment programs. In this section, the content of management issues is discussed and related to successful enrollment efforts. Consideration of content issues is particularly important to enrollment because so many involved in the profession were not really trained as managers when entering the field.

There is a great deal of potential that only needs to be informed as to the possibilities. Schools can benefit highly from careful attention to the ways in which management might best be done. The key issue is how resources can be directed to the achievement of enrollment goals.

One of the best ways to develop people's abilities is to share the possibilities for doing the job well and allow them to apply their best to their particular job and situation. Here, we will share the possibilities and their direct application to the management of enrollment. The reader can apply this in the most appropriate way possible to the problems on a particular campus.

Four primary areas will be addressed in regard to this issue:

1. Leadership and its importance in the enrollment area.
2. Using data and information in the development of enrollment efforts.
3. Preparing the enrollment master plan.
4. Developing the talent of staff members.

LEADERSHIP

It is in the areas of leadership and its influence that the biggest changes have occurred in enrollment management. The position of director of admissions is largely in the process of being replaced with titles such as vice president for enrollment management, director of enrollment management, and dean of enrollment services. The enrollment office is clearly one that represents the disappearance of certain types of positions and changes in demands on the individual who is chiefly responsible for meeting enrollment goals.

In fact, the proper subject for discussion might be enrollment leadership rather than management. The issue of management in the admissions office may be the wrong one to address. Without enrollment leadership, there is likely to be no progress in a program—even with the best traditional management ideas.

Enrollment influence is also another key point. Leadership and influence are obviously related. If one is able to lead, one must be influencing people. It is worthwhile, however, to view leadership and influence separately.

Many faculty and administration members at schools are very aware that changes will come to their organization. They are also very concerned about the rate of change and its effects. This can lead to paralysis and inaction on key issues that impact enrollment. To move beyond this, the faculty and administration may need to be influenced in directions they already are leaning toward—like a tree that has been partially cut and only needs a slight shove to fall. In the following example the impasse is unusually severe:

> Terri was running a fine enrollment program but for the last three years the results had been diminishing. This year the president wanted to turn things around and had been clear that there would be changes if it did not happen.
>
> Frustration was rampant for Terri as she tried to deal with the situation. She had been to conferences, heard speakers, read books, talked with her peers, and knew that new strategies would be needed.
>
> More letters would have to go out—more time would be needed on the road—telephone calls would have to be made—her staff's knowledge of the school would have to increase—and all of this at salaries that were lower than her peers'.
>
> Terri also knew that the business program at her school was populated by a faculty that everyone thought was in need of rejuvenation. Student evaluations had constantly rated the department at a low level and the word of mouth in the field was now poor. Thus, a continuing decline in business majors.
>
> With all of her knowledge and the demands of the president, she still was not planning or willing to change significantly. Her attitude was to stick it out as long as possible and then move on. It was not worth the effort.

Terri's situation is not unusual. The expectations of her were clear, but there was very little support for her from the president or the academic dean. The salaries were to remain low, the faculty in business would remain, and the president was unlikely to be available for the next three months as he devoted himself to the "important" task—fund raising.

Terri will not influence anyone because she does not have the experience or the support to take the kinds of risks that come with the turf. The essential failure is that she is not able to provide a sense of the issues for the people on the campus, and she will not be able to start the ball rolling to accomplish the tasks at hand. As a result, no one wants to make an investment in the enrollment situation.

Susan's situation is a similar one:

> Granite College had had a few bad years and it felt very much as if Susan, too, had reached the end of the road. She had been trying, for three years, to develop a better program and to in-

fluence the faculty to think about dealing with the adult learner. Susan had completed her doctorate in communication this year and was hoping that this would be the year she could turn things around.

There were problems, however, in that her staff turnover was very high and the school was not able to provide the resources she needed to do more than a superficial job of communicating.

The success of an enrollment program depends, to a large extent, on having a leader who can motivate and energize the institution in thinking about enrollment issues. But it is not enough to get people thinking—there needs to be action, sometimes on a broad scale. This means that the leader also must be able to influence people at the school, often the top management.

This is one of the key differences between the traditional director of admissions and the individual who is considered an enrollment manager. Leadership means being able to develop the energy of all so that they will set goals, develop strategies, and take the actions that are critical to enrollment success.

The enrollment leader must be able to lead and influence a wide diversity of people, many of whom have not been led and do not want to be led. The enrollment leader must be able to mobilize the college or university community to meet enrollment goals.

Good leadership strategies encompass recognition, support, goals, strategies, time, energy, and knowledge. The enrollment leader must be able to move people forward who deal with traditional, nontraditional, and graduate students.

USING DATA AND INFORMATION

What should be the content of the management information system? The system should consist of the following elements:

- The weekly report of results (Figure 7.1). This shows the status of the inquiries, applicants, confirms, campus visits, and other important information that enrollment managers need to have at their fingertips each week.

- The admissions counselors' weekly report (Figure 7.2). This tells how close the staff is coming to the contact goals and general activities designed into the program. This report contains such items as telephone calls, school visits, people seen, and general contacts.

- The inquiry report (Figure 7.3). This will tell how many inquiries are coming in and their distribution. Because having sufficient inquiries is basic to running a good program, this is critical data to have available.

From _____   Weekly report # _____ Ending _____
                    Director of Admissions

Activities	Week	Cum	Letters	Week	Cum
Inquiries received:			Pre-application:		
1. Phone			1. Mass mailer		
2. Mail			Group		
3. Walk-in			2. Information		
Total			3. Prospectus		
			4. Career		
Phone calls:			5. People		
			6. Financial aid		
4. 1st follow-up			7. Environment		
5. Other			Total		
Total					
			Post-application:		
Applications received:					
			8. Acknowledgement		
6. Next term			9. Status		
7. Following term			10. Interview confirm		
8. Other terms			11. Other		
Total			Total		
Counseling:			Post-interview:		
9. By phone			12. Accept—next term		
10. In person			13. Accept—following term		
Total			14. Accept—other terms		
			15. Rejection		
Interviews:			16. Tuition receipt		
			17. Succeed		
11. On-campus			18. People 2		
12. Off-campus			19. Orientation		
Total			20. Other		
			Total		
Campus tours			Grand Total		

A. Anything unusual in last week's activities?   No _____ Yes _____ If yes, please explain.

_____

_____

_____

B. Are we on top of things?   Yes _____ No _____ If no, please explain. _____

_____

_____

C. What is the most urgent to concentrate on? _____

_____

_____

FIGURE 7.1. EXAMPLE OF AN ADMISSIONS OFFICE REPORT.

- The word processing report (Figure 7.4), which tells how many letters and pieces of correspondence have gone out to students and influentials. This allows monitoring of communication flow systems.
- The goals and metastrategies that serve as part of the management information system. Looking at the actions that have been established will help to pinpoint where the potential problems in the program may be.

Name _____ Week of _____ To _____

Date	Time	Visits	Inquiry	No. Seen V	Prev-ious SR	New SR	TR	Other	Total Seen		Prev	PC-1	CVP	ACP	Other	PCS
						Inquiries						Phone activity				Total	
						New			Total							Daily	
SUN.										Student						
MON.										Student						
										Other Activities:						
TUES.										Student						
										Other Activities:						
WED.										Student						
										Other Activities:						
THUR.										Student						
										Other Activities:						
FRI.										Student						
										Other Activities						
SAT.										Student						
	Student assistant calls															
	Weekly totals															
	Cumulative totals															

FIGURE 7.2. EXAMPLE OF AN ADMISSIONS COUNSELOR WEEKLY REPORT.

- The midyear evaluation should be a summary report that will show how the program is going overall (Appendix). This report is developed in December prior to refining strategies for the rest of the year, and in April when the enrollment office is deciding what will be done in the next year.

	Seniors	Juniors	Other	Totals		
				TW	LW	TL
Date						
Miscellaneous						
Search						
Letter						
School Visit						
Application						
Walk-in						
Visit Day						
Bus. Poster						
B.S. Poster						
Test Scores						
Fine Arts Poster						
Ed. Poster						
N.S. Poster						
Gen. Poster						
F.A. Poster						
F.A.F.						
Daily Totals						

	Freshmen		Readmits		Transfers		Specials	
Applications	SI	FA	JI	RA	TI	TA	OI	SA
Weekly Totals	SI	FA	JI	RA	TI	TA	OI	SA
Com. Totals	SI	FA	JI	RA	TI	TA	OI	SA

FIGURE 7.3. EXAMPLE OF AN INQUIRY REPORT.

Flow	Week 1	Week 2	Week 3	Week 4
Inquiry Flow:				
Letter #1				
Letter #2				
Letter #3				
Letter #4				
Letter #5				
Application Flow:				
Letter #1				
Letter #2				
Letter #3				
Letter #4				
Letter #5				
Enroll Flow:				
Letter #1				
Letter #2				
Letter #3				
Letter #4				
Other Flow:				
Letter #1				
Letter #2				
Letter #3				
Letter #4				

FIGURE 7.4. WORD PROCESSING REPORT.*

*These are letters that are to be run in various enrollment systems. This report is completed each week as letters are produced and compared with expected flow.

This combination of data should help keep a program on target if it is evaluated on a regular basis. This will be especially helpful if graphs are used to keep track of key data. For example, it might be important to graph inquiries, applications, campus visits, and confirms on a weekly basis in order to avoid last-minute pressures. Take the following case:

Jeff was examining the inquiry data and it did not look positive. He was comparing the actual accumulation of inquiries for this year with the goals, and the lines were far apart.

The problem was that the inquiries would be very hard to generate in another month or two, and he needed to move now if he was to make up the difference.

Armed with the graphs and other data, Jeff went to the president and developed a plan to send a second inquiry mailing to all students on the list to try to gain some ground on the problem. Convinced by the data, the president gave the okay for a four-color piece and he also gave approval to the extra funding required in order to produce it quickly.

Jeff knew if he could just generate a few more inquiries, he could make up some of the problem in better conversions of inquiries to applications, but he was not likely to make up the whole difference without doing something special.

In this example, the management information database allowed the director to help others understand the need for action and get staff and management support for a special effort. The effort was ultimately successful and led to the enrollment the school needed in the fall.

Regular review of the database can help all staff members do a better job with the program and develop strategies that will address the gaps when they are found. In Table 7.1, particular types of data are indicated and related to the times at which particular reviews should occur. Following this type of approach—if done with the right attitude—can also increase ownership in the enrollment results.

MASTER ENROLLMENT PLANS: THREEFOLD PLANNING

The process of enrollment management is special because it requires so much from so many people at the institution. Activities to improve enrollment can occur in many and diversified areas, from the product to the institution's climate. Note that this process does not exclude such areas as publications. The enrollment management matrix approach simply includes many more aspects of the institution and their interrelationships in regard to enrollment issues. For these reasons and to stimulate involvement and commitment, the plan and the process of creating it are central to the success of the institution.

Given this fact, why do so many institutions have plans that are dust-covered and sitting on the shelf, out of reach physically and over-

TABLE 7.1. Management Information System Matrix

Type of Data	Weekly	Monthly	Semiyearly
Program data	YES		YES
Contact data	YES		
Metastrategies		YES	
Talent development		YES	
Inquiries	YES		
Goals		YES	
Letters	YES		

looked in the planning process? Some institutions lack a plan altogether, as in the following case:

> Diane had been running the enrollment program for several years and was beginning to face extreme pressures to accomplish one of the main desires of the president—to enroll twelve hundred new freshmen.
>
> They had not come close in the last three years but the president's desire had now become an obsession. He demanded it, and this year Diane knew that she had better come through.
>
> When asking how Diane was going to accomplish the goal, the president had gotten no answers and did not care. He only expected her to perform.
>
> Diane was now trying to explain to the consultants how she was going to do this, and she was not doing a very good job at it. In fact, she was getting very defensive. The staff was not aware of the situation and they did not answer any of the questions posed to them with any clarity. They did what they were told when they were told to do it. No more, no less.
>
> Diane was now almost hostile and finally said she knew what she was going to do. It was all in her head and she did not have time to write it on paper.

An isolated example? Not really. There are reasons why this kind of phenomenon exists and there are ways to approach enrollment management that will be as productive as possible. That approach must involve everyone in the planning process and must produce a plan that is used by a number of people.

DIFFICULTIES IN PLANNING. The following are a few reasons why there are problems as institutions try to plan for enrollment management:

- *Size.* The size of the task is immense. This can be true of almost any planning venture, but it is especially true for enrollment planning for even the smallest institution.

  Have you ever noticed how long it can take people to create a personal plan of action in their lives? The time to do it and the perceived benefits often do not match. The attitude of "why take the time to plan when we could be spending the time actually doing it" is often voiced. This is reinforced even further as the staff feels the pressure for results and the need to get into action. The number of items, issues, and people that must be dealt with in the enrollment plan often offers an even stronger excuse for not doing enrollment planning. It's just too big a job.

- *Complexity.* The complexity of the plan can also cause one to avoid the whole issue. There are a large number of factors and relationships involved in developing an effective plan. This can include resources, people, timing, inside and outside events, product impacts, and data needs. Sometimes it may seem as if the list could go on forever, and it often does. Just when one piece is in place, another needs to be added, subtracted, or modified.

There is usually a tendency to want to keep things as simple as possible. This can be a problem if all of the items mentioned previously are included plus the time factors that are often critical to the overall success of a project.

- *The need to be used.* These are plans that need to be applied. The plans must focus the energies of people on the enrollment programs.

  The size and complexity make it imperative that everyone who is involved in the planning process and its resulting actions does what the plan said should be done. If the plan gathers dust, many people are going to have problems. This means that everyone who needs to be involved gets involved at the right time, in the right place, and with the right attitudes about the process.

- *The need for flexibility.* There is a need in enrollment management to be able to change what is being done if the desired results are not happening. The plan must be such that it is easy to understand and not so hard to put together that it could not be changed if the situation has arisen. Flexibility will allow the people involved to do the right things now and in the future when the program may look very different.

All of these factors need to be taken into account in any planning process used in the enrollment area. To create an enrollment plan that will motivate, be flexible, and be used, a three-step planning process is recommended.

This type of planning process breaks down the creation of the plan into manageable "chunks" that can be undertaken individually. The end product will focus people and their energies on the total enrollment effort.

To make the planning process for enrollment management effective, the process of creating the plan can be divided into three steps. The *first step* is the setting of enrollment goals in total: this entails not only numbers but the many other characteristics that go into effective planning.

The *second step* is to develop the enrollment metastrategies. These are the overall strategies that are so important to the enrollment program that it would be difficult to direct the program without them. The *third step* is developing the activities that will ensure that the enrollment strategies are realized. In this case, the strategies cannot be set before the goals are known; likewise, the actions cannot occur until there has been an agreement on strategies.

An advantage of this approach is that the participants do not get involved in decisions that might block the process of managing enrollments until they are well beyond the goals and strategies. This means, for example, that the institution will consider trying things that may not have been considered if the focus were put initially on actions—actions they perceive are not affordable, approaches that they had tried before, actions that involve too many people, or actions that the school does not know how to accomplish.

STEP 1: SETTING ENROLLMENT GOALS.   Establishing number goals is difficult for many enrollment managers—and, therefore, often neglected. If the numbers are available, they frequently do not reflect the true budget numbers that are needed for the school to be really successful. It would be a shame to meet enrollment goals and still not be able to survive as a college!

The numbers are also often focused on one type of student—the new freshman. They often do not reflect the diversity of ways in which enrollment can be controlled, such as through nontraditional students and retention of current students and the enrollment of part-time students. The bottom line always seems to be the new freshmen. This is the way the faculty—and the media—evaluate the success of enrollment.

This needs to change. There needs to be a variety of goals for which strategies are developed. Energies must be focused on a diversity of issues including numbers that will really pay the bills and allow the school to do what is needed in such key areas as salaries and other resources.

Table 7.2 represents a goal chart for a school in the Midwest. It shows expectations for traditional and nontraditional students. The same approach also could include part-time, graduate, or professional students. These numbers will be needed for this school to reach financial goals for the year. Note that these goals could be set for any term of entry, not just the fall. It is important to point out that these types of goals will, in the future, reflect larger concern with part-time students.

TABLE 7.2. Example of Chart Showing Enrollment Goals

Status	Traditional		Nontraditional	
	New	Continuing	New	Continuing
Freshmen	500		120	
Sophomores	34	400	30	75
Juniors	120	320	67	56
Seniors	15	300	75	67
Graduate	0	0	0	0
Total	669	1,020	292	198
Total Traditional	1,689			
Grand Total	2,179			

By focusing on the total array of ways enrollment goals can be satisfied, the school is less vulnerable to sudden or long-term changes in the marketplace. It is rarely the case, however, that the numbers are the only criteria on which we should be focusing our energy. There can and should be a number of other considerations. These can include attribute or characteristic goals. The quality of the students is probably a consideration. The "A" student may have to be treated very differently from the "C" student in terms of wants and needs. On whom should these be focused? In addition, there are other issues such as age, geographic distribution, sex, and race. Any of these can and should be included in the goals statement. Type of student may be important at some schools, as in this case:

> The president and the faculty were very interested in finding students who were especially creative. They wanted students who could benefit most from a faculty who felt innovative and upbeat in terms of their disciplines and expectations.
>
> This proved to be particularly important to the theatre and communication departments. The theatre faculty wanted students who were willing to take many risks in a program that focused on both classical and street theatre—a challenge, to say the least.
>
> In addition, this faculty did not want any more baseball players. They had a preconceived notion that the baseball players were more rowdy than other students and were not as good in the classroom, a perception that was later proved wrong by the baseball coach.

These aspects of the goal statements need to be taken into consideration as the final picture is painted. This picture can be compared to the city at the end of a trip. The traveler will know that he or she has arrived at the right place when the people on campus are actually seen.

The focusing of energies is important here because the staff may, for example, have to treat new juniors differently from returning sophomores in terms of product, communication, and climate issues. The research used to define these goals also may be very different.

One more look at this frame of reference is necessary in order to view how enrollment problems may impact goal-setting. Figure 7.5 represents how the frame of reference has changed over the last few years and what could be the latest step in terms of framing goal-setting for enrollment.

Initially, enrollment management followed Model A, which was a model that focused mostly on full-time students without much effort given to returning students. This eventually evolved into Model B, wherein some attention was given to returning students while marketing efforts still continued for the new, full-time student.

This evolved to Model C, in which traditional students were worked

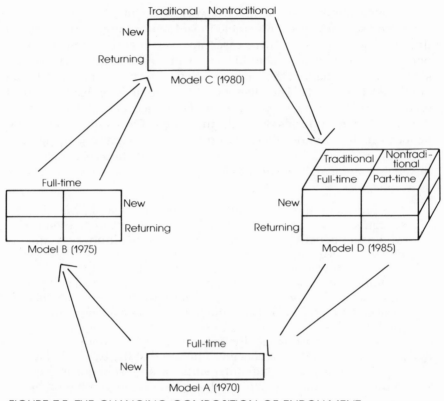

FIGURE 7.5. THE CHANGING COMPOSITION OF ENROLLMENT.

with extensively and nontraditional students received attention as well, with minimal efforts put into retention. This is now evolving to a new model, which is being seen in many colleges and universities today. Model D is an effort to represent the fact that schools are now working with full-time and part-time students, new and returning, traditional and nontraditional, trying to maximize enrollment in all four corners of this grid.

Model D represents a different set of management problems and issues. It means that goals, resources needed, content issues, and process issues are quite different. There will be different management and climate problems in using this model and different types of attitudes and beliefs to be considered. In this model, for example, we must be concerned about climate and attitude and belief issues as they relate not only to full-time students, but also to part-time students. This particular model may be put in the context of the previous goal-setting exercise.

STEP 2: ENROLLMENT METASTRATEGIES.   "John, what are the things that you need to do to conduct an effective program this year?" This is a standard introductory question used in the evaluation of an enrollment program. It can bring a very defensive answer or, at best, a very limited answer from the director of admissions and the enrollment office staff. In John's case, the answer was weak: "We need to visit the high schools, do a great deal of interview work here on campus, and try to keep up with the folders."

In John's program, there were not that many student folders to deal with, but the staff's attention was focused on the idea of leaving enough time to spend with each application folder. They felt that this would assure that prospective students were getting as much personal attention as possible. There were a good many things that were not occurring in the enrollment program that should have been happening. In addition, John did not have sufficient budget to deal with meeting enrollment goals.

This situation is not all that unusual. Admissions offices often are not able to elucidate the general strategies that should guide their thinking over the year. The program and the people in it flounder in terms of knowing what to do to succeed. The answer one would like to hear is a set of simple yet complete statements of the array of strategies needed to ensure that the enrollment goals will be met. These could be used for all individuals in the program to decide what they needed to do to be successful for the school; however, it is really the *role of the director to be able to identify the basic strategies that are important in the meeting of enrollment goals.*

Following are some important points about metastrategies:

- They are general. They relate to overall actions that are needed to accomplish enrollment goals.
- They are short and simple and can be related easily to enrollment goals.
- They are limited in number, usually no more than fifteen for a program annually.
- They are developed after the goals are set.
- They can be used as guides in keeping the enrollment program on target as part of the management information system.
- They lead to a set of actions that are obvious in terms of the enrollment metastrategy. (There may be content issues that are not so obvious, but this issue will be addressed in a later section.)
- When reviewed, they should result in a feeling that enrollment goals will be met.
- They include strategies that relate to the product of the institution.

- They include strategies that relate to the climate of the institution.
- When developed, they do not ask for actions and thus are designed to avoid the objection: "Yes, but we did that before; it just will not work."

This last issue is a key ingredient in this approach to enrollment planning. It is very difficult to do enrollment planning when almost every idea or concept is followed by the objection that it will not work. This drains energy from the most creative people and takes energy out of the process itself.

The use of the metastrategy approach can help identify the things that must be done, the actions that will make a program succeed. These are the items that you know are essential. You will not discard them before they are communicated to people, and others recognize the consequences of decisions not to follow them.

The following is a sample set of metastrategies:

1. To have 7,000 inquiries per year distributed to support the total enrollment goal and the desired geographic distribution.
2. To have adequate communication programs to convert generally interested potentials to inquiries, referrals to inquiries, inquiries to applicants (11.2%), applicants to confirms (45%), and confirms to enrolls (95%).
3. To have adequate professional and clerical staff to support the communications and office functions.
4. To have adequate computer hardware and software to support the communication and data functions of the office.
5. To develop and maintain a volunteer network to strengthen awareness and increase interest in the institution.
6. To develop and maintain a promotional strategy including publications and media materials to support the communication goal.
7. To develop and maintain a financial aid program sufficient to support enrollment goals. To communicate this program to potential students.
8. To develop and maintain an on-campus contact program that will support the enrollment and communication goals.
9. To design and implement a territorial management program for professional staff (closely related to goal 5).
10. To develop and maintain a management information system.
11. To develop and maintain office systems adequate to support enrollment goals.
12. To train and develop staff—professional, clerical, and volunteer.
13. To maintain the information base to support communications and general enrollment decisions.

MANAGEMENT OF THE ENROLLMENT PROCESS

14. To have an adequate budget to meet the enrollment goals of the institution.

15. To develop and maintain a process to keep the college community informed of and involved in enrollment activities.

Specific product or climate strategies might include these goals:

1. To enhance the advising program with the introduction of peer advisors.

2. To develop 20 percent more internship opportunities in majors outside of business.

3. To examine decision-making processes at the top level.

4. To conduct six miniworkshops to increase commitment to enrollment management.

The institution's *enrollment task force* (see Chapter 9, which is a discussion of this point) should develop the metastrategies after approving the goal statements. To have the best possible enrollment effort, strategies should be included for the areas of product, data, communication, management, and climate. The need to integrate several key areas is one of the main reasons for developing the task force.

Usually, there is the need for strategy development in several areas of the institution, and the matrix focuses attention on the issue of integration. The use of the task force focuses attention on the interaction of people who can develop a good plan that will impact enrollment from several directions. Because of the complexity, the metastrategies may need to be put together over the course of several meetings.

The strategies, along with the enrollment goals of the organization, should be sent to members of the institution so that they may review them and provide feedback to the task force. The material that is sent to the institutional community should be accompanied by a memo describing the purpose of the mailing, what is expected, and the time frames within which a response should be made. Once the feedback is received, revisions will need to be made. It may be possible that you will have to revise the goals of the program or the metastrategies after the information has been circulated.

It was clear in John's case that once the metastrategies had been developed, the president and the business officer were having some problems. They said, "We cannot afford this many publications. You can get along without the career brochure and the alumni piece. The parents brochure and financial aid are okay, but the others are really not possible, so let's not do them.

"You also will have to go easy on the telephone work because the telephone budgets for all offices will be held at last year's levels."

These were the comments of the president as she reviewed

the proposal that had been put before her for the year's work. She was cutting back and would have to take the responsibility for the program results if the goals were to remain unchanged.

After meeting with the president, John assembled the task force and shared the information with them. Upon doing this, they all had to review the goals that had been set because they were clearly going to be difficult to meet given the reduction discussion with the president. In fact, the committee had to respond by saying that the goals were now not feasible and would need to be revised downward by about 12 percent. With the strategies that were now in place, it would be impossible to support the original program goal.

While not pleased with this action, the president and the business manager now had the options clearly before them in terms of their enrollment future.

In this particular scenario, understanding has been developed about the reasons for particular actions. The "trade-offs" required may be better understood as well as the impact of decisions.

STEP 3: ENROLLMENT ACTION PLANS.   Once the metastrategies are in place, the next step can be undertaken. This generally should be under the direction of the enrollment task force but may require more resources than can be found in the committee. If the strategies call for actions that are the responsibility of one office (such as financial aid, career services, communications, or alumni), the appropriate offices will need to play a role in development of the action plan.

They should *expect* to do this because strategies have been communicated to them and they have had a chance to review them. In fact, they probably will have let you know already that they expect to be involved in the development of actions to impact strategy.

There were a number of problems in the computer area at Granite College. The computer people were perceived as not very responsive to most offices and their participation in the development of an enhanced financial aid program for the school had been abysmal. Now they were to play a key role in the development of a new enrollment strategy. Few people expected them to come through, but they now were ready to address the problem.

Sandy and Mark from computer services had gotten the message that this was important some weeks ago when they had seen the metastrategies from the enrollment task force. The whole group expected the computer staff to play a key role in improved results, and Sandy and Mark had no choice but to respond.

Now they were getting ready to meet with the committee to explain their side of the reasons why the computer area had been a problem. There were two sides to the story and now theirs was going to be heard.

The use of the task force and the metastrategies has the potential to bring people together on issues and makes it possible to find new solutions to old, long-standing issues. This process will help to define the actions that need to be taken in ways that will be more likely to get the job done (see page 147 for a discussion of development of action plans).

TALENT DEVELOPMENT

The content of the talent development program is an essential ingredient of the enrollment management effort. In the content of this important area, concern should be focused on both the way in which talent is nurtured and the specific areas on which the talent effort is focused. One of the most critical requirements is that the enrollment manager take seriously the role of the development of people. The manager needs to have the attitude that staff members can always grow in their field and that professional growth is a requirement for a successful program.

KEY AREAS OF CONCERN.   There are a good many areas that deserve attention in the development of the professional staff, but initially the individual should be hired for the enrollment program because he or she possessed some specific characteristics that are important to the job. In interviewing people, it is important that one of the first characteristics to be sought is the ability to produce rapport (see the discussion in Chapter 6 of the importance of rapport) and the right attitudes about the job and type of school for which they would be working.

There are many things that can be reviewed in selecting admissions people, including professional experience, the number and type of academic degrees, and the specific courses they have taken. The list can get very long and often the school will focus on only these items. The faculty or others will insist that certain quality factors be present. The fact is, the most important factors in producing enrollment success will likely be the ability of the person hired to produce immediate rapport with the student and influentials and that person's enthusiasm about the job and the school. It is this enthusiasm that excites and interests the prospective student.

In addition, if the admissions person is able to develop trust on the part of the student and influentials, the ability to work with that individual to understand wants, needs, and problems will increase. This gives the college a better chance of matching the institution to the student.

A person who can develop this level of trust and excitement about a school will be a great resource; identifying this personal characteristic is more difficult to do only if a "credentials checklist" approach to hiring is used. In this case, understanding can be developed of the specific ways in which the institution matches the expectations of the student. The representative also can deal effectively with problems and address the barriers that might prevent the student from even listening about the college.

Once the admissions person is in place with the ability to develop trust and excitement, the proper skills and knowledge need to be nurtured. A specific plan for each person should be developed that builds on an analysis of the strengths and weaknesses that may be present. This plan should include potential changes in the areas of knowledge, skills, and attitudes.

KEY FACTORS IN BUILDING INDIVIDUAL TALENT DEVELOPMENT PROGRAMS.   To simplify the understanding of the talent development area, one can divide it into three parts: skills, knowledge, and attitudes. Of these, skill and attitudes are likely to be the most difficult to deal with. In this perspective, attitudes can be most important in maintaining or improving an enrollment program.

Developing talent can be a way to gain a strategic edge over competitors. This is especially true in the areas of meeting student expectations and in terms of basic issues of relationship management. While the focus of the effort may be in the enrollment office, the talent development effort should involve everyone and every part of the organization. While it obviously cannot hit everyone, it should deal with the more key success areas of the institution. For that reason, this section will briefly discuss the areas of the registrar's office, the faculty, and enrollment office—one area because it is so often mentioned as a probem area (registrar), one area because it has an opportunity for great influence and contact (faculty), and one area because it is the first contact (the enrollment office).

First, the registrar's office, in most institutions, can play a key role in the retention of students. The challenges for this office may, indeed, be less in their technical capacity to handle records than in their ability to manage their relationships with people and be of service. But to accomplish this, the rapport among the office staff must be better than it is in the case below:

> The registrar was describing the fact that he had just conducted a training program for the office. They had discussed answering the telephone, being polite to students, ways that students might generally view the office, and several other issues that had appeared as problems over the last year.
>
> The registrar also said that the sessions had done very little to help the situation. There had been no change. When asked

if the office people had requested the program, he said no. When asked if they had role-played, he said no.

In fact, the talent development program had violated two main principles:

- Do not give people something they do not want.
- Always do some sort of activity that will cause people to *experience* the situation.

Role-playing in the office would have given the staff more of an idea about what behaviors are critical to success in relationship management. This would have been especially true if they recognized that there was a problem and had requested help.

Second, the faculty must be skilled at interacting with students. If they are not, then a training program needs to be initiated, as in the case below:

> The research at Plumpton College had indicated that the advising program was not working for the students. According to a survey, they were not getting enough time from faculty, and the advising was of the wrong type. The faculty were generally advising in terms of what courses to take, avoid, or put off—if they were advising at all. On the other hand, the students wanted help developing goals and finding ways to meet them.
>
> The chairman of the faculty senate had met with the dean of the college about the issue at the dean's request. The issue, according to the faculty chair, was not that the faculty did not want to advise. The faculty had met on the subject and concluded they were not rewarded for advising, so that caused the function to be given a lower priority. They also indicated they did not know how to advise. They wanted training if they were to do the job well. Rewards would not be enough if the training were not done.

In this case, while the faculty clearly did not want to be counselors, they did need to have some of the skills. They needed to understand how to help students set goals, develop actions, and evaluate progress. The faculty needed to be facilitators, not directors. This college solved its problem: a series of workshops followed by work sessions on these goals did the job.

Third, in the enrollment office, the talent development program becomes critical. The development of skills, knowledge, and attitude becomes critical. Development of knowledge in the areas of the market, the student, and the school, and of key attitudes in regard to work and type of work, are all critical. People rarely join the office of admissions with a realistic idea of what they will need to do. The office often needs to develop personnel in many directions.

TABLE 7.3. Overview of a Professional Staff Development Program

Topic	Knowledge	Skills	Attitudes	Concepts	Resources
				The following are concepts to be presented and used in the workshop.	The following are resources that can be consulted for further development of topics.
Enrollment Management	To understand the area of enrollment management and the counselors' role in this type of approach. These areas all require the same basic types of skills, knowledge, and attitudes. These will be summarized below:		Being able to deal with the limited role of the counselor in this type of approach.	General communication model. Product issues: • System concept • Levels	Data
Interviewing Telephone Presenting Working with influentials Using groups Follow-up Planning Stress management	Student School: • Faculty • Services • Programs • Financial aid • Environment • Process Market Self Stress management	Questioning Listening Integrating Planning Self management Stress management	Service Patience Persistence Winning attitudes Like school Like job Hard work is good	Service Four-box model Neurolinguistics Time use The warrior mentality Selling styles Buying readiness Sale Learn Advocating Follow-up Action research Winning attitudes Planning strategy: • Goals • Strategies • Actions Tai Chi Breathing movement	Data: National Database *The Marketing Imagination* Levitt, Free Press, 1984 *Situational Selling* Hersey, Center For Leadership Studies, 1985 *Fighting To Win* David Rogers, Doubleday, 1984 *Influencing With Integrity* Genie Z. Laborde, Syntony Press, 1984 Training Manual, The Ingersoll Group, 1983 *Psychology Of Winning* Dennis Waitley *The Tao Of Tai Chi Chuan* Tsung Hua Jou, Charles Tuttle, 1980

Table 7.3 represents an overview of a professional staff development program for an enrollment effort.

ATTITUDES.   To many people who are involved in schools, attitudes seem to be one of the key talent areas, and yet one of the least recognized and hardest to change. Some key attitudes that seem to often get in the way are those of flexibility, openness, and influencing. These often end up as difficulties because of the need to have these characteristics and the fact that they are often areas that have not been fully developed in the counselor's background.

Some of the most rigid people can be found on the faculty and in the offices of colleges and universities. At times when individuals need to be as open as possible to the options and opportunities possible, they may, at a particular institution, be narrow in their thinking and feeling about issues. Some examples are:

- Knowing ahead of time what students should do rather than listening and helping a student toward personal goals.
- Feeling that students need to be punished, one way or another, if they lose a key, card, or some other item. This can often be done informally by nonprofessional staff.
- Insisting on closing the office at exactly the right time even if people are still waiting to pay bills or complete registration.

At the same time, the school will need to be open to the idea of influence and competition. That is, the school needs to be open to the idea that it is okay to influence people and that the business of enrollment management will mean that a school is competing in the marketplace. The more a school is oriented around itself rather than the consumer or the competition, the more problems it will have in the future. Each institution should strive to identify its key *attitudes for success* and develop them to the fullest extent possible.

Table 7.4 summarizes some of the key skills, knowledge, and attitude areas that are essential to the success of the organization. Looking at each of these areas may help the institution develop an edge in the marketplace. In each case, a plan for talent development should be developed by the school, the office, or the individual as a way of coming out on top for everyone, including the potential and present students. This chart could help in developing personal plans for growth.

RESOURCES, CONTENT, AND PROCESS AGAIN: DEVELOPING ACTIONS.   Resources, content, and process issues need to be reconsidered now in terms of the enrollment actions and coordinating the actions in a way that will be effective in focusing on what needs to be done. Each

TABLE 7.4. Key Issues Matrix for Talent Development

	Product	Data	Communication	Management	Climate
Skills	(1) Advising Presenting Selling Relationship	(2) Analysers Selling Using Designing Breaking down Interpretation	(3) Questions Listening Selling Presenting	(4) Feedback Planning Control Time Reassembly Tearing down	(5) Communication Problem-solving Relating Feedback
Knowledge	(6) Curriculum Services Environment Options Possibilities	(7) Statistics Surveys Focus Groups Transforming issues Management	(8) Market Student College Staff	(9) Planning Analysis Problem-solving Teamwork	(10) Culture Climate Others Self
Attitudes/beliefs	(11) Product can be changed Package instead of program Change is okay	(12) Data can have impact Validity is important	(13) Influence is okay Like	(14) Control Plans	(15) Trust in the institution

These items are discussed by number as follows: (1) Skills, over and above basic skills, that faculty and staff need to have to do well with students—the competencies related to climate; (2) skills, mainly associated with the development of data, that will help a school have the right database; (3) basic skills in communication that could help professional enrollment personnel and faculty do a better job of meeting the needs of students; (4) basic management skills essential to building strategy, implementing strategy, and keeping it going; (5) basic skills for getting along and working together; (6) knowledge that is required to maintain strengths in a particular program, service, area, or relationship; (7) knowledge needed in key areas critical to developing an enrollment database; (8) key areas in which knowledge is required to function well in influencing students; (9) knowledge of how to build a plan and get it implemented; (10) key areas that may deal with institutional climate; (11) attitudes toward the product that can be fundamentally decisive in the future of the school; (12) key areas that may deal with institutional climate; (11) attitudes toward the product that can be fundamentally decisive in the future of the school; (12) key areas that may deal with institutional climate; (13) a key ingredient: with these attitudes, an enrollment effort may have great difficulty; (14) good attitudes needed toward these two agendas; (15) high trust levels save energy often wasted on unnecessary questioning of actions or ideas.

strategy will require certain resources. These resources can be people, equipment, facilities, materials, or funds that may or may not currently be in one's budget.

For some institutions, dealing with enrollment management may require a major infusion of resources of all types. This has been found to be true of community colleges which, until several years ago, did not have to do much more than take orders. Probably the primary areas of resource difficulty will be people-related. This can occur in terms of numbers of people or in terms of the attitudes and beliefs of people. Some items of concern are usually:

- Developing the word-processing resources to support use of personal letters in the enrollment program.
- Creating the number and quality of publications needed to support the communication strategy.
- Having the talent to run the program. For some schools, finding the right enrollment manager has been a challenge in itself.
- Finding staff people who truly like being in contact with a significant number of people each day. These must be individuals with specific kinds of attitudes that will excite students and produce the kind of relationships that will result in enrollments.
- Having sufficient people. Many enrollment programs are not set up with sufficient staff to meet the needs of the school or the potential student. This is especially true for staff who are in direct contact with potential students and their influentials. We usually try to assign one counselor for every 2,500 students in the inquiry pool.
- Having volunteers who will augment the enrollment staff in specific ways. In schools with very large inquiry pools, a counselor for every 2,500 inquiries is not feasible. Therefore, the effectiveness of the enrollment staff needs to be expanded through the use of volunteers.

CONTENT ISSUES: ACTIONS.   The issue of doing the right things in the right way comes up again under the area of content. Each of the actions undertaken will involve a content piece. For example, it would not be sufficient to have one counselor for every 2,500 inquiries if the people doing the admissions counselor function were not trained adequately or are not backed up with the appropriate resources.

Developing the capacity of the staff to do interviews and presentations, use the telephone, and generally work with students is essential to a program's success. Likewise, it would do no good to produce a viewbook for a school unless the messages were right, the design was excellent, the print quality was outstanding, and the photography was such that the pictures really sold the school.

PROCESS: ACTIONS.   The process of creating the enrollment master plan is one of the most critical areas of a successful program. The plan that is created should include strategies and actions that clearly will do the job of increasing enrollment. To this end, it is important that there be specific strategies and actions for the product area, data and information, communication, management, and climate. It is this combination of activities that will ensure success for enrollment efforts.

But this is not enough. To implement the plan requires people who understand what needs to be done, who are committed to the process, and who are involved in the process throughout the organization. The situation should occur that people are making the necessary product adjustments while the communications people are getting ready to publicize it—all of this resulting from the research and data that have been applied to the enrollment effort.

The following proposal for the development of a volunteer metastrategy may help illustrate the important issues of developing enrollment actions.

The intent of the action plan is to make sure that people understand or feel that a particular goal can be reached. It is critical to be certain that once we have read the action plan, we are sure the relevant items are in place and that the energy is there to make the program go. This means, as shown in Table 7.5, that the goals of the program need to be examined and the appropriate resources determined. The institution needs to be certain that any content issues have been addressed and that the process is in place. Let us look at each of these areas in more detail.

GOALS: DEVELOP A VOLUNTEER PROGRAM.   Goals are now needed for this metastrategy. In this case, the goals are specific objectives in terms of numbers for volunteer contact with students. These numbers must be sufficient to lead the school to believe that the goal will be achieved and will motivate the alumni in their effort.

In terms of resources, as indicated in the table, budget, time, a training program, and a plan for volunteer effort will need to be in place, as well as a coordinator for the program.

Key content issues generally revolve around the training program—making certain that one exists and that the training program will work, and determining the focus of what we want alumni to do. The key content issue of the volunteer action plan is that contact from the alumni is important. Alumni should play a key role in the management of the school's relationship with potential students.

Other content issues involve the general structure of the training program and the creation of a training manual. A final content issue is defining what alumni should do. For example, they should keep in touch with the school. They might make telephone contacts and conduct college nights, college fairs, high school visits, and receptions for the students. They should also keep good records on the people with whom they have come in contact.

Process issues involve selecting the people to be used, managing these people, and developing a recognition program. A key problem in using alumni is to have alumni who will really work. This means that rather than selecting the people toward whom the alumni director may feel most favorable, people should be selected who are willing to give time and energy. A process needs to be developed for this. A good process is to call people, ask them if they will work, mail them materials, and then recall them to confirm their decisions. If they have not read the materials or given much thought to them, they are obviously not going to be very helpful in an alumni effort.

Another issue in terms of alumni and volunteer efforts is giving recognition. Some funds, time, and energy need to be spent periodically in recognizing the people who are involved in this effort.

This is an example of the detail with which an action plan should be worked out to support a metastrategy. By the time the plan is done, almost anyone reading it should be able to feel that the program is going to work.

THE TASK FORCE APPROACH.   Getting commitment, involvement, change, and action have led to heavy use of the task force approach in developing the enrollment program. An enrollment task force can best tackle the job of dealing with the development of an enrollment master plan for an institution if the institution desires to tackle the task of enrollment management systematically. This approach is also critical if it is likely that the school or the system will need to change to a substantial degree.

If the school feels that the task of enrollment management is taken care of merely by creating some new publications or by hiring a few more staff people, the task force approach is not suitable.

WHY IS THE TASK FORCE SO CRITICAL?   The task force will serve as a critical connection to the institution. Ideas that are discussed in the committee also will be discussed in the institution. The ideas of the people in the institution at large will be brought back to the task force. This diffusion of agendas is the key ingredient to the success of a task force approach.

In addition, the task force allows more creativity and commitment to be developed around enrollment as an issue and can lead to the successful implementation of ideas, even when the ideas have involved a considerable degree of change.

TABLE 7.5. Example of a Meta Strategy for a Volunteer Program to Improve Contacts with Students*

Action	Resource Issues	Content Issues	Key Dates	Responsible Person	Process Issues
Appoint an enrollment coordinator.	Someone needs to be responsible for the effort.	Many programs are not successful because someone does not have full-time responsibility for the program.	01/04/85 to 01/31/85	Director of Enrollment Management	Make certain that the person has the skills, knowledge, and, most importantly, the attitudes to do the job.
Create the budget.	A specific budget for the volunteer effort.	A second major reason why many volunteer programs may have difficulties.	02/04/86 to 04/05/86	Director of Enrollment Management; Coordinator	Involve the president and other key people. Do not start the program unless there is financial commitment.
Develop the volunteer plan.	Time and knowledge.	Make certain this spells out the way in which this program will succeed.	05/01/86 to 06/01/86	Coordinator	The rest of these activities are part of the plan. Circulate for review. Involve the alumni, faculty, and students.
Select volunteers.	Lists and the cooperation of people who work with alumni, students, and faculty.	Make certain to select people who have the attitudes and the time to do the job.	06/01/86 to 10/01/86	Coordinator	This is critical at this point in the process. Take the time to develop the right group of people.

Develop training materials: manual, on-campus programs, off-campus programs, quality control	People, publications, letters, flow. Asking what we want them to do. Role-playing. Examples.	These people have to believe in the school. This will help all of the volunteers to feel good about what they are doing. This activity must be limited in actual objectives of contact so that the volunteer can accomplish it.	06/01/86 to 10/01/86	Coordinator	Be certain to have some on-campus time built in. Use a training program similar to that used for the professional staff.
Develop management system.	Management reports, notification forms, return forms.	One of the ways of focusing the staff's energy and the volunteers' energy is to make certain that people know what needs to be done.	06/01/86 to 07/01/86	Coordinator	Be certain to explain this item carefully and use it in the program. This is the most critical aspect of sustained efforts—all process and critical.
Recognition program.	Letters, visits to the alumni, newsletters, ceremonies, meetings, scholarships.	Recognition is always a key issue when working with volunteers. A great deal of time needs to be spent letting them know that we know they are there.	06/01/86 to 10/01/86	Coordinator	

* This form is a simple way to develop an overview of the critical things that must be done in implementing a meta-strategy. These forms would be developed for each piece of the program. The form would normally include many more items than included here and would include the use of students, alumni(ae), and faculty.

The use of the task force accomplishes several purposes:

- provides a mechanism for gaining involvement of the institution in enrollment management;
- develops commitment of the entire institution to the process of enrollment management;
- provides an arena for finding opportunities to deal more effectively with enrollment management;
- is a group of people who can do problem solving at times of crisis or in time of normal planning for enrollment.

KEY ISSUES TO CONSIDER.   There are several critical issues that need to be addressed for the task force to be successful. These issues include task force membership, having knowledge about enrollment management, and having a process that will bring out the best in people doing the job.

Membership selection for the task force is a more important issue than the size of the task force. The concern often encountered is to keep the task force to a manageable size. Task forces as large as fifty and as small as ten have been effective in dealing with enrollment issues. It is not the size that is critical but rather the people who are in the group.

The people who will most likely be involved in the enrollment management process need to be included. The task force should also include faculty, key administrators—except the president and academic deans—and, in some cases, students and board members.

The key is to have people who are involved directly in enrollment management, who will spread ideas to the organization, who will bring ideas back from the organization, who will be supportive of the whole process—and who, if not involved, could possibly create barriers that might stand in the way of progress. This group of people will be most productive.

LEARNING ABOUT ENROLLMENT MANAGEMENT.   In discussing enrollment management with a group of faculty who were having trouble dealing with enrollment management, questions were posed as to whether they could build a Piper Cub airplane if they were given all of the parts and the tools. The answer to this question was obviously no. Even given the blueprints, the faculty was certain it would take too long to build the plane to be worthwhile, and then they were not certain they would want to fly it. The same holds true for the enrollment task force. People on the task force must have some background development in terms of enrollment management before the job can be done.

The matrix can serve as a good organization strategy for the development of the committee's knowledge on enrollment management.

Discussions or presentations on the matrix can be helpful, especially for development of the task force members' attitudes and beliefs about this key agenda for the school.

A more detailed discussion of this approach is found in Chapter 9 in the discussion of the enrollment task force.

CLIMATE AND ENROLLMENT

The climate of the educational institution is, more often than not, one of the most critical variables in managing enrollments. This is true because it is likely that the institutional climate determines:

- The way in which and the extent to which users of the institution's services benefit from their association.
- The degree to which the institution is able to respond to enrollment opportunities or threats.
- The degree to which the institution can effectively solve problems.
- The amount of real creativity that exists for identifying solutions to problems.
- The degree to which the institution is cohesive in times of adversity.
- The degree to which people in the institution will consider different points of view with openness and enthusiasm.

An example helps to illustrate this point:

Jan's enrollment program had been in trouble for the last three years. The numbers of applications were off badly, and conversions to enrolled students had dropped 10 percent.

In addition, the retention of students had fallen dramatically. At this point—Christmas—the news was given to Jan that only about 50 percent of the freshmen had registered for another term at the school.

The faculty was now pointing fingers and placing the blame on Jan and her staff. The staff had worked harder each year, but the results were dwindling faster than they could make contacts.

The Board was putting pressure on the president, and he had to find a scapegoat. Academic programs at the school were very limited, and the faculty wanted only the liberal arts and the best students. This was a small, isolated school that was really not attractive to those very bright students who would select the pure liberal arts as an option.

Blaming and finger-pointing continued, and the main concern of the dean of academic affairs was her personal survival, which she saw as threatened by anything the faculty did. In addition, the trust level between the president and the faculty was not high, since the president had not been on campus for several months and the last real raise people had had was three years ago.

In the meantime, Jan was in trouble and so was every student attending the school.

This discussion of the climate factors that can be involved in enrollment situations includes the ways to take action to improve a situation where the climate of the institution negatively impacts enrollment results.

GOALS

The goal of climate management is *to maximize the flow and the effective use of information at an institution in order to improve the capacity to obtain and retain students.* Information is the substance upon which actions, feelings, beliefs, fears, joy, and the energy of individuals in the system are formed. When each person receives and can process information well, there are many more options on which to develop actions. Without information, a large part of the "food" that provides the energy to complete tasks for the organization is lost.

Information flow occurs between people, between offices, and between organizations. When the flow of information is blocked in some way, the direction of the system can be altered. Maintaining the flow in all directions is critical. Getting information to flow through the system is the first key step in dealing with the climate aspect of enrollment issues. The information may never influence the individual or group if it cannot be absorbed.

Information processing also must occur if data is to be useful. It must be digested and the useful pieces retained while the "garbage" is discarded. If the processing of information is defective at any level, the possibilities for action diminish. Certainly, the possibilities for taking the *right* action are decreased substantially. If one is hiding any substantive array of information and discounting the good, barriers are created to effective action. If data is interpreted as a threat when it should not be, actions will not be taken when they may be very necessary.

Information use is the final key agenda. Once the food has been taken in, it has to go to the muscles and organs of the organizational system and be utilized in the right way. If the individual or office, for example, has purchased some information and understands the vital elements but does not know how to use it, the institution is vulnerable.[1]

Many climate issues can be traced to these few basic ideas on information flow. Our discussion will focus on examples of how information flow is impacted by climate.

CLIMATE RESOURCES

The resources that are needed in the climate area are primarily the people in the organization and the knowledge, skills, and attitudes of these individuals in relation to their tasks and interaction. If these are managed well, the ability of the school to deal with enrollment issues will be significantly enhanced. These are, perhaps, some of the more complicated resources that must be managed on the road to a successful enrollment program.

PEOPLE

People at all levels are involved in creating the institutional climate. This includes students, faculty, administrators, other staff, alumni, and outside supporters. There is probably no one who could not contribute to a bad climate if so inclined. On the other hand, it may take a large number of people and a great amount of energy to correct a poor climate. In any case, it is people who are the primary resource.

KNOWLEDGE, SKILLS, AND ATTITUDES

The skills and knowledge needed by people can be easily identified. These include skills and knowledge in areas such as decision-making, listening, hearing, problem-solving, and creativity. It should be noted that these items can be directly related to the flow of high-quality information through the organizational system.

Another skill area is the ability to acknowledge and support people. If people listen well to each other, clear indications are given that what people are saying is important. This contributes to the flow of data in an easy fashion, the ability to exchange views, and ultimately to effective problem solving and decision-making.

Attitudes and beliefs that are important include feelings that the climate is important and a belief that climate can impact the ease with which an institution attracts and keeps students. Associated with this

[1]The metaphor of information use as nourishment is from *Grow or Die: The Unifying Principle of Transformation* by George T. Lockland (New York: Random House, 1973).

is an attitude of trust. The most formidable barrier to a healthy climate is lack of mutual trust between the leadership of educational organizations and the people in those organizations.

A final resource of critical importance is a good problem-solving process. This should be a process in which the climate skills of the institution are creatively directed toward dealing with the complex problems of enrollment. The problem-solving process should not be ad hoc but should reflect a systematic, easily understood scenario in which everyone can participate.

THE CONTENT OF CLIMATE

There is a problem. Most efforts at dealing with organizational issues tend to start with the identification of something on which the institution wants to work. Frequently, although schools might wish this were not so, these issues start out as problems—elements causing the world to be other than the way people would want it.

Certainly enrollment could be classified as a problem area that arises frequently, whether for a department or for a school. When the numbers are down, most people recognize that a problem exists and then the activity begins. Because the problem exists for many people, they must deal with problem solving—difficult enough on an individual basis—on a group or organizational level.

The problem, low enrollment, is frequently not the core problem, but is a symptom of other issues. This is the point at which an institution with a good climate has an advantage. This institution will begin the process of trying to identify the problems and the development of possible solutions without the defensiveness and game-playing that may go on at other schools. The school with a good climate can develop valuable insights on many issues, including how they work with students over the long run.

In this situation, the climate becomes critical to the success of the organization. When there are problems, there should be reasoned analysis—the development of creative options to deal with the issues, the development of strategy, the implementation of actual strategy to impact the area, support and recognition of key people, and trust.

Steps to effective solutions usually can be better taken by a group than individually, and can be best accomplished if there is free flow of information. This is especially so if there are changes to be made. And it will be even more true if there are some fundamental changes that need to occur in the organization such as changes in focus, mission, programs, or large-scale reallocation of resources.

THE PROBLEM-SOLVING PROCESS

In order to develop the best insights into dealing with enrollment issues, the problem-solving process needs to be carefully structured. Dealing with problems is often more effective if it starts with the definition of two areas—the present state and the desired state.

The problem exists and can best be restructured by identifying some condition that should exist if things were the way they should be. This is a definition of a desired state as perceived by those involved in the problem-solving process.

In identifying this desired state, a definition or description of a present state is required. This is the view of the world as it currently exists in regard to the problem issue and how it currently impacts enrollment. Frequently, the institution starts to deal with issues but does not know what the present state is. Going forward is not possible without doing the analysis of both states.

With these two states defined, one can begin to address the gap between them and the matter of how to move from point A to point B. Following is an example of present versus desired state:

> Granville College, which has been in existence for more than a hundred years, is suffering what appears to be a potential enrollment disaster for fall. They are down approximately 25 percent in applications, and they have no deposits for next year.
>
> Visits to the campus also are down. The director is very worried and wants to make contact by sending out some 5,800 brochures. The director, however, has a limited professional staff, although the number of staff members is greater than at neighboring institutions. The director has asked for help from alumni, students, and faculty, but is not receiving it.
>
> In fact, the request for help from faculty has incensed them to a point where they are asking for a dismissal from the program. The director has had nothing but letters from faculty indicating that it is not their job to do recruitment, but hers, and she'd better get on with it. The dean of the college, who has been in his position for about four years, is worried about losing faculty support. As a result, he is publicly siding with the faculty, although he personally agrees with the director that additional help would be appropriate. The director reports to the academic dean.
>
> Students have been difficult to organize because many of them are not on campus during the day and because they are listening to the faculty; they don't understand why their help is needed.
>
> The development program is also under a great deal of pressure and the alumni function reports through them. The alumni have been identified as key to development support,

and although their giving is minimal, the alumni director will not give time to the admissions director for this type of effort to support enrollment.

The president has not been critically aware of all of this, as he has been spending a great deal of time away from campus for fund raising and is presently on a three-week vacation. The director has had little experience in dealing with top administrators and does not know how to deal with the president.

Therefore, a large number of inquiries exist with limited capability for personal contact at a time when it is most needed.

The desired state for this program is to have high-quality contact with a larger number of inquiries and to be able to sustain this contact through the process of application, deposit, and enrollment.

This high-quality contact would include 500 calls a week during January, 250 calls during the spring, and sufficient contacts to give a yield of 3.4 percent from inquiries to applications, 63 percent from applications to deposits, and 95 percent from deposit to enrollment.

RESTRAINTS AND DRIVING FORCES AND THEIR USE

The next step in the problem-solving process often is an analysis of the forces that keep the system in the present state and the forces needed to help move the program to the desired state.

These forces may best be sorted out on the basis of restraining forces and driving forces—restraining forces being forces that keep the system from moving into the desired state and driving forces being those that might push the system into the desired state. Each of these forces exerts an impact on the system, and the present state represents the combination of these forces.

In this analysis, several concepts are important. The restraining forces are inhibitors and, if weakened, allow the system to move away from the present state into a more desirable position. Sometimes all that is needed is the weakening of these restraints and the system begins to move.

It is important to note that not all restraining forces need to be addressed. It can be very frustrating to see so many problems as a school acts on issues. It may be that weakening one or two of the restraints will be sufficient to allow the system to move into a new position. This means that the restraining forces need to be prioritized and addressed individually as to the benefits of addressing them. Sometimes, trying to deal with restraining forces may make the issue worse. In this case, recognition of that fact will be helpful.

In a similar way, driving forces help the system to move toward a more desired state. These are factors that push the system in a more productive direction.

But, as with restraining forces, not all of the driving forces are equally powerful. Some will be more influential than others and some will be easier to address than others. Making good decisions about the factors to tackle often will spell the difference between schools that are successful and those that are not.

It should be clear that the combination of weakening some restraints and giving more strength to some driving forces often will be enough to move a system in the direction of the desired state. In essence, as with other items of the Enrollment Matrix (see Chapter 2) there is an advantage to thinking about synergism rather than trying to tackle a single problem and hoping it will remedy the situation.

The following are some of the restraining forces for Granville College:

- No history of direct experience of people on campus with volunteer contact efforts.
- Lack of understanding of the complexity of enrollment management.
- History of downward trends of enrollment and fear created by this trend.
- Lack of contact by the director with the faculty and other staff members in previous years.
- Lack of support from the academic dean.
- Staff members' inability or unwillingness to have as much contact as they should with potential students.
- Lack of presidential involvement in the enrollment effort.
- The tendency to blame others.

The following were identified in an initial list of driving forces:

- The director understands that contact with students is important.
- The director is generally a good organizer and has done some training of staff.
- The president is usually decisive once she understands the problem.
- There is clearly a need for more contact.
- There is sufficient time to have an impact on the enrollment effort.
- There has been a large number of inquiries.
- There are a few key current students who are interested in helping the effort.
- There are some key faculty who are interested.

In this list of restraining and driving forces, there are some that will have more force than others in meeting the desired state. The idea is to select the restraining and driving forces that will have the most impact on success.

With the restraining forces, the most pressing issue is creating presidential involvement in the effort. Certainly, the downward trend and the lack of understanding will take time to address. If the president becomes involved, the issue may at least be easier to deal with in the short term.

In terms of driving forces, it seems clear that Granville should try to make certain that the president understands the situation and that the students who are interested are helping to be successful. In this case, some additional driving forces could be created by getting faculty involved and motivating them to do the job.

SUPPORT FACTORS FOR PROBLEM SOLVING: KEY CLIMATE AGENDAS

There are factors that, if present in the institutional population, will cause the process of building the desired state and working with it to be more effective. These are part of the climate area and need to be worked with, on occasion, to ensure that the process of dealing with problems is possible. These are factors related to individuals and groups that, if developed, can lead to a more effective result. The more important characteristics include *trust, communication, creativity*, and *decision-making* processes. These factors need to combine with solid institutional goals that can orient individuals and groups in the right direction. Moreover, they have to do with the ability of the individual and, ultimately, the group to take in and process information. In order to work effectively, the individual or group must be able, like an organism that needs food, to absorb information. That same individual or group must be able to process the information successfully and somehow translate the information into effective action. Where these processes do not work well, the system can suffer something akin to starvation or indigestion as it tries to function.

One of the key issues in some schools is the lack of data for decision-making. The school may have lived in isolation and not have the informational resources to deal with problems. Likewise, schools may be flooded with information yet paralyzed in using it. These institutions are not any better off than the schools that are starving. The information may be present, but the process for dealing with it effectively does not work well on an individual or group level.

The support factors ensure that finding information will happen and using the information is possible. Each of these support factors can arise from and interfere in one or more steps of this process. Consider each of these terms individually and then examine a scenario that demonstrates how a good climate helps a school to succeed.

TRUST

Trust is a basic factor that is needed if an enrollment management program is to succeed. Trust is too often found at a moderate to low level at many schools. The amount of trust in the educational system and its people seems to be declining in recent years, and the academic world is a harsher one because of its absence. Here, the president whose word is constantly challenged can be recognized, as can the department that is protecting its territory and looks on all issues as a battle for turf; as well as the individual instructor who is certain he or she will not get tenure and feels neglected in this process, or the admissions staff members who lack enthusiasm because they are certain that the faculty is not able to deliver on the promises being made.

> The feedback had become depressing for June, the director of enrollment. The word was out that students were not treated very well on the Olmstead campus. The amount of counseling time that students could expect was apparently very limited, and the treatment of women at the school was particularly bad.
>
> There was word of long-standing conflicts between the faculty and the administration, and the feeling in the outside world—and with some of the newer faculty—was that time was being used in this area rather than in dealing effectively with students and their needs. As a result, enrollment goals were not met and retention was at an all-time low.
>
> The enrollment staff had been trying to deal with falling enrollments. The problem was now being compounded because the falling numbers were causing budget difficulties that in turn were causing blaming and finger pointing and intense competition for resources—which was creating bad feelings on the campus.

This is not an unusual problem today. The climate may not be a problem until a crisis comes. When the problems arise, the cracks begin to appear and just when all of the energies should be focused on moving ahead successfully, the school ends up in a pattern of behavior that only feeds the negative situation. In this case, trust may be a major issue.

REASONS.   There are several reasons why trust may become a problem in developing an enrollment program. These can include the following situations:

- One individual has to do a lot of follow-up because he or she does not have confidence in the other person doing the job. This slows down the process of implementing any changes.

- Extra work may be involved in a project because one of the participants takes responsibility for all of the work.

- Too much time may be taken to develop a program enhancement because people do not believe that it can or will be done.

- A program fails to improve because people do not trust the others to do the work or to do it in the right way.

- The president is not able to sell an idea because the people in the organization do not trust him or her.

When distrust is felt toward the higher levels of administration, improvement attempts may become completely blocked:

"The president wanted to improve the enrollment situation and had a consultant in to determine what the options were. The consultant ran into a brick wall because the people he talked to were not being open. People were friendly and pleasant but he was not finding answers to any of the questions he had asked. The enrollment situation was critical, but these individuals were not about to share anything of importance."

At supper, the consultant was told the reason why from the dean of women. At the end of the meal, she said, "You know you are wasting your time here. The people will not tell you anything."

She said that anyone who disagreed with the president or who the president saw as a problem would end up being verbally abused and likely terminated as soon as possible. The examples she gave were numerous, and a check of the records of the employee turnover in the school indicated that something was certainly abnormal and people might have good reason to fear reprisals of one sort or another.

In two days, nothing was learned except that people were not willing to share or do anything that might raise the anger of the president. In this case, it was difficult to give even this feedback to the president, as he might react to his people in general in terms of having let him down.

In this case there was just no way to deal with the problem—it was a real no-win situation.[2]

---

[2]As managers have become more concerned about trust as a critical climate factor, they have become familiar with the work in this area by Jack R. Gibb. In a book entitled *Trust: A New View of Personal and Organizational Development* (Los Angeles: Guild of Tutors, 1978), Dr. Gibb develops the relationship between trust and organization success. The insights presented here may be helpful as institutions encounter the potential danger of the trust agenda in managing enrollment efforts.

THE INDIVIDUAL.   Tables 8.1 and 8.2 represent the impacts of trust and nontrust on the performance of individuals.

Here it can be seen that virtually every aspect of an individual's ability to deal with information can be impaired:

- Motivation: the focusing of energy on the issues of dealing with enrollment change.
- Consciousness: the ability of the individual to be aware of what is going on around him or her.
- Perception: abilities to pick up critical information.
- Emotionality: the ability to react to information critically.
- Cognition: the ability to use the data and to think about issues.
- Action: the ability to do something with information that will help deal with the situation.
- Synergy: the ability to work together to an effective solution to problems.

This collection of areas in which lack of trust can impact the ability of the individual to function indicates the way in which the issue of trust can seriously impair the best-designed efforts to deal with enrollment.

GROUPS.   The issue of trust also can impact the whole system. Table 8.3 represents a summary of the thinking of researchers on the issue of defensiveness as it is represented in low-trust environments.

Here, the processes or behaviors used in defending systems are presented and represent significant barriers to enrollment success. If these behaviors are being played out in the environment, it is likely to impede changes needed for the solution of enrollment problems. Likewise, it is likely that these behaviors will be seen by present students—and they are likely to be concerned by what is happening.

How much easier the process can be in an environment where the trust levels are high, and cooperation and nondefensive behaviors are the norm! While an environment of complete trust is rare, a better trust environment is possible if this is valued by the institution.

GENERAL COMMUNICATION

"We have poor communication"—an overused phrase often put forth as a reason for difficulties. It is an explanation that is not very helpful when the wolves are at the door and there are serious problems to address. This is, however, usually one of the issues that is raised when things just do not seem to be working and answers are needed. Communication as a concept can be hard to deal with because it is so general. People using the concept need to be more specific about this issue so that the solutions can be pinpointed. The answer needs to have more meaning when the president or others say, "We have got to get it together here." What often is labeled a communication problem cannot be dealt with because the underlying difficulty is lack of trust, lack of intention, and lack of commitment.

The following are some items affecting good communication once trust is present. These are skills that need to be examined at any institution in developing successful solutions to enrollment problems.

LISTENING AND HEARING.   Listening and hearing are skills that most people in the organization feel they do well. Actually, it is often the case that many people who make decisions are not very sensitive to each other largely in terms of these two very important characteristics. Yet listening carefully would solve many of the problems that occur among various groups. Faculty/administration and faculty/student relationships could be improved greatly through development of this skill.

Listening and hearing can impact the enrollment effort in many ways. The following people are adversely affected by a deficiency in these qualities:

- The faculty members who are fixed in the way that they want to do a job. They already know the best way to do this and will not have their minds changed about anything.
- The administrator who spends the time with staff but is obviously tuning out the situation.
- The advisor who does not have time for students.
- The student who is not heard and thereby becomes a prime candidate for loss from the school. Often all the student wants is to be listened to. This can supply the only motivation the student needs to be satisfied that the school is taking care of his or her problems.
- The student who does not listen in class. Such students may end up saying that the professor is not doing the right job, yet the students are not doing their part.
- The board member who listens and then goes away with previous perceptions of the school's situation unchallenged. The frame of reference has been a business one and the president has not changed the feelings that are preventing the school from getting action from the board.

These are only a few examples that provide an idea that the core of many issues will be the poor listening or hearing abilities that develop early in educational experiences and carry over into professional or student/faculty relationships. In each of these situations, the problem is a combination of deficient listening and hearing. The words often are being

TABLE 8.1. The Tori Discovering Processes*

Discovering processes	Orientation of the person	Proactive energy focused on:	Personal wants
TRUSTING—(T) BEING	Being me — discovering who I am	Accepting self and others	Love — giving and receiving love
Personing	How do I create me?	Trusting	
Centering	What is my uniqueness?	Expressing warmth	
Accepting		Seeing differences	
Warming			
OPENING—(O) SHOWING	Showing me — discovering how to reveal myself to others	Spontaneity	Intimacy — giving and receiving intimacy and communication in depth
Letting in	How to let you in and share our space?	Impulsivity	
Listening	How to show you how I feel and see?	Rapport	
Disclosing		Tuning in	
Empathizing			
REALIZING—(R) ACTUALIZING	Doing what I want — discovering my wants and how to realize them	Searching	Fulfillment — giving and receiving personal fulfillment
Asserting	What matters to me?	Fulfillment	
Exploring	What is my life for?	Life enrichment	
Evolving		Allowing	
Wanting		Achievement	
INTERDEPENDING—(I) INTERBEING	Being with others — discovering how to live and work with others	Interacting	Freedom — giving and receiving freedom
Integrating	How do I create my freedom?	Participating	
Joining	How do we transcend our own beings?	Cooperating	
Sharing		Giving and getting freedom	
Synergizing			

*Source: Jack R. Gibb, Trust: A New View of Personal and Organizational Development (Los Angeles: The Guild of Tutors Press, 1978).

TABLE 8.2. The Tori Defending Processes*

Defending processes	Orientation of the person	Defensive energy focused on: Punishing self and others	Personal needs
DEPERSONING Coding Role-ing Detaching Appraising Observing	*Finding a role* — discovering and creating a role What is my role? How do I compare with others?	*Punishing self and others* Evaluation Distrust Moralizing	*Punishment* — giving and receiving punishment Need to manage warmth
MASKING Closing up Distancing Filtering Strategizing Covering	*Building a facade* — discovering a strategy How do I protect me? What is my best covert strategy?	*Strategizing* Circumvention Distortion Formality	*Distance* — giving and receiving social distance Need to manage intimacy
OUGHTING Influencing Persuading Parenting Coercing Manipulating	*Finding my needs* — discovering our demands and expectations What should I do? How do I change me or you? How do I get power?	*Persuading* Influence Passivity Resistance	*Influence* — giving and receiving influence Need to manage motives
DEPENDING Controlling Submitting Leading Dominating Rebelling	*Controlling me and you* — discovering rules, boundaries, contracts How do I protect my turf? What is the law?	*Controlling* Dependency Management Rebellion	*Control* — giving and receiving controls Need to manage relationships

*Source: Jack R. Gibb, Trust: A New View of Personal and Organizational Development (Los Angeles: The Guild of Tutors Press, 1978).

TABLE 8.3. The Wants Hierarchy and the Environmental-Quality Phases*

Phase theme	Ascendant want, sustaining the phase	Secondary wants that enrich the basic and ascendant want during the phase state
I Punitive	To survive	To be secure, to punish and be punished, to be moral and to impose morality, to fight, to withdraw
II Autocratic	To give and gain power	To control, to be controlled, to maintain order, to get status, to obey, to rebel, to have authority, to evaluate
III Benevolent	To protect and to be protected	To help, to teach, to parent, to be cared for, to rescue, to be dependent, to give and receive warmth
IV Advisory	To understand and to be understood	To consult, to give and get advice, to be rational, to be aware of order, to gain wisdom
V Participative	To join and to be joined	To collaborate, to encourage involvement, to persuade, to influence, to be a member, to be included, to include others
VI Emergent	To be in community	To be part of a whole, to touch, to be aware, to be self-determining, to be close
VII Organic	To feel and to express feelings	To get sensory gratification, to create self, to get new experience, to be impulsive and spontaneous
VIII Holistic	To be whole	To find my roots, to create a free will, to have voluntary control over all bodily functions, to expand self

TABLE 8.3. *continued*

Phase theme	Ascendant want, sustaining the phase	Secondary wants that enrich the basic and ascendant want during the phase state
IX Transcendent	To transcend	To be egoless, to be need-free, to be born anew, to move into new areas of being and awareness
X Cosmic	To join the universal all	To transcend self, to be want-free, to transcend need for separateness

Source: Jack R. Gibb, *Trust: A View of Personal and Organizational Development* (Los Angeles: The Guild of Tutors Press, 1978).

said and the words are reaching the ears of both parties, but after that, things run amok.

People may be hearing something different from what is being said. And this is causing each to respond in inappropriate ways. This can be a circular problem that gets worse as the years go on—especially true when there are groups of people who do not listen very well to each other. Poor listening combined with lack of trust can be devastating and can undermine many of the potential impacts a faculty member wants to have on the student. The relationship between faculty member and student may never develop.

CREATIVITY/INNOVATION

Creativity is a subtle skill that most people also claim. In the case of an institution that must survive in a competitive situation, it can be the difference between success or a lingering feeling that things are never going to be good.

Creativity is important in many situations, including some of the following:

- The development of ways to fund enrollment enhancements. They cannot always come out of the budget, as this may decrease the school's ability to offer the programs that will be successful in the future.
- Educational programs that sometimes have to be very different from the way they were in the past. This can include a whole curriculum or it can include the enhancements of a program through such strategies as internships, co-ops, and outside mentor relationships that

make a program successful. The development of these options often depends heavily on creativity.

- Relationships between students and faculty—finding new ways to build a solid relationship on which enrollment success is based. This can include a faculty member knowing how to deal with people in a more productive way, and it may mean that the faculty member or administrator will have to be able to change over to behaviors that will make him or her more successful in the marketplace.

- Finding new ways to deliver and thus motivate people about curricula that are fundamentally important but that do not receive the attention they should from the student or the school. This is the case for some schools in terms of the liberal arts. Creative representation of the benefits of a liberal arts education is sometimes all that is needed to interest the student.

DECISION-MAKING

Decision-making can become a key issue in developing more effective enrollment programs. Colleges and universities have generally tried to produce a democratic model of management that allows for a great deal of input and a wide dispersion of decision-making responsibilities. This means that many people get involved in deciding about what to do, without necessarily having to deal with the results of a decision. This can be harmful if decisions are of low quality or if decisions are made too late to deal with the issues.

The crippling effect of this factor can be seen in a situation like the one below.

> Defective decision-making processes are usually a combination of all of the climate factors. When these climate factors all come to bear on one process, however, it can mean a catastrophe in the making. Such a catastrophe came to a small service-related college in the Midwest, which was forced to close its doors.
>
> Decision-making can become most apparent when it brings about the closing of a school—especially a school with great potential and with a product that is now needed, more than ever, in the marketplace. The faculty and administration, looking back, could hardly believe the disaster. They gave excuses:
>
> "If only someone had said something earlier, this all could have been avoided."
>
> "A month is just not enough time."
>
> But in reality the school had brought this fate upon itself through a series of decisions that did not include all of the people in the organization. It might open again, but the very fact of closing is now going to make it extremely difficult to reopen.

The school had erred in many different areas:

- By overexpanding its financial aid program in hopes of attracting more students; by not communicating well with either the faculty or the admissions office, thus making decisions that did not bear fruit;

- By not supplying the resources or the personnel to the enrollment office so that the programs could be adequately promoted; whereas, this school should have recognized that it had to compete heavily and the program was not adequate for this task;

- By not raising the expectations of the development group and by not dealing with the assumptions of the development group that the goals could be obtained;

- By not including the community of the school in the process from the beginning, and in this way applying the energy of the whole institution to the process of its survival.

This example represents how many areas of climate can impact a particular process of the organization.

MACROFACTORS: STRUCTURATION AND CO-ORIENTATION

Macrofactors are those factors that, in a group of people, combine to produce effects that keep the ability of the school to reach its goals at either a very minimal or a very high level. These combined factors can best be represented in the concepts of *structuration* and *co-orientation*.

Structuration refers to the idea that the people in the institution may not all experience the same climate. The climate of the faculty may be very different from that of the students and the administration. This means that interpreting the feeling of the people in the community may be puzzling because the various groups cannot really appreciate what is happening for the others. This is an example of the "walk a while in my shoes" phenomenon.

This situation can occur when the institution is a resident college/ university in which the faculty do not spend a lot of time on the campus except in teaching their classes. This means that the students will have a total experience in terms of time with the organization, while the faculty may experience the school only as a place to work. While some of this may be natural, it may become destructive when one or the other group completely loses sensitivity to the needs, wants, and feelings of the others.

Co-orientation occurs when one group has a certain type of feeling

TABLE 8.4. Faculty and Student Ratings of College Expectations*

	Present Students	Faculty and Administration
1. Preparation for grad school	49.28	32.89
2. Move into career	87.56	53.95
3. Communicate effectively	67.70	94.74
4. Be an expert	39.04	8.00
5. Variety of experiences	50.84	42.11
6. Personal advising	46.27	64.47
7. Make more money	27.64	1.33
8. Awareness of philosophies	39.42	76.32
9. Depth of knowledge	82.49	62.67
10. Academic advising	36.45	40.79
11. High academic quality	80.86	92.11
12. Intercollegiate athletics	20.24	21.33
13. Religious growth	31.65	44.74
14. Intramural athletics	18.66	51.32
15. Fraternities/sororities	6.00	.00
16. Broadly educated person	78.95	92.11
Average	47.69	48.68

* Values of very important—responses from students in a typical survey at a small liberal arts college.

about a topic and others share in it. This is especially critical when dealing with issues that are at the core of the institution's success.

This chart indicates some differences of opinions between faculty and present students in terms of:

- Preparation for a career.
- Being an expert.
- Becoming a broadly educated person.
- Learning how to communicate effectively.

The faculty want one thing and the students another. In this case, the issues should be discussed so that a better match can be made or a different population of students can be recruited. One of the key roles for the task force is to evaluate this type of situation and develop the strategies that will create a match (see Chapter 9). The better the match, the more the student will feel that wants are being met.

INSTITUTIONAL GOALS AND LEADERSHIP

Two of the most important characteristics are the factors that can tie all of the people in the organization together, if it is at all possible. These are the issues of institutional goals and leadership.

INSTITUTIONAL GOALS

If everyone is committed to the organization, the institution can more easily move forward to a successful future. Unfortunately, the goals and directions of the organization are too often only words on a piece of paper. They are not something that people have had to really strive, struggle, and fight for. They are words and not beliefs, and therefore there is insufficient commitment to the organization. Without this commitment, there is a limited chance that people in the organization can have the energy that will keep them moving. *But they will keep moving.* If it is not over positive goals and issues that will produce mutual success for everyone, it will be on negative items that happen, perhaps to benefit one person or group but not another.

The faculty can be motivated often to act for a person or an issue but seldom to do the very best job possible, at whatever cost, to be successful with students and other potential users of the services of the organization.

The university faculty clearly felt it was the best available in its region. The evidence was presented in terms of research grants and publications. They also wanted to focus on doing graduate work and research. To accommodate this, they desired to deal only with those students who were at the top of the class and would require the least amount of time and energy to educate.

The problem was that the top students wanted some things that the faculty, in this case, could not or would not give. The students wanted:

- Faculty who were available to them on a regular basis.
- Faculty who were concerned about students.
- Faculty who were excited about their subject areas and who were excited about the idea of working with undergraduates.
- Teachers and not researchers.

The problem was that the top students wanted this more than did the average students. The desires of the faculty were not focused on meeting the needs of the top student, and it was now showing up in the enrollment results.

THE KEY ISSUE OF LEADERSHIP

None of the necessary changes or improvements will occur unless there is support and encouragement from people who are leaders or influencers. One definition of a leader is one who is able to influence. These can be the top people at an institution or those people who are able to influence, regardless of their levels in the institution.

If the leaders at an institution believe they will be able to improve, the chances for a project's success are great. If they do not believe, the project will not have a chance. The institution needs to be certain these people will be available in terms of their time, their support, and their efforts at making certain that the resources needed are available.

This point is developed extensively by Warren Bennis and Burt Nanus, authors of a study on leadership.[3] This study analyzes issues of leadership in organizations in general, and in particular it makes the following assertions, which are critical to enrollment management:

- A critical issue of organizations today is their incapacity to cope with the expectations of their constituencies.
- There is a lack of commitment to the organizations by their employees.
- Organizations are now very complex in terms of their issues. "There are too many ironies, polarities, dichotomies, dualities, ambivalences, paradoxes, confusions, contradictions, contraries, and messes for the organization to understand and deal with." (p. 8)
- Lack of power is a key issue in all of these agendas. This is viewed as the need to be able to initiate and sustain action toward a goal.

This translates, for these authors, into a lack of leadership in educational organizations—the lack of a person who can influence in a way that brings out the best in people as they pursue the goals that lie before them.

INDIVIDUALS AND GROUPS.   The influence that is needed may come from individuals or groups. Certainly, it should be relatively easy to identify the individuals who can influence. These people should be worked with early in the game. Getting them on board will greatly facilitate the flow of information in the system.

PROCESS ISSUES

The process area is most critical to the success of climate work. The process of working with climate includes such tasks as making certain that it is important to address climate issues, assessing climate, and changing climate. If climate has a critical impact on the enrollment area, then one would need to be very careful to determine if it is necessary to be concerned with it and what to do about it.

This is doubly important because changing the climate is very difficult and because people are generally very sensitive about the climate

[3]Warren Bennis and Burt Nanus, *Leadership: The Strategies for Taking Charge* (New York: Harper and Row, 1985).

area. The problems one can cause in doing the wrong thing can make the enrollment situation even worse than it might have been had nothing been done. "Opening the can of worms" can create more issues than everyone wants to deal with—especially for the president.

ASSESSING CLIMATE

The assessment of climate can be done in several ways, but there are two approaches that are most useful. The first is to experience the climate and honestly process that experience.

The second is to use an instrument and discussion to bring out others' views of the institutional climate and its potential impact, to use this process to develop insight about climate, and to develop strategies to deal with it.

> The ashtrays were dirty and the snow was not shoveled from the sidewalk to the apartment. The consultants had arrived on campus after waiting for the pickup by the dean for almost an hour. As they pulled up to the school's apartment, they were forced to wade through the snow and carry their luggage into a cold and somewhat dirty apartment.
>
> When they mentioned the problem of the ashtrays and someone's leftover breakfast still being left in the apartment, the dean was somewhat upset—not at the fact that the apartment was not ready, but at the fact that the consultants did not appreciate at least the effort.

This was the beginning of a bad experience for everyone. During the interviews, the consultants found that the students felt uncared for by the school. They felt they were not the customers in any sense, but were constantly having to fight for any consideration by the faculty or the administration. The retention levels were very low and likewise turnover of the faculty was high.

In this case, the climate was very clear in the beginning and the experience of the consultants on the first visit could have predicted the problem. Likewise, this could be predicted by people on campus as they did—or did not—do their work each day.

THE CLIMATE WORKSHOP.   As a part of the overall assessment of the institution's readiness to manage its enrollment, an evaluation of the climate can be done. In fact, the enrollment workshop (discussed in Chapter 9), if evaluated carefully, gives one a feeling for the climate at the institution and helps indicate whether potential for improvement of the enrollment picture lies within this area of the Enrollment Matrix (discussed in Chapter 2).

If the participants resist the workshop, this may indicate that the institution will have problems with change and with the issues involved in addressing enrollment issues effectively. Often this will indicate a commitment to a series of values inconsistent with the attitudes and behaviors that would meet the wants and needs of the users of the school's services.

An example of this is the faculty who cannot accept the idea of meeting other people's needs. This is a faculty who has all of the answers and is certain that enrollment management is only a problem of finding students who agree with them. It is a faculty or administration with little flexibility about how the educational process should be done.

This position can be even more of a problem if the individuals involved have not changed their thinking about education since the first class they took in grade school. Yes, there are many of those people in attendance. These individuals are often reflecting educational philosophies that represent the limitations of their parents, grandparents, or mentors.

On the other hand, if the workshop goes reasonably well, people want to know some things about themselves and are ready to listen, the workshop can be an excellent first step to a significant improvement in enrollment potential.

In this approach, the participants—a sample of the college or university community—are asked to complete an instrument posing various questions related to the climate of the organization. The approach that they take, their answers to the questions—individual and group, and the way in which they process the materials are all-important in developing an analysis of the climate area.

Figure 8.1 represents a composite result of several such workshops. Two facts should be noted for the group of people participating. They agree on some very important enrollment issues that the institution has to cope with, including the need for high creativity, good communication, leadership, good decision-making, recognition and support, and awareness of goals. At the same time, this group disagrees that these exist at their institution. They are saying that they would like to deal effectively with enrollment in a situation where there is low creativity, poor communication, defective decision-making, lack of awareness in terms of goals, and lack of adequate support and recognition of people in terms of enrollment.

This does not usually make a great deal of sense to the participants at this point. If they are willing to believe what they are seeing or feeling and know that it is linked to long-term enrollment success in the future, there are some changes to consider.

The school that identifies these characteristics in a survey, but later denies that they exist or are important in terms of enrollment management, will continue to struggle. Such a school does not see the relationships that are critical to future success.

	Strongly Agree				Strongly Disagree	Don't Know
1. High levels of risk-taking would be required of staff and faculty in creating a good enrollment program.	1	2	3	4	5	6
2. The level of risk-taking in my college by staff and faculty is high.	1	2	3	4	5	6
3. If tasks are not getting done, it may indicate problems.	1	2	3	4	5	6
4. Tasks generally get done at my institution on a timely basis.	1	2	3	4	5	6
5. High creativity on the part of college staff would be important in meeting enrollment goals.	1	2	3	4	5	6
6. Creativity among faculty and staff is high at my institution.	1	2	3	4	5	6
7. Good internal communication would be associated with creating a good enrollment program.	1	2	3	4	5	6
8. I am generally satisfied with my communication with people in my organization.	1	2	3	4	5	6
9. Strong leadership by senior management would be important in meeting enrollment goals.	1	2	3	4	5	6
10. The people in midmanagement positions in my institution will say that their opinions generally are heard by senior staff.	1	2	3	4	5	6
11. Trust levels are generally high at my college:						
a. between students and faculty	1	2	3	4	5	6
b. among faculty	1	2	3	4	5	6
c. between faculty and administration	1	2	3	4	5	6
d. between students and administration	1	2	3	4	5	6
12. Having a good decision-making process in place would be important in meeting enrollment goals.	1	2	3	4	5	6
13. Decision-making processes generally work well in my institution.	1	2	3	4	5	6
14. People in my institution generally feel supported in their work.	1	2	3	4	5	6
15. People at my institution generally would be willing to tell me if they felt I was NOT doing something right.	1	2	3	4	5	6
16. Having clear goals for the entire organization would be important in meeting enrollment goals.	1	2	3	4	5	6
17. The institutional goals at my college are generally clear and understood by most people.	1	2	3	4	5	6

FIGURE 8.1. COMBINED RESULTS OF A SURVEY OF CLIMATE AT SEVERAL SCHOOLS.

EVALUATING THE POTENTIAL IMPACT OF CLIMATE.   Let's look at one of the issues in the chart and see how it might impact enrollment. Lack of an effective decision-making process will likely be a final stumbling block, if not an initial one, for managing enrollment successfully.

It may be that the school will not even consider that a problem exists. They have a feeling that something is wrong but are not willing to make any decisions to investigate it completely. Many people want to go on with an investigation of the issues, but no one will initiate it. The president, who usually will need to support and initiate the process, can start or stop such an inquiry quickly.

Later, when solutions have been forthcoming, converting them into action will be unlikely to occur unless the appropriate decisions can be made on resources, content issues, and process. Even before any decisions have to be made, the flow of information and the processing of this information will be stopped if there is poor communication; the best that can be expected will be business as usual, because the flow of relevant information has been blocked. Upon examining the potential impact of the decision-making process on enrollment, the school might decide to address this issue as part of the enrollment management process.

CHANGING THE CLIMATE

There are several critical factors to consider when evaluating the climate data and the actions that are needed. It is important to assess things carefully at this point, since changing the climate is not an easy process. It seems appropriate that the area that may have the most impact is also often the most difficult to deal with.

Dealing with climate may not be critical for short-term success but *is* critical for dealing with long-term success for a school. This is represented well in the following scenario developed for Hood College:

> Between the fall of 1972 and the spring of 1975 . . . the faculty had become increasingly restless as they watched what they termed the "collapse of collegial governance." Budget preparation took place in the president's office behind seemingly closed doors. The fourteen persons who reported directly to the president appeared to be sparring with one another for attention and resources. Only in June of 1975 did the trustees become aware that the college budget had crossed the line from black to red in 1974. The use of reserves and [other] monies masked this situation from most observers. In fact, the trustees, who by now had decided to replace the president, learned that same month that the new president would inherit a budget $300,000 in the red rather than what they had thought would be a budget $300,000 in the black. What had happened? Short-term responses had worked, but at a cost to the morale and finances of the college. Longer-term strategies would be required to stabilize the college and complete the turnaround.[4]

Climate difficulties should be addressed if there is a clear connection between the difficulty and the long-term enrollment success of the institution. To merit a specific strategy, the phenomenon being studied must prevent the school from really being successful. It must indicate difficulties for the school in terms of enrolling or retaining students. This means that the school does *not* try to address other issues that may be difficult but do not impact enrollment.

A part of this analysis prior to action must include a development

---

[4]Janice Green, Arthur Levine, and associates, *Opportunity in Adversity* (San Francisco: Jossey Bass, 1985), p. 239.

of a sense of the accuracy of the data found. Often this is not difficult and people will agree readily that the phenomena are true and that they have existed for a long time. They also will agree readily that the issues being addressed can readily impact enrollment at the school.

In other cases, there will be great disagreement and denial of the data. This denial is often not rational and the approach to challenging the data becomes game-playing or loaded with feelings that are blaming, protecting, or limiting. This is often the case when the issues are very frustrating or explosive. The following quotes are important in considering changes in climate:

- "We in organizations need to be self-conscious about what we are doing so that organizational action is enlightened action—but how?"
- "Success has something to do with deliberately exploiting, or at least prizing, multiple realities instead of treating different realities or different interpretations as 'communication problems.' "
- "Since we all come to problem-solving situations from a particular place in time and space, and from a discipline, our knowledge is always limited and fragmented. Somehow organizational practices need to encompass and embrace diversity in order to reintegrate knowledge."[5]
- "The challenge of dealing with multiple realities can present significant opportunities for the organization. It can be a significant barrier to success."

In other instances, there will be a reasonable challenge that is felt as helpful, clarifying, and aimed at making certain the situation is correct before proceeding. This can be felt as a reasonable effort at collaborative problem-solving with the aim being to understand and not avoid.

Often, then, observers can tell about the accuracy of the data from a school's reaction and approach to the information and its use.

If managers have agreed with the data and want to change the climate, they must look at the process, including the steps already taken in a positive direction, by examining the climate. Building on this first step will likely now be relatively easy after getting through the first critical steps. One can now begin to change things in the rest of the system through the wise use of a task force, if the school has taken the right directions in terms of the task.

In order to get a change effort going, it is important that people see that there is a positive consequence of change. This is especially true since there will need to be changes in behavior that will require a great

[5]Linda Smircich, "Is The Concept of Culture a Paradigm for Understanding Organizations and Ourselves?" in *Organizational Culture*, P. J. Frost, L. F. Moore, M. R. Louis, C. C. Lundberg, and J. Martin (Beverly Hills: Sage, 1985), p. 55.

commitment. Without a vision of the positive payoff of the project, there will be little chance for success. These positive impressions can be developed through meetings with various people on campus and through newsletters or reports that describe the needs for change and the benefits.

An even better way to facilitate change is to talk with people. Working with individuals and describing the consequences of needed changes can help to spread the word throughout the organization. This is especially true if they also recognize the need for change.

The task force is a vehicle to make certain that there is sufficient discussion about the needs of the organization to change the system. As people in the organization see the results of better work of the task force, they will begin to try to obtain the same results and benefits. Modeling of effective behavior is a powerful tool to use in this regard.

A LOOK AT EACH OF THE KEY TASK FORCE ISSUES

This is what makes the structure of the task force so important. The group must be of sufficient size and influence to impact the organization. The people on the task force should be able to demonstrate to a large enough portion of the organization that things are better.

Working with the task force, then, is critical. The enrollment manager needs to use this group at all levels and make certain that they recognize the importance of modeling to the community. This group needs to be willing to work on better processes for interaction, processes to deal with increasing creativity, and the development of better decision-making and problem-solving capacities.

The people on the task force will need to be recognized and supported by people in positions of influence in the organization. They also may need to learn how to recognize and support themselves more positively.

INSTITUTIONAL ISSUES

What is being sought in terms of achieving progress is to deal with issues of co-orientation and institutional goals.

The more people in the institution are together in terms of the goals, the easier it will be to deal with successful futures. Of course, one cannot expect—nor is it desirable—to have agreement on everything. But it *is* important to have agreement on the key issues of service to students, as well as identifying and meeting the expectations of students and the organization.

Of course, a part of this cooperation is developed through agreement on what the goals are and what the successful pathway would be for the college or university. The clearer the understanding of the goals, the easier it is to make changes.

These goals can be formulated in several areas, including:

- The quality of students.
- The type of students in terms of attitudes and beliefs.
- The mix of students from a geographic perspective.
- The mix of students from an ethnic/minority perspective.
- The mix of students from a program perspective.

These goals tend to describe the desired conditions which, if people can visualize them, will motivate thinking and actions to achieve the desired results.

–9–
THE ENROLLMENT TASK FORCE

Dealing With Change and Climate to Improve Enrollment

The use of task forces in enrollment efforts has proven effective because of the role of change in building an effective enrollment program, and the need to deal with climate issues as enrollment problems are addressed. More and more, enrollment managers and senior staff members are faced with implementing changes at various levels as institutions attempt to move toward a more successful enrollment future.

The task force must develop strategies and plans for each of the key variables of the Matrix, including product, data, communication, management, and climate. The right composition is required to deal with any critical issues to enrollment that may occur in these areas.

CHANGE AND THE TASK FORCE

Effecting changes related to enrollment can be difficult. These can be changes in how some particular procedure is done—such as sending a publication or implementing a different type of on-campus program. They also can mean the wholesale changing of structures and attitudes about enrollment management within the institution. In an institution where enrollment is failing, the basic situation is already disquieting and the prospect for change even more so:

> The director was presenting the enrollment data to the faculty, and they were more than a little upset.
>
> The enrollment was not going up, and this would now be the fourth year in a row that the numbers were down. The fac-

ulty could not see spending any more money in the enrollment area. The director, however, knew that the recruitment program would need a better salary schedule so that staff members would stay, and considerably more money would need to be spent on the publications and materials.

From the faculty perspective, there was only one problem. The director and her staff were not selling the school. The faculty wanted nothing to do with more or better publications—they wanted results with no better materials. After all, there must be a great many students out there waiting to come to the school.

One of the enrollment staff members, when making a presentation to the faculty, was hotly attacked by the faculty and was driven from the room by a barrage of questions and what felt like personal attacks.

Changes often spread from the enrollment office to other parts of the institution. The changes that are needed can be found in many areas of the organization. The faculty, the services, the president, the deans, and the staff may be involved in change issues. Because of the depth and scope of the potential change efforts, colleges and universities have to pay attention to several issues associated with change:

- Is change needed or not?
- Is the change related to improving or altering the enrollment picture at the institution?
- If change is required, what issues need to be addressed in a systematic way?
- How does the institution develop the intent to change?
- How is intention converted into reality?
- Does the change involve individuals, groups, the organization, or groups of organizations?
- How can the institution make changes in the most productive way?

CLIMATE AND THE TASK FORCE

The area of climate has a special importance in the enrollment task force approach. The climate of a school (discussed in Chapter 8) has a unique place in developing effective enrollment programs. It is critical in terms of enrollment of students, both new and returning, and the climate, if a problem, can be very difficult to improve.

One of the main roles of the task force in the development of effective enrollment programs is creating better understanding of climate issues and of opportunities for changing the climate.

UNDERSTANDING

The task force is a microcosm of the institution. It should represent all of the issues that are preventing the school from being successful. It surfaces these issues in a small group that can develop understanding about the key issues important to climate. In the following case, a very specific problem had to be recognized before improvements could be made:

> The enrollment at Paxton University had been declining for three years. New students were getting harder to find, while present students were getting harder to keep. The situation was very visible to everyone.
>
> One of the causes of the problem was a denial on the part of key faculty members that the problem was going to require them to change their ways of doing things. Some had been teaching the same way for twenty years and saw no need to change.
>
> The second problem was that it was not much fun anymore to teach. Most of the faculty had been around for a long time and the thrill of the task had left. They were spending less time on campus and more time getting ready for retirement.

This was the scene that had to be addressed as the school tried to cope with its enrollment. The faculty felt the admissions office should be changed and that the only ones not to blame were the faculty members themselves.

The task force at the school contained many of the faculty and staff that contributed to the prevailing morale on campus. The first two weeks of task force work were difficult, but then they began to make progress. The implications of the data were inescapable. The problem suddenly belonged to everyone, and everyone needed to deal with it.

CHANGING THE CLIMATE

There is no simple way to change a climate at an institution. The inertia of doing things in certain ways by certain people must be addressed, and overcoming this requires patience, time, and skills which people may or may not have.

The climate cannot be changed with a workshop or two, with reading some books, or with an external consultant who spends a few months working for the school. Changing the climate requires that at least one key group of individuals develops better ways to deal with climate difficulties and that these skills gradually be transferred to the rest of the organization. The task force can develop styles of feedback, communication, recognition, support, and decision-making. The task force members can serve as models as others observe the results of the work.

Lack of trust is a potential negative at many institutions that can be addressed by the task force. The trust levels in the task force can become very high, so that the importance of trust will be appreciated. This trust level can become contagious as people begin to appreciate the feelings of trust and commitment to the institution that evolve over time. Eventually, a new inertia can be developed that will support a good climate and allow change to occur productively.

FACTORS IN TASK FORCE SUCCESS

When the task force approach becomes an important part of the enrollment effort, having an effective group depends on several critical factors. These include the composition of the task force, successful diffusion of new ideas, development of strategies, education of task force members, rewards and recognition, support, absence of penalties, and having a process that works well.

COMPOSITION OF THE TASK FORCE

Selecting the right task force composition is an important first step in creating an effective enrollment management program. It can best start by defining what is not critical in the makeup of the task force.

It is not important that it be a specific size or that certain key people automatically be included in the group. Prior rules at the school for developing committees or composition of present committees should not be the basis for the formation of this group of people. In fact, this is a good opportunity to establish some new relationships for people who need to be a part of the process of enrollment management. This may represent an opportunity for people who feel isolated to become a part of the school. If there are traditional ways of creating a committee, or if there are specific norms for building committees, they should be avoided. For this reason, it may be better that the initial task force be an ad hoc group that will eventually decide what the final group should be as they conduct their initial work for the school.

The composition of the task force is related to the following issues:

- The need to create enrollment plans for the key areas of the Enrollment Matrix (discussed in Chapter 2): product, data, communication, management, and climate.
- Developing positive inertia around the management of enrollment.
- Establishing an effective mechanism for change of the institution.
- The need to improve and develop the climate of the institution.

- Motivating people at the institution with regard to enrollment management.
- The need to have a continuing source of energy and resources for enrollment management.

The size and composition of the task force must contribute to the effectiveness of the group in each of these areas. The right members must be present to accomplish the goals of the work.

The composition should include faculty, administration, staff, and students. At times, the task force also will need to include board members or alumni. The number of representatives may vary, but the task force should include representatives from each of these groups.

If the advising program, for example, is thought to be a potential problem for the organization, the task force should include those people who can impact this area. This could be faculty, students, or staff members who are particularly interested or knowledgeable in student development.

The actual members may be individuals who will be instrumental in developing people in a positive way. Or an individual may be included who frequently has been a barrier to change:

The bursar had always been a problem at Windstar College. Every student had to pay a bill, and that meant that every student had to deal with the bursar and the staff.

The office was notorious for giving people a hard time. Closing the payment window in the faces of students who had stood in line was standard procedure. If it was time to call it quits for the day, it did not matter who was there.

Students paying bills were treated as if the university were doing them a favor. The office hours were inconvenient, especially for the nontraditional learner.

This office—and this person primarily—had been a problem for years and was unlikely to change. Thus, John was on the task force. It was hoped that, somehow, through insights into the magnitude of the problem, he would change.

In summary, key issues are to gather the right people in the right numbers who will:

- Be able to create the right influence to get things to happen.
- Be influenced in some way by the work.
- Be able to create and aid in implementing the plans for the key variable areas.
- Be able to assist in building the climate that is needed for enrollment management.
- Need to be involved in any change process that is apt to occur.

DIFFUSION

The process of diffusion is familiar to any individual who has taken a good science course in high school or college. In this process, a small amount of a material spreads so that it is distributed throughout the system.

With the task force, it is hoped that the members diffuse ideas and feelings about enrollment management throughout the system. One person is encouraged to talk to another, move ideas through the system, and draw ideas from the system into the task force. In this way, the ideas of people on the task force can be presented to the community and be evaluated. The impressions of the institutional community members should also become the substrata for consideration of the task force.

EDUCATION OF TASK FORCE MEMBERS

The education of task force members is essential to the development of an effective program. It is unlikely that the task force will create an effective program without some knowledge, skills, and attitudes about the task.

For example, building a plane is, in anyone's terms, a very complex job. To assign this to a college committee would be clearly recognized as foolish and impractical. It is unlikely that any one person or group of people on campus would have the expertise to do this—and they would readily acknowledge this if asked.

Constructing an enrollment master plan is almost as complex as building a plane. And yet people launch the project without much background in the concepts and processes of tasks that are involved. To do this will ensure that the project will be mediocre at best and will not develop the high-quality improvements that a school wants, needs, and deserves. Development of insights about enrollment management is essential to constructing an excellent program.

THE PROCESS OF EDUCATION.   A first priority is to make certain that members understand the need for education in enrollment management. The task force leader will have to do some selling of the idea if the seriousness of effort is to occur. If issues of time, recognition, and support already have been addressed properly, it is likely that the idea of education will be acceptable. A few good examples of education will probably suffice to get cooperation from the group.

One of the best ways to start is with the Enrollment Matrix (discussed in Chapter 2). Orientation and discussion of the principles involved in the matrix can be an easy way to develop discussion on the key issues. This can be done through the use of slides, overheads, reading, discussion, presentations, or especially through the use of workshops focused on attitudes about the matrix.

WORKSHOPS.   The workshop approach is a very positive method that can communicate to the group as a whole the issues on which understanding is good and the areas where further thinking and experience are required. This can be particularly helpful regarding the variables and the impact of attitudes and beliefs on enrollment management.

Not all of the attributes are difficult to conceptualize. The ideas of goals and resources for each area are relatively easy to grasp. Developing the goals for the product is something about which most faculty members feel good. The ideas of process and content are more difficult. The workshop approach allows us to use specific techniques to develop understanding of these last two areas.

The issue of *product* is analyzed in Table 9.1, which is a survey that might be used in the product section of a workshop. Note the different areas of the product that have been included and the issues that might prompt discussion as the survey is completed.

The issue of *content* can be examined in the workshop context by asking questions about how a particular area is seen or constructed. Content, as we have seen, means that there are right and wrong ways to approach anything associated with enrollment management. This includes such areas as:

- The development of an advising program.
- The career counseling and placement program.
- Financial aid.
- The computer major, and other career-oriented programs.
- The ways in which faculty should or should not interact with students.

The way that each of these is carried out for a school may involve unique considerations. People on the task force will need to understand, at least minimally, the various options that are possible for each of these areas in terms of content.

REVEALING ATTITUDES AND BELIEFS OF THE TASK FORCE.   Attitudes and beliefs ultimately can serve as serious hindrances to the success of a school's enrollment effort, and often represent the first barriers to the progress of an enrollment task force. Identifying members' beliefs and those that may be helpful or a hindrance to enrollment management is an important step in the education of task force members.

Common predispositions include such assertions as these:

- Faculty should not have to be involved in enrollment management.
- There are too few funds.

TABLE 9.1. Product Survey

	Strongly Agree				Strongly Disagree	No Opinion
1. The product that a college has to offer is critical to meeting enrollment goals.	1	2	3	4	5	6
2. The environment of a college is very important in enrolling and retaining students.	1	2	3	4	5	6
3. My college offers good services that meet the needs of students.	1	2	3	4	5	6
4. Faculty are the most important appeal in the product area in terms of meeting enrollment goals.	1	2	3	4	5	6
5. The area of student services is a critical aspect of the product.	1	2	3	4	5	6
6. Academic programs and curriculum are the most important part of the product area in terms of attracting and retaining students.	1	2	3	4	5	6
7. We will have to *evaluate* our product carefully to see that it best fits potential student markets.	1	2	3	4	5	6
8. We may have to change the product we offer if we are to meet enrollment and retention goals.	1	2	3	4	5	6
9. We will have to compete harder in the marketplace to meet our enrollment goals.	1	2	3	4	5	6
10. My college offers an excellent student life program that focuses on personal and social skills development.	1	2	3	4	5	6
11. My college has good facilities and modern equipment that meet the needs of students.	1	2	3	4	5	6
12. Changing our product will be relatively easy.	1	2	3	4	5	6
13. My college generally prepares students well for their careers.	1	2	3	4	5	6
14. Students tend to pick the college that best meets their educational and career goals regardless of cost.	1	2	3	4	5	6

- Students should come to our school without this much effort.
- The administration is our enemy (from a faculty member).
- The faculty members are our enemies (from an administrator).
- My opinions are not important (from a student on the committee).

REWARDS, RECOGNITION, SUPPORT, ABSENCE OF PENALTIES

For anyone serving on the task force, there must be ways for that person to be recognized and supported for the effort.

Frequently, people do not feel recognized for their service on various committees and groups. It becomes a just another task to do at some schools. It represents an obligation or part of the grind for the individual involved. This cannot be the case if the enrollment task force is to do well.

The president, department chairpersons, deans, and students need to be encouraged to support the task force members in various ways. The task force participants must feel that their efforts are important and are needed in setting the course of the organization. This group must clearly be seen as unique in contrast to other committee or group assignments on campus.

Likewise, there should not be penalties for serving on the task force, as would probably be the case if this faculty member felt pressed to do so:

> Joan was up for tenure and had been asked to serve on the enrollment task force. She was having difficulty giving her time, and when the chairperson asked about this, she indicated she was having problems with her department head.
>
> The issue was research. Joan was being evaluated for tenure on the basis of her research productivity and the teaching evaluation of her students. The department head looked upon her work with the task force as unimportant and perhaps something she should not be doing. Certainly, it should not interfere with what was truly important—teaching and producing a research paper this year.

Even though the president had indicated both a strong interest in this committee's doing quality work and the importance of its work to the school, the prospect of joining it was not positive for Joan.

INTRODUCING THE ENROLLMENT MANAGEMENT PROCESS

We have found, in our work with many schools, that there is a need for a systematic process for introducing successful enrollment management into a college or university. Since the enrollment management idea involves the integration of several areas of the school and the involvement and commitment of people at many levels, the process of introduction becomes critical to success. Introduction of the task force into the process at the right time can increase its effectiveness and the commitment of people to work in this group. If the process is not carefully carried out it can create more problems than existed originally and can set the enrollment effort back. Example of problems that result from lack of attention to the process include:

- Development of databases that ultimately sit on the shelf and have little impact on the enrollment program.
- Development of databases that have little relevance to the problems being addressed by the school.
- Discouragement and hostility on the part of the campus community due to lack of immediate success in enrollment.
- Requirements for action on the part of the campus community outside the enrollment office that are ignored.
- Data or information that cannot be used for improvement of communication because the capacity to use databases and delivery systems is not in place.
- Introduction of the task force into the process before there is much that it can do. Individuals on the task force who were excited at first find their enthusiasm dwindling when they have little to do.

To avoid these types of results it is wise to look at the process of introduction of enrollment management as occurring in several stages with the final stage being the implementation of strategies that will achieve the desired enrollment state. These intermediate stages can be viewed as transition stages that allow for a reasonable progression from one step to the next in the process. One step can lead to the next such that a solid building of enrollment success occurs. In this case people on the campus can see that progress is occurring and focus not on immediate number increases but rather on solid progress toward a successful enrollment future. If the people on campus understand the process they will know what to expect and when. There will be more patience if the process makes sense.

In the enrollment management process it is especially important to recognize that a significant amount of time will be required. It is reasonable to expect that the correction of the enrollment problem will take time. Often the enrollment problems occurred over a long period of time (see Figure 9.1) and will likely take a long period of time to correct. In the case of this school, the decreases had occurred consistently during each of the last five years. In this case, the turnaround required a great many changes that took time to introduce.

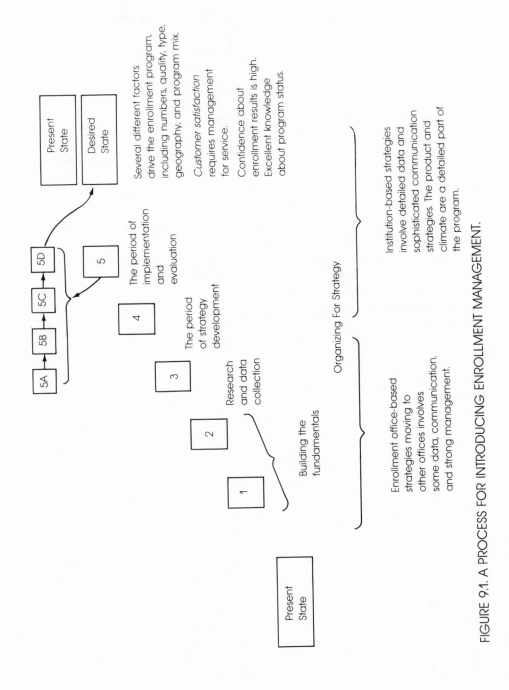

FIGURE 9.1. A PROCESS FOR INTRODUCING ENROLLMENT MANAGEMENT.

A SUGGESTED PROCESS

The general process for introducing enrollment management is illustrated in Figure 9.1. The process begins with a definition of the present enrollment state and then moves to the building of enrollment fundamentals. This is followed by the development of the database. The process then moves to strategy development and implementation. In the process one step should likely occur before the next. In the end, the desired enrollment state of the organization is achieved and a process is in place that can keep the institution focused on achieving this desired state year after year.

In fact, a desired enrollment state, however preliminary, should be in place before the process starts. If this is done, the actions required to move forward become more meaningful and can be targeted more effectively. Once the school is ready to move toward an enrollment management mode, it should then begin the introduction of better fundamentals—assuming that these are not being done well. The preliminary desired state will likely change as more information becomes available, but this state will begin the process and serve as an initial focus for the research design.

The enrollment fundamentals would include actions in areas generally associated with the communication and management sections of the enrollment matrix including:

- Development of effective communication programs that can use the database for enrollment and effective word processing.
- Development of the ability to communicate personally with potential students.
- Implementation of a training program that could be used to develop staff and others in their contact with potential students (discussed in chapter 7 page 146).
- Implementation of an enrollment master plan including a preliminary desired state and key operational strategies (discussed in chapter 7 pages 133 to 141).
- Implementation of a management information system (discussed in chapter 7).
- Formation of an enrollment task force that can participate in the development of the research strategy that would be used to develop the database.

If these actions can fall into place, the development of a database and the subsequent enrollment strategies can be productive. The data will actually result in actions that will improve the enrollment situation at the college.

The second phase of introduction of enrollment management would be the development of the database. While this might be started during the period of dealing with fundamentals, it will likely not be completed until after the fundamental actions are working to improve the enrollment results. In this phase the full set of surveys, focus groups, competition studies, and environmental scans would be completed. With these results the fundamentals will be even more targeted and the task force can become involved in the development of enrollment strategy and the targeting of the desired enrollment state.

The final phase of implementation of enrollment management would be the implementation of strategy. The strategies would be targeted at the consumer, the competition, the institution itself, and the businesses or environment around the school. This combination of overall tactical strategies, when implemented, spell the end of the process and very likely the achievement of the desired enrollment state.

Of course, by the time the school has arrived at that point, a new desired state is likely emerging and the process will usually start over again at the level of data collection. It is likely, at that point, that enrollment management has become an institutional way of doing business and one that will continue to be of value to the institution.

TASK FORCE INVOLVEMENT.   The best point at which to introduce the task force into the process is the research stage. The task force, with its basic knowledge of enrollment management, can be involved in the research plan, the development of surveys and focus groups, the subsequent refinement and solidification of the desired state, and the strategy development that will lead to enrollment success in the future.

At the database and following stages, the task force has a critical role in communicating the work of enrollment management to the institution and insuring that the appropriate people and parts of the institution are included at the right time and place.

AN OVERVIEW OF THE PROCESS.   Table 9.2 presents a scenario that was played out for one of the task forces that we have worked with in the enrollment area. This will provide an idea of the sequence of events and some of the things that can happen as enrollment management is put into place.

TABLE 9.2. An Outline of the Key Issues and Milestones for an Enrollment Task Force

Issue Area	Observations or Actions	Comments
Is there an enrollment problem?	The following was observed about the enrollment program at Granite College: • Enrollment was off by 26 percent over a three-year period. • The downward trend was interrupted only by one or two years over the last eight years. • The college was much less selective the last five years. • The college had been giving out much more financial aid over the last three years. • There had been releases of faculty and staff over the last five years. • The retention of students was at its lowest in the last two years. • The satisfaction of students revealed in initial focus groups was very low. • Several strategies had been tried to turn things around but the trend continued. • There had been five directors of admission in the last four years.	There was an enrollment problem in several areas. There was no disagreement that the problem was serious.
Is this a problem that will require change or work with climate?	The following observations indicated that changes would be needed and that there were likely to be some climate issues: • Trust levels were low. The administration had little credibility. • Confidence levels were low everywhere. The faculty did not trust the staff or the	This combination of issues indicated that the task force approach would be essential.

TABLE 9.2. *continued*

Issue Area	Observations or Actions	Comments
	administration and they did not trust the faculty. • The students were caught in the middle. • Understanding was hard to obtain. Very few people wanted to listen to what was happening. • Resource allocations would need to change. Some people might see themselves as losers and some as winners. • The president did not interact with anyone, least of all his own people.	
Getting people involved in education.	The first workshop was held. This was for the whole faculty. The thinking was that before the task force was formed there should be overall acceptance of the idea of enrollment management before moving into the task force work. It was felt that we had to verify the need to have a task force involved. The agenda for the first workshop included: • Development of the day's objectives. • Introduction to the Enrollment Matrix through the use of a survey that developed the main points of the concept. This survey was developed for the college. • Discussion of the responses to the surveys as they were completed by groups.	The workshop went well. The enthusiasm of the participants was very high and people were ready to go to work on the problems. People generally agreed that there was a set of issues that needed to be addressed and that the whole community should be involved.

TABLE 9.2. *continued*

Issue Area	Observations or Actions	Comments
	• Comparison of individual survey responses to group survey responses.	
	• Development of key restraining and driving forces.	
	Observations of the day:	
	• The participation was excellent except for the academic dean, who slept through the event on both days.	
	• The dean of student affairs was not able to mix well. People avoided him and he avoided them.	
	• People showed up on time and stayed late.	
	At the end of the second day:	
	• The president entertained the idea of a task force.	
	• Three days after the workshop, the president appointed the task force, including faculty, students, staff, and board.	
Organizing the task force	Organization sessions were held. In these sessions, the following important agendas were undertaken:	
	• Establishing desired outcomes for the task force. What will happen if the work of the task force is successful?	
	• Development of key restraining and driving forces in regard to the desired outcomes.	
	• Development of strategies for the achievement of the desired outcomes for the task force effort.	

TABLE 9.2. *continued*

Issue Area	Observations or Actions	Comments
	• Negotiation with the president and the board over decision-making processes. • Separation into separate work groups. Separate groups were developed for each of the areas of the matrix.	
Setting goals	The task force subgroups met to develop enrollment goals for each of the areas. The goals were developed and considered by the complete task force. Once these goals were accepted, they were circulated at the college and returned to the task force. Revisions were made and the goals sent to the president and the executive committee.	
Developing strategy	The task force subgroups considered strategies and followed the same process of circulation of materials for review. One of the strategies called for an evaluation of the academic dean and the dean of academic affairs. These people were aware of the concern of the task force. The president and the board reacted to the task force recommendations. Within three months, both the dean of academic affairs and the academic dean had been replaced. Strategy and goals were in place.	To reach the end of this state required six months. In this period, the task force had become very close and the process began to give the participants some feeling of ownership and control over the outcomes of the college's future.
Developing actions	Over the next few months, various offices and the task force worked on	During the time of developing actions, several issues arose

TABLE 9.2. *continued*

Issue Area	Observations or Actions	Comments
	specific action plans and timetables to achieve the strategies developed by the task force.	around the availability of resources.
	The actions included an upgrade of the dorms and the development of a new curriculum based on the social services and the importance of experiences as a part of every student's program.	In general, these issues were resolved with few problems. In some cases, there were feelings of loss, but these could be put into the perspective of gain for the whole college.
	Several program and service changes were suggested with the majority of them implemented.	Several actions required faculty commitment. These were generally taken on with little problem.
	New administrators were hired and, for the first time in several years, a college picnic held over the Memorial Day holiday was attended by almost everyone.	
Wrap-up	The enrollment master plan was accepted by the task force, the president, and the board in September. This included a permanent task force that would evaluate the enrollment program each month and report to the college on progress toward implementation of the program.	
Evaluation and restart*	The task force continues to evaluate and will repeat the process of plan development in the spring.	

* Each school that has used this approach has had a different sequence and outcome. On the whole, however, their experiences were positive and moved the institutions toward better climates and toward a more positive implementation of desired change.

-10-
DEVELOPING
ENROLLMENT STRATEGY
An Application of the Matrix Approach

There are two general types of enrollment emphasis that are needed by schools. The first is the need for localized efforts in the office responsible for enrollment management. This office needs a great deal of work and, because of this, work in enrollment from a total institutional perspective is not advised.

In the second approach, the solution of enrollment problems involves the total institution and will be strategic in nature. In this second case, there needs to be widespread institutional involvement at all levels directed at resolving enrollment issues. Examination of these two phenomena provides insight into the use of the Enrollment Matrix. In the second case, issues of market segmentation become important, as does the use of market segmentation in strategy development, as discussed in this chapter.

In the office-centered approach to enrollment management, much of the effort concentrates in the communication and management section of the matrix. In the following scenario, the institution was not doing the fundamentals well, and no amount of market data or product attention could therefore have had an impact. It is likely that the climate area of the matrix may have been involved in the solution of this enrollment problem as well:

> The president of Miner College had just received the results of an enrollment audit. As he read the observations, he noted the following:
> - There was no functional enrollment master plan.
> - There was no management information system for enrollment.

- No one knew the number of inquiries.
- The campus visits were down.
- There had been no training of the enrollment staff.
- Mailings were not going to students on a regular basis.
- The number of junior inquiries was unknown.
- Staff morale was low, and the director was very defensive throughout the audit.
- Faculty confidence in the enrollment office was at a low level.

The list seemed to go on and on. The faculty had lost touch with the program and had very little confidence in the director. He knew it and they knew it, but they had not been able to talk about it (a clear climate issue). Little cooperation could be expected from faculty members or present students in terms of contacting potential students for fall.

At this school, the problems of planning, training, staff morale, and faculty confidence would need to be addressed before any significant look at product or data would make sense. Research would, at present, be totally out of the question. Institutional change could not occur until the enrollment office had been addressed. This school needs to work on the fundamentals (see chapter 9, page 336).

STRATEGY

Strategic approaches to enrollment issues are a relatively new phenomenon. They have been brought about primarily because of external factors at schools, including demographics, changes in consumer attitudes, and increased attention to each student by many schools. All of this adds up to more competition. As there are fewer students to be distributed among institutions, someone will end up losing students if another institution gains. Therefore, strategic initiatives are called for.

Strategic initiatives can be defined as a set of actions on the part of a school to differentiate itself significantly from competitors or to respond, through strength, to the disturbances in the environment and thereby meet enrollment goals. These can be generally targeted at the consumer, the competition, the institution, and the environment of the school.

The keys to this definition are the words *set, initiatives,* and *strength.* In times of stress, the institution needs to react and not let the marketplace determine in a negative way the fate of the organization. The institution should take the initiative through strength, which may mean taking some immediate initiatives while conducting research and developing long-term strategies.

In addition, the strategy will involve creative actions on several fronts, which implies the use of a matrix approach. In such cases, the Enrollment Matrix (shown on p. 13) is an excellent tool for helping in strategy development and implementation.

THE MATRIX AND STRATEGY

Four basic agendas emerge from the matrix when it is used in a strategic sense: the product strategy, the communication strategy, the overall management strategy, and the climate strategy. The data area of the matrix is used to provide overall information for the institution in developing strategic initiatives: the appropriate effort obviously involves a data strategy for each action.

The enrollment task force develops a set of interlocking initiatives designed to provide the institution with an overall advantage in the marketplace. The following pages explore the use of the Enrollment Matrix in developing strategic enrollment initiatives. This analysis is followed by a discussion of the development of segmentation and strategic actions.

PRODUCT STRATEGIES

Product strategies generally involve a combination of actions that can include programs, curriculum, people, services, and the environment of the institution. These types of strategies commonly involve such actions as reduction/addition of majors, forming alliances, developing services, or moving into more advanced financial aid programs. Too often, however, an institution will try to overcome its problems without reference to the product. For many schools, this will mean the selling of what the school has, regardless of fit with the marketplace or fit with the competition. This "take it or leave it" philosophy is more widespread than many would like to believe. It is evidenced by such strategies as going into nontraditional markets without fundamentally changing the school's programs.

SOME VIEWS OF PRODUCT STRATEGIES.   Product strategies can include actions in any or all of the attributes of the matrix, including goals, resources, content, or process. Possible strategies for all these attributes are demonstrated in Table 10.1. It is also characteristic of this area that it is very dependent on data for development and on the climate area for implementation. In the following case the data was available, but the climate made its diffusion difficult:

> The database for Hilton College indicated that students were particularly concerned about advising, goal setting, and men-

TABLE 10.1. Sample Strategies for Attributes in the Enrollment Matrix

ATTRIBUTE	SAMPLE STRATEGY
Goals	1. A shift from serving graduate and professional students to serving students moving directly into careers. 2. A concentration on high-quality students. 3. Strengthening of the ability to serve students from a particular country. 4. Development of a program emphasis on quality and mentorships.
Resources	1. Accumulation of the funds to develop strong responses in the co-op and career areas. 2. Developing resources to place special emphasis on computers. 3. Developing additional scholarship funds.
Content	1. Special training of advisors in a relationship strategy. 2. Reducing the number of majors to concentrate energy on strong programs. 3. Developing new majors. 4. Developing a special emphasis on career counseling. 5. Developing programs and curricular options to work with nontraditional students. 6. Developing a better advising system and approach. 7. Using special advisors for new students.
Process	1. The development of a service strategy that maximizes positive outcomes from student contact with people at the school.

toring. Upon discussion and work with this data, Hilton developed the concept of goal-focused advising as a unique product strategy.

After much discussion, and as people began to understand the concept more completely, there was considerable resistance by the faculty to the idea. People in the student affairs office had developed the concept but not shared much of the information with the faculty. As a result, the faculty was unclear about what was needed. In the end, the idea did not work because the school could not get cooperation from the faculty about who would do the job.

SYSTEMATIC PRODUCT STRATEGIES.   Levitt's idea of a system rather than a specific program or major offering (see pp. 38 and 39) represents an example of a potential product strategy. As discussed in Chapter 3, where this idea was introduced, the institution following this approach would be valued for its ability to package a group of items to meet student expectations. The value would be in the strength of the package and not in the individual majors. The strategy is a good one when a small school finds itself working against bigger institutions.

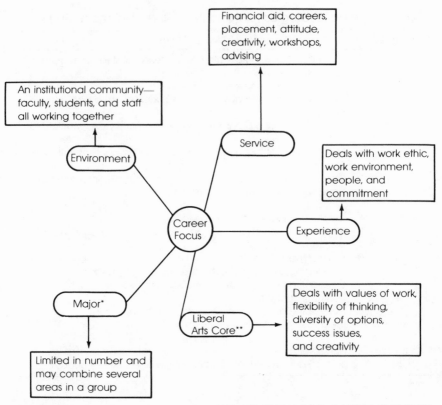

FIGURE 10.1. EXAMPLE OF A SYSTEMATIC STRATEGY FOR CAREER SUCCESS.

*This may be a limited number and in no way represents the core.
**This does not imply a set of majors in the liberal arts. Rather, it is a set of courses and other approaches that produce a sense for the liberal arts as related to a career outcome.

A sample package emphasizing career success is represented in Figure 10.1.

In this package, no piece is judged to be more important than the other to the central issue of a career focus. The experiential, service, or environmental components are headed by the most qualified people possible and they work as a team in developing career emphasis programs complete with special placement opportunities. The career focus could be on a generally recognized career area as business or teaching, or on areas such as graduate or professional schools. The career emphasis could also be in such areas as history and English. In this type of package, the key factors for success would be the school's ability to place its students and produce support courses and opportunities for the program emphasis.

MORE GENERAL STRATEGIES

Another way of viewing a product strategy might involve a dyad construction. The model below represents a dyad between quality and personal attention:

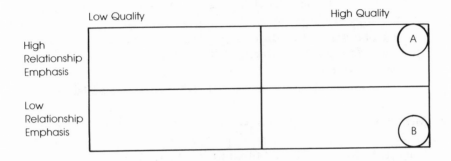

Here, institution A is of high quality and has a high relationship emphasis. (Using the term relationship management rather than personal attention is critical to the concept.) The school that emphasizes relationship management is one that values advising, time between students and faculty, mentoring, and having all of this done by the best faculty available. Because this is a defined product initiative, funding, training of staff and faculty, and use of time and evaluation would be based on these items. The key point is to maintain the traditional quality resources of the product while adding the relationship dimension. The relationship aspect would need to be managed as well as any other part of the program.

COMMUNICATION STRATEGIES

The chapter on communication (chapter 6) presented a formula associated with the enrollment of students. In this formula, there are eight key communication variables, including such items as the use of messages, awareness, and image. In this case, the communication variables are the items to work with in developing enrollment strategy.

To realize the product strategies, a well-developed communication strategy needs to be put in place at the same time the school is dealing with the product issue. Doing this will greatly enhance the possibility of success for the product option. Showing that the product option can meet students' wants and needs is critical. This can best be done through accurate messages and personal contact with the student around the product.

In the previous example, a product strategy option was selected that included becoming identified as a school that was a high-quality and high-relationship institution. To this end, the communication strategy should clearly reflect these important issues.

The themes of the communication strategy would include:

- Emphasis on the campus visit.
- A well-developed campus visit program that reinforces the idea that relationships are important.
- The use of letters; letters from department chair persons and present students would be very effective (a tone and style of copy that reflect personal attention).
- Messages in initial publications that reflect quality and faculty relationships.
- Messages in later publications that reflect the total institutional environment and its ability to support relationships. These would be delivered through copy, photographs, and design.
- Training and skill development for the enrollment staff to build abilities to deal with relationships.
- Follow-up by volunteers that reinforces the quality of the school in terms of its current students and graduates and the importance of relationships. Volunteers would be used heavily to provide support and keep commitments in place.

CLIMATE STRATEGIES

Climate strategies can be linked with a successful product strategy by looking at the key areas of climate: commitment, competence, and consistency.

The product strategy—even if it makes sense in the marketplace—will not succeed if there are low levels of commitment to the effort. This can be seen in many of the books that are available on curricular changes. Too often, a positive product change is dropped before it gets a good start. Building commitment should be considered carefully as the new product strategy is constructed. Involvement, meetings, internal sales, leadership support, and special presentations are all critical to having the strategy work in the long run. Building commitment requires free flow of information—one of the ingredients of a good enrollment program.

Competence is another key climate issue. The strategy may, as in the case of the relationship strategy mentioned earlier, depend heavily on the development of new skills on the part of faculty and staff. Often the motivation of the faculty and staff is not included in the consideration of the cost and time needed to implement new strategy initiatives, as in the following case:

Johnson College spent the better part of two months examining ways in which it might develop a more competitive niche in the marketplace. Being small and facing a large number of competitors, it needed to offer an educational option that would stand out.

The strategy developed at Johnson College was to offer a better and more integrated student development program. This would include more *time* with the student, specific work on helping the student set goals, and assistance to the student in developing strategies to meet the goals. Much of the effort would depend on the faculty doing more work with students and having the time and skills to help the students sort out their directions.

The program was introduced, publications were prepared, and finally the faculty were asked to attend a series of workshops to develop the knowledge or skills to do the job. The faculty indicated, as a body, they did not want to be developed, did not want to do the tasks, and felt, initially, that the program was not reasonable or workable. After two years, the program failed. The strategy was excellent, desired by potential students and not offered anywhere else, but it was not a strategy that was helpful to Johnson College.

MARKET SEGMENTATION: STRATEGY IN THE MANAGEMENT AREA

In the management area of the Enrollment Matrix, the issue of market segmentation plays a large part in the development of strategies. To use market segmentation, the market is divided into specific clusters, and the efforts of the institution are targeted at one or more of the clusters. This is done to give the institution a specific advantage with a particular group of people.

In the use of market segmentation, there are several general patterns to consider. In Figure 10.2, Cluster #1 and Cluster #2 are market segments that are very different in terms of their characteristics. These might be age or ability segments. Managing the enrollment of both these groups might prove to be somewhat difficult. There is a large gap between the clusters, and the resources of the institution, from the product side, might have to be spread too thinly. Limited resources might be stretched even farther as the needs of these two groups are served. Communication with these groups also might prove difficult. The farther apart the clusters are, the more difficult it is to manage enrollment.

In terms of Cluster #3 and #4, there is some overlap which might make the development of product and communication much easier. Resources can be shared in meeting the needs of a new group of people. In this case, the matrix can be very helpful in making the appropriate adjustments.

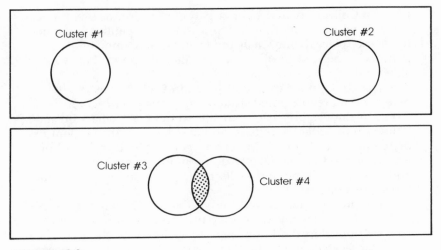

FIGURE 10.2.

SEGMENTATION AND THE MATRIX.   There are two considerations in developing a *segmentation* strategy: the *matrix variables* that might be selected for attention, and the attributes of the variables that are considered.

There are five areas in which changes are made most often in terms of the matrix:

- *Product goals.* What is the primary focus of the product that will serve student needs as determined through research?
- *Product resources.* Are there any new or additional resources that might be needed?
- *Product process.* How will the school's behavior change as the segment varies?
- *Data content.* Are there any new questions that have to be asked to develop strategy?
- *Communication content.* Are there changes in messages, amount, or type of communication that are needed?

These parts of the matrix might be specific targets for thinking when developing enrollment strategy. Following is an examination of segmentation variables and the use of the matrix in segmentation.

THE KEY SEGMENTATION VARIABLES.   A specific scheme for segmentation of potential students is represented in Figure 10.3. Here, the major segmentation variables are:

- *Type of student.* With which types of students does the school want to deal?

Segmentation Description	Do Not Know	Low Ability To Meet Students' Needs	High Ability To Meet Students' Needs
Type Of Student			
Traditional			
Nontraditional			
Graduate			
Undergraduate			
Professional			
Major			
Attribute Descriptors			
Male/Female			
Geographic			
Age			
Income			
Academic			
SAT			
ACT			
GPA			
Rank			
Race			
Program Preference			
Attitudes And Beliefs			
Expectations			
"Ideal"			
Attractive			
Single Sex/Co-Ed School			
Value Orientation			
Basic			
Extended			
Student			
Family			
Orientation To Others/Self			
Parents			
Peers			
Friends			
Other Influentials			
Self			
Behavior			

FIGURE 10.3 KEY SEGMENTATION VARIABLES.*

*In this form people at the school would complete the statements to the right according to their knowledge of the segmentation variables.

- *Attribute descriptors.* What are the key physical, academic, or income descriptors?
- *Attitudes and beliefs (expectations).* What are attractive and "ideal" characteristics?
- *Value orientation.* What are the basic and extended value descriptors?
- *Orientation.* What characterizes potential students' orientation to influentials—peers, parents, friends, and others—and to themselves?
- *Behavior.* What does the potential student actually do?

These are the major factors to be worked with in identifying the market segments for meeting enrollment goals. Within these, of course, there are subvariables of importance.

TYPES OF STUDENT VARIABLES.   The major types of student variables include:

- Traditional
- Non-traditional
- Graduate
- Undergraduate
- Professional
- Part-time
- Full-time
- International
- Minority
- Male/Female

As the matrix is examined in these terms, the best approaches to deal with these groups should emerge. Each variable represents a potential way to target students and influentials. These are the opportunities to determine which potential students to deal with and how to form an extensive relationship with them in terms of understanding the school. These groups of students have different expectations, find different things attractive, have different problems they face in terms of their education, and, in some cases, have very different values. Consider the following case:

Greg was a typical traditional student. In his interview with the admissions staff, he indicated that he was looking for a school that could provide the quality of education he was looking for and could specifically prepare him for a career. Greg was going to have to pay for much of his own education. He knew that there would be debt involved, and he would need a job soon after graduation.

As a result, he was quite interested in how much time faculty members would spend with him, and if they were excited enough in their work to motivate him, since he felt it would be difficult for him to concentrate on his work. As Greg moved through the decision-making process, however, his interest shifted from the faculty to the type of student life opportunities that were available, particularly the theater program.

Sally, on the other hand, was a non-traditional student who came to the admissions office during an evening session wanting to pursue a degree program which she had given up shortly after marriage. She needed about two years of college and had thought a great deal about going back to school, but was worried about how she would fit in and whether she would be able to do the work required. A great deal of time had to be spent in examining these problem issues before Sally moved on to the issues of cost and how her family would react to the idea of her attending college.

These two students exemplify the ways in which different aspects of the individual become important in the enrollment management process. The communication strategy, the ways of introducing people to the school, and some aspects of the product can be tailored to the concerns expressed by Greg and Sally.

As the type variables are examined, there are not sufficient ways to segment them efficiently unless more detailed descriptors are used. The list of variables must be expanded through the various other descriptors on the list in Figure 10.3. In time, as competition increases, finer segmentation will be needed.

ATTRIBUTES.   After deciding on a student type, the attribute group should be the first filter that is applied. Attributes are basic physical, demographic, and other easily identifiable factors. In this group, the strongest traditional descriptors are related to academic, economic, race, and program preferences. Items such as male/female or geographic differences do not show large variances in terms of expectations, what the students find attractive, or the characteristics of the ideal school. Differences in students described by these categories seem to be minimal until nontraditional students are examined.

This means that it will be difficult to target this group of people with any messages that might specifically cause them to be more interested by a particular school. Messages such as quality, career preparation, and concern would be attractive to the whole group, and the differences between schools would largely relate to how the school developed the message (the communication strategy) and how good the product was in terms of its focus on key expectations and resources devoted to the effort.

TABLE 10.2. Student Expectations*

STATEMENTS	MALE	FEMALE	EAST	WEST	19	21+
Prepare for a career†	86	91	90	87	88	30
Concerned faculty‡	78	83	81	83	80	45
Up-to-date faculty	84	86	85	84	85	80
Career placement	66	77	75	73	73	58
Leadership development	31	35	37	33	33	—

* Source: "1986 National Student Database." Prepared by The Ingersoll Group, Inc., Denver, CO.

† Percent who said very important.

‡ Percent who said very attractive.

TABLE 10.3. Factors Preventing the Nontraditional Student from Pursuing More Education*

FACTOR	PERCENTAGE
College entrance requirements	10.03%
College program requirements	5.87%
Cost of education	51.05%
Family responsibilities	46.10%
I am too busy	27.53%
Program not available	14.41%
I have not really thought about it	12.59%
Transportation	7.71%

* Data from a survey of nontraditional students in a midwestern state.

AGE.   There are differences among age categories that can be used to differentiate between schools. With the nontraditional student, for example, there is often concern about barriers rather than a positive expectation, as seen in Table 10.3.

Nontraditional students also will typically want more help as they come into the institution. The care and feeding of the entering student may be critical.

GRADES AND INCOME.   Grades and income may allow the institution to begin to segment in a more productive manner. Here there are differences in terms of grade levels and income that the school must consider. Meeting wants and needs or gaining a competitive advantage will depend on which market segment the school wants. It is interesting to note that there seems to be a strong link between SAT scores and income (see Figure 10.4). The higher the income, the more likely grades are, on the whole, to be high. Understanding student wants, on the other hand, needs to be as closely linked to the student characteristics as possible (see Table 10.4).

In these cases, product content in terms of having a faculty who works with students is critical. The "A" student expects to have faculty who are available to meet every need in a superior way. This requires of the faculty a high-quality program, being available, being up-to-date, and being accessible. The school also will need to be able to provide a library that students perceive to be up-to-date.

In addition, there are concerns about time and place issues for some students. The nontraditional student is more likely to want courses and programs at night or on weekends. The nontraditional student also will want courses that are concentrated over one or two periods a week rather than spread into short periods several times a week. All of these are issues that relate directly to product content. These are areas in which the school can, if it wants, develop an advantage.

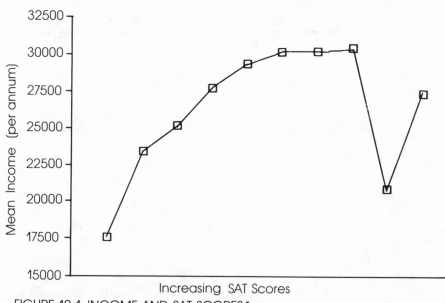

FIGURE 10.4. INCOME AND SAT SCORES.*

*Adapted from Admissions Testing Program of the College Board, *College Guide to ATP Summary Report 1981–82,* page 36.

In this type of data, it is interesting to note that the graduate student is very eager to have time with the faculty. It is important not to over-emphasize the amount of research the faculty is doing. While research represents an opportunity for the graduate student to be involved, the more research there is, the less faculty may be available for contact time with the student.

The potential graduate student also is interested in what types of services are available. This is increasing in importance. This is certainly true in terms of financial aid and is becoming more so with career de-velopment and placement. The recent M.B.A. and the history Ph.D may

TABLE 10.4. Attractive Features and Attribute Descriptors*

	GRADES		HIGH/LOW INCOME	
			$50,000 TO $100,000	LESS THAN $10,000
	(A)	(C)		
Prepare for a career	86%	95%	93%	94%
Concerned faculty	82%	76%	81%	82%
Up-to-date faculty	82%	72%	85%	78%
Career placement	61%	76%	68%	79%
Leadership development	32%	47%	35%	45%

* Data from a national survey of high school seniors conducted by The Ingersoll group, Inc., each year.

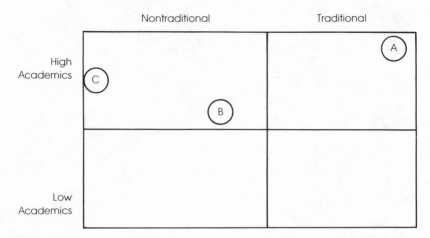

216   RONALD J. INGERSOLL

FIGURE 10.5.

be very concerned about getting a job. The school—especially one that wishes to compete—that can offer the student help in finding a good job will have an edge. A school with an M.B.A. program that is not well-known must have some sort of placement service. The placement service will be seen as an augmented product by students and a positive in terms of the school's position in the marketplace.

FUTURE DIFFERENTIATION: ATTITUDES AND BELIEFS.   Attitudes and beliefs contribute a great deal to the ability to segment markets and to differentiate schools. They provide a way for the school to demonstrate how it can meet student needs and develop a competitive position. The school can target its basic communication to the attitudes of a selected group. Attitudes and beliefs also should be used to determine the fit of the product the school has to offer to the wants and needs of both students and influentials. The better the basic fit, the easier it will be to communicate the value of the school.

Figure 10.5 shows three types of schools. These schools are separated on the basis of whether they deal primarily with traditional students or nontraditional students and also whether the students attending the school have strong or weak academic backgrounds. The schools are each located generally toward the high academic area, but they are quite diverse in the types of student they attract in terms of traditional/nontraditional.

School A enrolls traditional students of high academic quality. These students will expect a great deal of concern from the faculty and a faculty with a great ability to help students understand materials. Students of high academic quality seek faculty who are very teaching-oriented and who are willing to spend a lot of time with students. This school will not have to be as strong in terms of student services, but will have to deal with more diverse expectations in terms of career preparation or graduate school. These basic conclusions come from a review of attitude and belief data associated with the Ingersoll Group's National Student Database for 1986 (included in the appendix).

School B, on the other hand, serves both traditional and nontraditional students. This puts complex demands on the faculty and administration. The faculty members will need to be prepared to develop their courses and programs for a diversity of times and for a variety of styles. The demands in terms of personal time will be very high—both with students who are limited in the amount of time they can spend with their work and with students who have high expectations of using faculty members as resources.

School C is depicted as dealing with a high number of nontraditional students who are fairly well prepared academically. This type of school will probably offer a large number of courses in evening or weekend formats. Faculty will be teaching a rather different style as compared with the faculty of School A. Faculty in institution C will present fewer lectures and more experiential material and are likely to be putting their course materials into one or two evenings rather than spreading them out over an entire week.

In this institution, services will be rather limited, and new approaches will be under examination in terms of student involvement with the organization. Note the differences in the content of the communication program *and* product resources for the different types of students that attend these schools.

The same grid used above to compare types of student and academic background can be adapted to other purposes. For example, schools can be compared in order to examine faculty concerns about students, quality of department networking, and overall support services (see Figure 10.6).

In this group, college A would be very appealing to nontraditional students if the support services were appropriate; college B would have less appeal for the nontraditional student even though its services might be good; college C would have less appeal because its services are weak.

SELF- AND OTHER-DIRECTED STUDENTS.   Another way of segmenting the market is through a consideration of whether the potential student is self- or other-directed. In these terms, the segmentation is based on whether the school is involved in an effort to influence and meet the needs of one student or whether the wants and needs of others need to be involved. In all cases, some work may have to be done with influentials, but in the case of the other-directed student, considerable attention may have to go to the influential. If the enrollment program is dealing with influentials, the enrollment management issues are more complex.

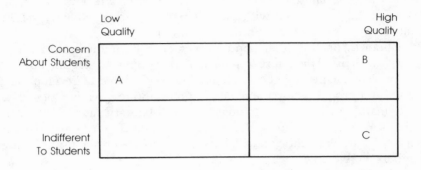

FIGURE 10.6. POSSIBLE POSITIONS ON SELECTED ATTITUDES AND BELIEFS.

INFLUENTIALS.   The influential (a person who advises or in some way directs the decision-making process) may be any one or a combination of the following:

- Parents
- Peers
- Friends
- Girlfriend/boyfriend
- School counselors
- Children
- Spouse
- Pastor
- Faculty
- Other schools
- Other relatives
- Alumnus

The task of influencing and meeting expectations needs to include these individuals. This will cause the school to expand its enrollment management efforts to deal with the following types of situations:

- Heavy peer influence that causes many students to go to one school because of the enrollment of one member of the group.
- The influence of peers on the student who has made a choice of a school but may waver because peers do not approve of the choice, or they ridicule it.
- The husband or wife who may feel threatened by the spouse going back to school or getting further education in general.
- The minister who can be helpful (or harmful) in the extent to which he or she participates in your enrollment program.
- The high school counselor who recommends only certain types of schools.
- The faculty member in an undergraduate program who recommends graduate schools to his or her better students.
- The parents who insist that their son or daughter go to *their* alma mater.

These are some ways to consider the Enrollment Matrix when preparing strategies to deal with these situations. These issues can be of concern for all types of students—traditional, nontraditional, graduate, and professional. The use of the matrix, adapted to the present discussions in Table 10.5, will involve primarily (1) Product resources and content that are used to meet students' (or others') expectations; (2) Communication content in the messages and themes that focus on the wants and needs of potential students.

TABLE 10.5. Adaptation of the Enrollment Matrix to Issues of Self- and Other-Directedness

	PRODUCT (CONTENT/RESOURCE)	COMMUNICATION (CONTENT)	DATA (CONTENT)
Self-directed	Expectations are only those of the potential student. A clear understanding of these leads to enrollment success. Augmented products are surprises only to the student.	Messages and contacts can be concentrated on the student. This may lead to better understanding and matches between the school and the student.	The information collected can relate only to the student. This simplifies, to some extent, the collection of data.
Other-directed	Generic product may include a great many "fantasies" of past experiences by the influential. Expectations of several populations need to be met and these are usually complicated. It is sometimes difficult to tell where expectations dominate. Expectations of the student may change once he/she is outside the influence of a secondary person. Product segmentation may be helpful (finding a school that is good yet safe). Once the student is at the school, attrition may result if the student's expectations are not met.	Messages, amount, and type of contact increase dramatically. Communication needs to be carried out at several levels with all influential. Expectations of several communication efforts changing over time as knowledge needs change. Communication will need to be carried out (often) with influentials. Communication may be more difficult to help the student know how the school can meet needs and thus may lead to a higher loss (attrition).	Attitude and belief data needs to be collected on a large array of people. Survey and focus group data collected on all parties involved. These are used in development of strategy. Questions are complex because the school is looking at what the influential wants and what the student wants.

VALUE APPROACHES TO SEGMENTATION

Another approach to segmenting students and influentials is through the use of values. This is an old method in the sense that this is a way that many people select their options anyway, and it is new in that the school can control or frame it so that it will be possible to take advantage of this important characteristic. As schools begin to compete more, they will need to consider these types of options.

There is good and bad in this approach to market segmentation. In some ways, it is difficult for enrollment managers and faculty to accept that they can, indeed, try to understand people's values and take advantage of value systems. It is acceptable to these people if it happens in a natural way, but it may be difficult in terms of using, with intent, the known or hypothesized value systems in influencing enrollment decisions and retention.

The good news is that the institution can get closer to what is important in terms of "fit" with the student. The student who selects a school on a value match may remain longer at the school. If the values of the people being recruited are better understood, the understanding may produce better decisions based on product "fit" and may be used to create improved communication programs. A better value fit may lead to better retention.

VALUES IN THE DECISION-MAKING PROCESS.   The value system of the student and the influential is a large part of how they view the world. The filters that allow certain information to get through and other information to be blocked are largely related to values of either party. This means that what the school wants to say in its communication program may be blocked if it is not acceptable, from a value standpoint, to the student or influential. The following are some examples of value-related issues.

> Tom was a survivor.[1] His background was not one that would have supported high achievement. He came to the institution from a rehabilitation program looking for just one more chance to do well. Tom had needed a great deal of support just to get started, and the school had found him by concentrating much of their enrollment effort one year on students who were in various programs within the city. It had taken a great deal of effort to get Tom going and a great deal of support to make sure that he continued with the work he was so pleased with. This type of student may be the resource for many schools in the future.

[1]Terms such as "survivor" will be developed in the following pages. Full definitions may be found in the book *Nine American Lifestyles* by Arnold Mitchell (New York: Viking Press, 1983).

Jane, on the other hand, was very interested in sororities and fraternities. She was wondering what she would do while she was on campus and what kinds of students she would meet, and her family was interested in the type of background of the people who attended the school. As she made her decisions, it was clear that the academic abilities of the present students and the teaching abilities and resources of the faculty were not as important as locating the right sorority.

Samuel was looking for the way up. He was analyzing what he would gain if he came to the school and began to look for a better place in life. It had been difficult for Ivy College, a very small, rural school, to interest Sam in their programs. He couldn't see how going to this school was going to produce a slot for him in a prestigious law firm as he went on to law schools in the future. Sam viewed his education as a way to climb the career ladder and not be in the same place his parents were.

A SYSTEM FOR EXAMINING THE IMPORTANCE OF VALUES.   A framework that works well for the examination of values is one developed by Arnold Mitchell. The typology that he develops, and one of several that are currently used by institutions marketing with values, is represented in Figure 10.7. As this figure shows, people may be divided into the categories of need-driven, outer-directed, inner-directed, and integrated.

Among need-driven people, the *survivors* are the most difficult to work with—unlikely candidates for many schools. These are students who do not have the drive to develop additional skills and knowledge. Their priorities rest in other places, and they do not see more education as a reasonable way to get ahead. The *sustainers,* however, are a real opportunity. These individuals are the people whom the school would have to reach at a very early stage. This would include early identification programs that many schools develop to work with students from the eighth grade on.

Programs in engineering and technology are good examples of this type of approach. A reason many students cannot take advantage of these opportunities is poor advising in high school. This can include taking the wrong courses as well as developing a poor attitude and low motivation. The college or university attempts to deal with this by developing specific programs to work with the students through advising, summer programs, seminars, and time spent with the students.

The offerings a school can make to this group may be extensive, but the school will have to be prepared to deal with frustration, fear, and desire to move forward on the part of the student. The services available to this group and the development of faculty to understand the student will be critical.

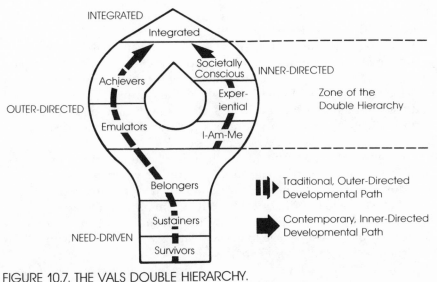

FIGURE 10.7. THE VALS DOUBLE HIERARCHY.

Source: Nine American Lifestyles by Arnold Mitchell (New York: Viking Press, 1983).

The sustainers frequently need to be told how well they are doing. This is a group that needs to feel progress, and they need to focus on the future so they have a sense of direction. This may be difficult, given the other issues with which the students are concerned. Advising and time spent with people at the school are critical.

Let us consider next the group described by Mitchell as outer-directed. What others think often guides the actions of these individuals. This is a large group—68 percent of the population over eighteen—and one that many schools are actually marketing to at present. This student is influenced by peers, influentials, and evidence of what other people have been able to do with their education. This type of student may be less inclined to act on inner wants and needs and to be swayed by the things that the school may say.

The outer-directed students are likely to be much like the students that many schools already enroll. These are the individuals who respond well to the crowd, are less likely to challenge the rules, and do not respond to the schools' desires that they be more aggressive, motivated, or educationally oriented in their activities.

It is clear that working with these students requires that some specific actions go to the influentials. The way to change these groups—if that is a need—is to be certain to plant the seeds with the right people and hope that these seeds will ripen into change. The individual faculty member working with a small group of people over a fairly long period of time may be able to change the nature of the student in some way. In most cases, however, the curriculum and ways of working with students demand that the program be fairly conservative and direct. Change or innovation will not work with this group.

The communication program needs to fit carefully the expectations of these people. The messages, photographs, and copy must be designed to impress these people and, in some cases, fit their view of the world closely. This group will relate strongly to the campus visit *if it goes well* and the campus is tradition-oriented. Photographs and off-campus programs will be very effective as long as they are not far from the student's fantasy of a college or university.

The inner-directed student, on the other hand, is a person who will act on values that are internalized. These can be experientials or society-conscious individuals. These are the students whom many of the faculty would most like to be with or teach. When dealing with the experientials, colleges need to be certain that they understand what these students desire, and they must be able to deliver. These are the people with whom staff members might have to spend the most time.

The society-conscious are very analytical about what is offered them and how it will help them to be better at the process of dealing with life and others. These are the people who may be the least impressed with the great buildings and external offerings. In fact, these may turn this population off.

Product fit is a key issue here. This is more of a challenge since the population of students is a mix, with the inner-directed being a minority. This will not be true, of course, if a school has been able to design its programs to attract these students. In most cases, the school will have no choice but to accept a larger share of the outer-directed individuals.

The inner-directed student will require more time and can be expected to contribute more to discussions, seminars, and independent study. These are individuals the school will have to find ways to stimulate and motivate without alienating the other students. These individuals are easier to influence on a one-on-one basis than through the process of planting seeds in the crowd.

Finally, there are the integrated students. Integrated students are independent and will use the capacities of both the inner- and outer-directed individuals to make their decisions about the college experience. These people look at all sides of the product offering and base their decisions on how the school fits them on many characteristics.

These individuals require a great deal more than a few publications to enroll them. They require the best a school can offer in identifying their wants and needs and showing how their expectations can be met. During their campus visit, the time spent with faculty will be critical, as will the efforts of dedicated alumni.

THE ENROLLMENT MATRIX AND VALUE SEGMENTATION.   The Enrollment Matrix is a very important tool in the development of products for value-oriented marketing and communication programs. Messages to each group need to be different, and the degree of personal contact, how the personal contact is used, and the amount of time needed in contact will all vary depending on the segment sought.

The research base must include some different types of questions if enrollment management work with this group is to be adequate. The whole potential student population can be sorted on value characteristics if the right type of instruments and questions are used in the research.

The areas of the matrix that change most with value segmentation are the product in all areas, the content of data, and the content of the communication variable.

-11-
RETENTION AND OTHER ISSUES OF ENROLLMENT MANAGEMENT

In this chapter, the issue of student retention is covered as an application of the use of the Enrollment Matrix, introduced on p. 13, Chapter 2. Retention provides a good illustration of the use of this matrix to develop a coordinated and effective approach to an institutional issue. Let us consider the following enrollment problem:

> Wayside College had fallen on hard times in the last three years. In September, new student enrollment was holding steady, but retention of freshmen into the sophomore year had dropped to 56 percent.
>
> In the spring of the previous year, there had been a great deal of trouble in the dormitories. Alcohol had become a serious issue, and the problems related to this caused bad feelings among students and faculty. It was felt that this situation had caused much of the retention difficulty through word of mouth that was not entirely positive.
>
> In addition, research in the spring indicated that the faculty and students were far apart in their expectations. The faculty did not want to give the time or energy to serve a group of students who were below average in terms of ACT scores and who were not interested in graduate study or traditional academic outcomes.

There were several knee-jerk reactions that could occur as a result of this situation. Fingers could be pointed at the faculty, the student affairs office, alcohol, careerism, or even at the parents who should have brought up better children. These reactions would not have gone far toward solving the problem, but they would have assigned blame very clearly.

A more productive approach would be to examine the institution systematically to understand the various ways the present situation could be improved immediately and for the future. The matrix can serve as a way of conducting this overview.

AN OVERVIEW OF RETENTION FROM THE PERSPECTIVE OF THE ENROLLMENT MATRIX

Table 11.1 represents an overview of the retention area from a matrix perspective. This adapted matrix represents possible approaches to retention before arriving at a final plan to address the problems associated with the area.

In a task force approach, this document might serve as the initial framework for developing an overall approach to retention issues. An alternative approach would be to develop the chart through initial brainstorming sessions with time devoted to each part of the matrix. This approach works well when the group is large enough to be broken into smaller subgroups that can address specific sections of the matrix. This also works well if the group is knowledgeable about enrollment management. Let us now analyze student retention, using the matrix as a guide.

PRODUCT

GOALS. It is unproductive to think that an appropriate goal for a school can be to retain every student for four years. In a two-year school, it is likely that many students do not enroll with the intention of staying even the maximum two years. Student commitment to a school is not high, and may change quickly if other educational options become available. Thus, the appropriate goal may simply be to retain the student who benefits from time spent at the school.

RESOURCES. The resources that are included in the retention goals consist of the people at the institution, especially the faculty, and the relationship management efforts of all individuals at the institution. Resources also include the service package, meeting expectations, and the characteristics of the entering class. Of all of these, the characteristics of the entering class are the most important, followed by the service package.

The institution cannot hope to control retention if the characteristics of the entering class are too distant from the nature of what the institution intends to do in terms of an educational goal. If the fit is poor, it will be only a matter of time until the student becomes sufficiently dissatisfied and leaves the institution.

Of course, this is very closely tied to the expectations of the student and the expectations of the faculty and staff who service that student. These expectations are usually very complex, but relate to students' expectations of the faculty and overall expectations of the school and its

TABLE 11.1. A Matrix for the Analysis of Retention

	PRODUCT	DATA	COMMUNICATION	MANAGEMENT	CLIMATE
Goal	To retain the student who benefits from the offerings of the school.	To understand the status of the relationship and the service package. Are we meeting expectations?	To ensure students get feedback on how the institution helps faculty and staff to get information.	To focus energy and action on retention.	To guarantee a smooth information flow to and from the present student population.
Resources	• People • Relationship program • Service package • Meet expectations • Entering class	• Surveys • Focus groups • Entering class • Departing class • Observing	• Newsletter • Personal letters • Recognition sessions	• Data • Retention plan • Advisor training • Staff training	• All institutional personnel • Information network • Political network • Culture network
Content	Show the student that expectations are being met.	• Questions • Frequency • Clarification	Continue marketing a critical issue, expecially for low commitment situation: how? what?	Content of staff training and advising.	The components of information flow and beliefs are most critical.
Process	Relationship and service issues are very strongly based on good process.	Conduct withdrawal interviews on a continuing basis. Encourage action research.	Especially critical are the first six weeks and times of testing.	Conduct training on a regular basis. Develop and feed back data on a regular basis.	Demonstrate value of good relationships in all interactions.

personnel. When faculty meet student needs, positive results are frequently the outcome, as in the case below:

> John had become very discouraged with his relationships on campus. He seemed to be getting nowhere in his calculus class, and he had not been able to spend the time in the tutoring sections that he needed. It seemed as if he was getting in deeper and deeper with no place to go.
>
> In addition, he was physically exhausted from trying to keep up. The efforts at holding a job and going to school were really beginning to take their toll.
>
> On John's worst day, Professor Phillips had invited him to eat lunch in the office. Bag lunches were his specialty, and he had packed extras on everything. A long talk ensued in which all of the situation came out—the course, the job, and the general discouragement.
>
> After lunch, the professor and the student decided to take the afternoon off. They went home and relaxed over a rerun of one of John's favorite movies, had a long supper, and a long session of calculus (thanks to Mrs. Phillips, who taught mathematics at a neighboring university). The time off and the activities broke the chain of events, and John went on to complete the term with reasonable success.

This was not an isolated event at this school. Its faculty valued their ability to know where a student was and to react to special situations. If John had not found a sympathetic ear when he was discouraged, his case might have ended like the following:

> "That's it!" said Darleen as she started packing her bags. This had been a bad week, but she was now being held out of class because she had not paid a campus traffic ticket—which she believed she had not received.
>
> Security insisted that she had, and this afternoon had told her that all students tried to get away with as much as they could and she was no exception. This was just not worth it, and she packed her bag and left.
>
> She did not come back—another problem in a long line of dissatisfied students at this college. The chance to find at least one good relationship was lost, as was the student.

CONTENT.   The content of the product area that impacts retention can be focused on the five main areas mentioned in the resource section of the Retention Matrix, especially *people* and the *service package*. The "people" area includes, above all, the faculty at the institution. Although many people will come into contact with students, it is the faculty that can have the greatest impact. It is important to remember that it is not the academic degrees or the papers or research that are important to the average undergraduate, but rather it is the relationship that the faculty member has with that student. This determines the satisfaction and is the ultimate determination of whether many students will go or stay. The amount of involvement a faculty member has is critical. The commitment of the student to the institution is determined, then, by the concern, availability, and overall interaction the faculty has with students.

In the service package, the institution is concerned with the contacts that people at the school have with the student on a day-to-day basis. These are the moments of truth that determine the satisfaction level of the student at the end of each day's experience with the school. These can include such items as the tone with which a question is answered, problem solving, reactions to requests for help, dealing with complaints, and overall style of interaction with the student.

Of course, the fit between the institution and the entering class each year plays a significant role in the number of students who return to the institution. The closer the fit, the better the chance that the institution has to maintain levels of satisfaction and commitment. If levels of attrition are very high, it is a good first step to examine the characteristics of the class that was recruited. For example, it would be wise to review the expectations of students as they entered. What did they want—and what has the institution given them?

PROCESS.   Once the expectations have been met, it is likely that a great deal of the impact the institution can have on retention is through the process area. It is through the interaction of people that the job really gets done. Process here includes all of the critical elements of interaction. This involves the service package, faculty interaction, and overall interaction between the school and the student.

DATA NEEDS IN RETENTION

GOALS.   The goals of the data area in terms of high retention are to understand the status of the relationship and service packages and to understand how well the institution is meeting expectations. Clearly, this can be understood only by collecting information from present students and students who choose to leave each year and not return. The use of this database should help the institution in developing overall retention strategies.

RESOURCES.   Data resources will include a database that contains information from surveys, focus groups, and conversations with entering and departing students. In the collection of information to deal with retention, two factors become important: obtaining the data in a timely manner, and having reliable focus group information.

Timing issues are particularly important in regard to retention research. Retention problems can arise quickly and can cause problems internally and externally. If issues are not resolved, the departing student can impact other students at the institution and potential students through word of mouth in the marketplace. This issue can be especially important for community colleges. These institutions recruit students within a close range of the college. This means that word of mouth can have an impact in a very short period of time. Combined with low commitment, it does not take much to cause a problem, as in the case below:

> The drop in the number of returning students was dramatic. Twenty percent fewer students enrolled than were expected. It was a surprise for everyone. But it made sense after the analysis was done.
>
> Alcohol consumption and problems in the dorms had become dramatic. The faculty had heard about the problem but had not become concerned. It had an impact on performance in the classroom, but people were afraid to confront it.
>
> Students went home, talked about it, and influenced their friends to stay home.

Reliable information must also be obtained from focus groups. In matters of retention, it is important to understand the meaning of terms and to be able to probe beyond the immediate responses. This type of need demands a thorough interview or focus group approach. The proper methodology in this approach allows the person conducting the session to ask clarifying and probing questions that can frame answers in a way that makes them useful. If the student expresses dissatisfaction with advising or some other service during the focus group, one can obtain a true understanding of the meaning of the problem. Even where the issue may be lack of funds or problems at home, the student can get a chance to clarify and provide more useful information to the school.

CONTENT.   Questions are at the core of all of the content issues relating to data. It is through the right questions that the institution can arrive at information that will help correct the problems of retention.

The institution needs to be certain that the questions are framed around the key issues that can be used in developing a solution. This would include questions about expectations and attractive features of the college. In addition, the school will need to analyze interactions with students by all people on campus and be able to say that the contact of the student with the school is positive. What do the students feel good about? What are they having problems with?

It is important that the questions be carefully constructed so as to develop clear insights into the key issues that are impacting the students. It is not sufficient, for example, to understand that the financial aid program is a problem. It is important to understand further whether this problem relates to:

- Treatment in the office.
- Improper packaging strategies.
- Lack of funds.
- Lack of understanding of the nature of the financial aid area.
- Insensitivity to students' concerns about money.
- Lack of communication with students in general.

The problem could, indeed, be in any of these financial aid areas and could be used as an excuse for some other point of dissatisfaction with the school.

Clarifying and probing questions are the tools that are used to deal with meaning. The researcher will have to be able to use these tools carefully to extract the best information possible and to link the information to enrollment strategy.

Regular use of research information is critical. A systematic approach to gathering this information must be in place for data to be useful. It should be the policy of the school to study every student who leaves in one way or another. All graduates or people who leave and return should be studied. This may require a great deal of persistence on the part of the school, but it will pay rich dividends.

PROCESS ISSUES.   Three issues are involved more closely with process than any other data aspect of the matrix. These include the issues of action research, the use of data and information, and keeping people informed about the project as it relates to retention.

The more people know about what is being done and why, the more likely they will be to cooperate during the process of collecting data and later using that data to develop retention strategy. This basic posture is important in the retention area because without it, people will find it difficult to understand why they should take the time to participate in the data collection process. This is especially true if the individual being studied is someone who is dissatisfied with the school.

It is here that individuals on campus need to understand the following basic information:[1]

1. A service is produced at the instant of delivery; it can not be created in advance or held in readiness.

2. A service cannot be centrally produced, inspected, stockpiled, or warehoused. It is usually delivered wherever the customer is, by people who are beyond the immediate influence of management.

[1]From Karl Albrecht and Ron Zemke, *Service America: Doing Business In The New Economy* (Homewood, Ill.: Dow Jones Irwin, 1985).

3. The "product" cannot be demonstrated, nor can a sample be sent for customer approval in advance of the service; the provider can show various examples, but the customer's own haircut, for example, does not yet exist and cannot be shown.

4. The person receiving the service has nothing tangible; the value of the service depends on his or her personal experience.

5. The experience cannot be sold or passed on to a third party.

6. If improperly performed, a service cannot be "recalled." If it cannot be repeated, then reparations or apologies are the only means of recourse for customer satisfaction.

7. Quality assurance must happen before production, rather than after production, as would be the case in a manufacturing situation.

8. Delivery of the service usually requires human interaction to some degree; buyer and seller come into contact in some relatively personal way to create the service.

9. The receiver's expectations of the service are integral to his or her satisfaction with the outcome. Quality of service is largely a subjective matter.

10. The more people the customer must encounter during the delivery of the service, the less likely it is that he or she will be satisfied with the service.

From this data, it can be seen that the institution should be very happy when people complain. If the institution understands, there is a chance to correct the problem. Surveys or focus groups are opportunities to turn a complainer into someone who is a bit more positive or to make a person who is basically satisfied even more impressed with the institution. Understanding these issues and how data will be used to help increase student satisfaction can make the process of collecting data smoother.

In terms of data use, clear rationales for the impact of information on enrollment results at the institution can help people in making the decision to cooperate. With the matrix approach, it is relatively easy to show how the information can be used to create better product fit, develop better communication with present students, and develop the enrollment strategies that will produce a long-term commitment. The climate area can be greatly improved if the impact of institutional attitudes and beliefs on students is understood. The process of using the data must be clear from each of these points of view. Developing tactical and operational strategies in each part of the matrix is the key.

The following are some examples of operational strategies that are climate-related:

- Better answering of telephones—prompt and friendly.
- More approachable departmental commitments.

- Willingness to keep a bookstore open evenings for nontraditional students.
- Scheduling flexibility in light of the demands exerted on the time of adult learners.
- Meeting with students once a week to improve the flow of information.

These are all actions that have been undertaken by schools after focus groups were conducted.

Finally, collecting data by doing research with every telephone call and every personal contact can help a program do better. In the following case, a telephone call, though frustrating, provided valuable information about improving the school's enrollment program:

> The telephone call was a routine follow-up to be certain that Jamie was still going to be present in September. After a great deal of small talk, the admissions counselor for Middle College felt something was wrong.
>
> After testing the waters, he asked if Jamie was going to attend. And the answer was no.
>
> This came as a shock, as the school had been working with Jamie for several months and had no sign that she was not going to be attending. The deposit had been sent, the room had been assigned—and now a change of mind.
>
> At first, the reason given was the cost, and Jamie said she was going to a school closer to home. But on further probing, it was determined that she was going to a private school of the same church denomination in the same state. The coach had visited a week ago and convinced Jamie that her experience at Middle College would not be a good one, and that she would not be challenged athletically or academically.

This experience was one that Middle College could do little about. But there apparently was enough weight in the idea that Jamie would not be challenged that she decided not to attend. Middle College had not come across as the right institution, and the issue was challenge.

This simple telephone call led to other research that caused Middle College to change its strategy dramatically for its first communication piece. Now they emphasize the faculty and the right degree of challenge. Action research, then, means making every contact and using every opportunity to gain valuable information.

COMMUNICATION

GOALS.   The goal of the communication program for retention is to maximize the conversion ratios of new to continuing student. This can include new freshmen to sophomore or the reentry of students who have left the institution from one to several terms ago. The assumption is that the experience may not be sufficient to maximize the student's continuing with the school. The experience may require some overall interpretation.

The following might be the retention goals set by a school in this process:

STATUS	CONVERSION
Freshman	85% freshmen to sophomores
Sophomore	85% sophomores to juniors
Junior	90% juniors to seniors
Senior	95% seniors to graduate
Reentry	20% graduation rate

In this example, the percentages give the institution some specific targets in terms of the return of a particular population. In most cases, it will be helpful to target specific populations in the organization, including part-time/full-time, commuter/resident, traditional/nontraditional, and graduate/undergraduate.

RESOURCES.   The resources for the communication program for retention can include print materials, media use, and personal contact with people on campus. The print area can include such items as brochures, newsletters, personal letters, or other documents that are given to the student. This area is not nearly as effective, however, as solid personal contact. Yet it should be a part of any solid retention effort.

The management of personal contact is by far the most productive item in the communication effort. This can include personal contacts by faculty, and larger sessions that focus on recognition of students' achievements and progress. In essence, every contact every day is a chance to influence retention for better or for worse. It is important to consider the quality of the contacts each day. Classroom contact, advising, social events, and informal sessions can all impact the effort to retain students.

CONTENT.   Content issues of special concern involve the communication formula covered in the communication chapter, (chapter 6) and the issue of continued formal communication after the student has arrived on campus.

In terms of the models used to understand the status of the student and his or her relationship with the school, two steps stand out: commitment and apprehension. The student who made and followed through with the decision to enroll at the institution moved from being apprehensive to making a commitment to attend. In many cases, the student may fluctuate back and forth between these stages over a period of time.

This seems to be particularly true of the community colleges where the students may first enroll because of location and cost and may have a low level of commitment to the school and the process of education. Without a reasonably high level of commitment, it is easy to become apprehensive.

To produce more commitment and maintain it, personal contact with faculty and others must remain the front line of effectiveness. To increase the likelihood that this will happen, the institution can deliver the right messages through the print and media channels that will assure the student that the right direction is being followed.

Brochures and letters can be used to let the student know, for example, of the quality of the faculty and how they give time to students. Letters and brochures can be used to promote the quality, prestige, and effectiveness of the college or university in meeting students' expectations.

Sometimes this kind of information can help the student to make sense out of the things that are happening around him.

In the end, however, it is the attention of the faculty, staff, and peers that will make the difference. Involvement and meaningful relationships will hold the student through the rough times and periods of changing perspectives and challenge, as in the case below:

> The president was discussing his goals for the college. He said that there should be done nothing that would lower the self-esteem of people associated with the school. The school, he said, would have to challenge each student but, at the same time, provide the right amount of support.

This statement captures the essence of a positive relationship strategy that can maximize the recruitment of each person until his or her association with the school logically ends. It is also essential that the institution meet students' expectations and that students be aware of this. This is easier to do if the school has enrolled students who fit with the overall beliefs of faculty and staff and if the school continues to ask questions about how good a job it is doing.

This means that the institution should have in place a communication effort with present students, especially during the first year. The main focus of this effort is to maintain commitment to the school and the faculty.

PROCESS.   The communication area will rely heavily on the service package as a key ingredient, and this is purely process.

The management of those "moments of truth" encountered each

day by each person interacting with others can make a significant difference to the student. The student who leaves the school because of a bad interaction with the bookstore, the bursar, a faculty member, or a fellow student, has probably had other problems—but the negative interaction has become the precipitating event. That experience causes the dissatisfaction that ultimately tips the balance in favor of leaving or staying.

Understanding the importance of contact and managing the contact successfully is critical. It is in this area that management must make its expectations about the treatment of people very clear.

MANAGEMENT

GOALS.   The management of the enrollment effort has the distinct need to focus the energy of the institution on retention issues. A goal of the management of the retention program is simply that—attention to retention.

RESOURCES.   The resources needed for the management of the retention effort include a tracking program, a retention plan, training and development programs for advisors, and training and development programs for staff members. Note particularly the emphasis put on the training and development of people. In future years, the amount of energy put into this area by schools is likely to increase dramatically.

The tracking program for managing retention must include a system to identify the student from the point of entry to each point of exit. In the tracking system, it is essential to identify exactly when the individual has left for what may be the final time.

Increasingly, the final time will be in question because the school will not really know when a student might return—even after graduation. Alumni programs can be developed to continue the learning that has been accomplished during students' tenure with the school.

CONTENT ISSUES.   The database for tracking, the content of staff development programs, and the operational strategies of the management plan for retention should be the primary areas of content concern.

The key content issues for *tracking* are the database for each student and developing the capacity to track on an individual student basis all of the entry and reentry dates for the individual from entry through departure. It is also key that the school is able to use this information on a regular basis for developing retention strategies in both the short and long term. Data must be available for analysis of leaving or reentry based on attributes of people and their attitudes and beliefs about their relationship with the school. Knowing this information, the school can

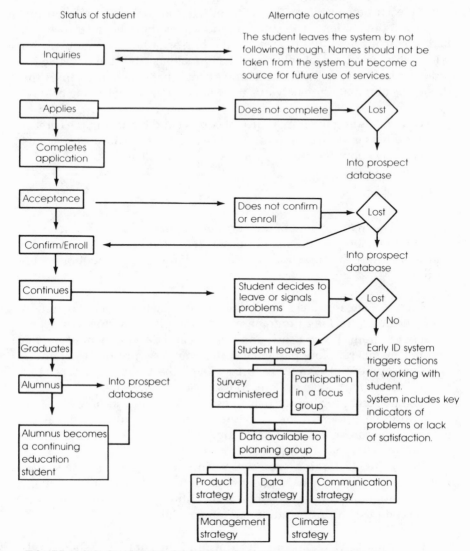

FIGURE 11.1. FLOWCHART OF STUDENT TRACKING THROUGH AN INSTITUTION.

better control the flow of students each year. The tracking pathway might contain any of the features or events depicted in Figure 11.1.

TRACKING PROCESS TO DEGREE.   Another critical aspect of the tracking program is identifying in some formal way the meeting of expectations and progress toward a degree.

The student's grades, attendance, commitment to work, and attendance at meetings with advisors or others may give indicators of a tendency to leave. Conducting surveys similar to those to determine fit or communication messages can help to make clear if the school is generally meeting the students' needs. The data collected will be essential to the management area in doing the job of minimizing attrition.

In this process, the institution has kept track of the student throughout his or her career to date. At each point at which the individual left the system, the tracking program kept the minimal data on file and managed to bring the student back. It could be hypothesized that the person could, at any time, become a candidate for further education or use of institutional resources. With effective management, the school could predict the use of the institution by graduates, and this should become an ever-increasing pool.

The training program (page 146) can be very much like the one addressed in the chapter on management. In the training program for retention, however, the effort is much more directed at problem solving and working with identification of student issues in terms of satisfaction, expectations, and meeting of needs.

The training program also would focus on aspects of the service package. This could include such items as being sensitive to the student who gives signs of dissatisfaction or preparing to leave. Early warning signs are likely to be present long before the action of leaving is taken. The early identification and communication of the signs to the advisor or counselor by staff or other faculty may be very important.

CLIMATE

GOALS.   If the information flow to and from the student is excellent, the right climate for retention exists. In cases of poor retention, the student may have become dissatisfied because he or she misunderstood some important factor about the school. The goal of the climate area is to maintain an environment in which the students' commitment to the college is reinforced. A large part of this effort should involve the flow of information to students on all levels. In the following case, a faculty that was well trained academically failed to provide its students with an adequate climate:

> The faculty in the department had proven themselves to be particularly insensitive to students. The faculty challenged but did not support. To work with this faculty was to be set up for criticism and put-downs.
>
> The last set of exams was particularly unrealistic in the students' minds. Yet, when challenged, the faculty did not want to discuss the issue.

People were working on the issues but the students did not know this. As a result, students left in large numbers between the semesters.

RESOURCES.   The important resources here are all of the people on the campus. Retention is an issue that relates very directly to the contact that each individual on the campus has with students each term. Thinking the contact through will give the individual more choices in terms of having an impact on retention. It is true that every individual has an impact on retention in the organization. In short, the people and the contacts are the resources of importance in the climate area.

This is where the issue of involvement as suggested by Astin,[1] or the significant other as proposed by Noel,[2] influence the retention figures.

CONTENT.   Content for the climate area is the way in which the contact is done. If the contact of people at the school with the student is made through a caring, concerned process, the students and others feel that they are wanted and are an important part of the school.

The flow of information to the student must be excellent. The student needs to know about all relevant facets of the organization. The student should be among the first to become involved in and aware of the decisions that will have an impact on his or her life. The information flow needs to go both ways—to and from each student.

The beliefs and cultural factors that the student strongly holds should be respected and supported by the faculty and staff. If the students' beliefs and the faculty and staff beliefs are too far apart, the comfort and support level for the student will decline rapidly. This is true on issues of meeting expectations academically, socially, or athletically.

Likewise, the student should feel that there is a true political base upon which he or she can have influence. If the students do not believe that there is an avenue for impact on key issues that are important to their interests, problems can ensue that may make everyone uncomfortable.

PROCESS.   Of course, process is the core of the climate area. There needs to be a strong, supportive, and constant attachment of the school to the student. The stronger the bond, the less likely it is that students will be lost. The better the interactions between people, the better the retention results. The process should be heavy with involvement for the student with the school.

[1]Astin, Alexander. *Preventing Students from Dropping Out*, San Francisco: Jossey-Bass, 1975.
[2]Noel, Lee; Levitz, Randi; Saluri, Diana; and Associates. *Increasing Student Retention*, San Francisco: Jossey-Bass, 1979.

VARIED ISSUES IN ENROLLMENT MANAGEMENT

There are some topics that deserve special treatment in the use of the Enrollment Matrix. There will be readers who will say, "This is an appropriate topic for a certain type of student, but not for my students or for my school." This may be the response of the graduate dean or the individual who works with nontraditional students. These will be the responses of individuals who often want help but do not have the time to think things through to the basics.

For these people, the following may be helpful in focusing on some special issues of the matrix. It will prove to be more profitable, in the long run, for any educational program to take the systematic pathway— at least as systematic as one can make it. In the following, some of the key areas of the matrix that seem to be very different for special cases will be reviewed. Not all of the areas of the matrix are included, since a specific agenda for a given situation may not include a particular section of the matrix.

PUBLIC/PRIVATE INSTITUTIONS

In looking at a comparison of public and private institutions, product, communication, and climate issues are the key areas in which the matrix variables may differ most.

PRODUCT.   Theodore Levitt (*The Marketing Imagination*, New York, 1983) identifies four key product variables, one of which is the generic product of an institution. This is the view of the school that is present in the public's mind regardless of what the institution tries to convey. Without any effort at communication, the institution has to deal with this vision. For public and private institutions, this perspective may be a key area of concern.

The public institution may have the initial vision of low cost and size to contend with. While cost images are not necessarily a problem, the size variable may produce an image that will require special attention by the school.

The public institution also may have to contend with issues of being perceived as nonpersonal and of lower quality merely from the point of view of being a public college or university. While this may not be the case in reality, the image will be present in many people's minds. For example, it is not unusual for focus groups of senior high school students to identify the faculty of the state institutions as being unavailable to students. This may be the opinion even though the students have had little, if any, personal experience with the school. Many of these opinions come from word of mouth or from parents' and influentials' feelings about what they have read or heard.

On the other hand, the private institution frequently will have to deal with images of being expensive but offering a better-quality education than the public institution. While the public schools are rapidly making a case of offering quality, the private institution—unless it is very small—will have an initial advantage from this belief.

COMMUNICATION.   In dealing with communication, one of the principal models in use by enrollment professionals is that developed by Hersey (Dr. Paul Hersey, *Situational Selling: An Approach For Increasing Sales Effectiveness*, Escondido, California, 1985). In this model, it is assumed that the consumer goes through several stages in the process of moving from being uninterested to being an enrolled student. These include:

- Being uninterested and uneducated about the institution.
- Being interested but uneducated about the institution.
- Being educated and apprehensive.
- Being educated and committed.

This model may have a real impact on the communication strategies of the private or public school. Many public institutions, particularly two-year schools or local institutions, enroll people who have less commitment than others to remain at the school until matriculation. The public or local institution may be perceived as a good place to start but not the one for the ultimate academic degree. There is reason to believe that the student going to this institution cycles between being apprehensive and committed and may enter the school with less overall commitment.

If the public institution wants to influence students, it will need to consider more effective communication at the stage of overcoming apprehensions and will need to continue to communicate with the student after he or she has enrolled. This communication is very important in the early stages of the student's enrollment.

It is at this point that the service package comes to the foreground as a part of the communication program. The services will communicate the institution's desire to meet expectations and student needs.

In terms of resources for communication, it is often the case that the public institution does not devote the resources that the private colleges do to the communication program. Spending rates for the public schools will need to increase in this area as institutions try to deal with influencing students. The amount of personal communication for the public schools, particularly in terms of individual professional counseling, will have to increase and become more effective.

Because the commitment of the student to the public institution may be soft, these institutions should have the strongest service package. Ironically, it is at these institutions that the service packages may actually be very weak.

MANAGEMENT.   The amount of energy and funding directed toward the enrollment programs at many public institutions is not high. This is reflected in lower cost-per-student figures for these organizations. As these institutions begin to explore enrollment management, major questions may arise about funding.

Private institutions, on the other hand, have been putting a great deal of energy, time, and money into this area for a long time. Staffing, planning, information systems, and training are generally given a great deal more attention in the private arena.

To balance this, in the future the public schools will be looking at additional commitments of staffing in the area of enrollment management. This will include individuals devoted to the student contact function and individuals dealing with data input and output for purposes of communication and program management. As this occurs, the need for training and development of personnel will increase, with better results to follow.

This cycle will benefit students as public and private institutions begin to compete more effectively with information and contacts with students and influentials. This has the potential to provide better options for everyone.

CLIMATE.   Political forces, a primary ingredient of the climate area, seem to be stronger on public campuses than private ones. Unions, legislatures, governors, and local boards all combine to increase the difficulties of these schools. This is especially true if changes are needed or if the institutions need to move in directions that are contrary to the desires or ideas of the important supporters. Issues of winners and losers become critical.

Cultural forces—attitudes and beliefs about what is important—are likely to be central issues on all types of campuses. The understanding of these areas will need to increase as their impact on enrollment efforts becomes more critical. It is common, however, for these to exert more influence on the private campus than on the public. Strong feelings about such issues as preparing students for careers can raise barriers to meeting students' needs very quickly.

LARGE/SMALL SCHOOLS

When looking at issues of small and large schools, there are special points to address in each area of the matrix. While the dividing point between large and small is difficult to fix, the following discussion deals with schools that enroll fewer than 1,200 students (very small), those that enroll 2,000 to 4,000 students (small), and those which enroll more than 4,000 students (large).

PRODUCT.   Two critical considerations in these schools are the generic product and the package concepts, which have been covered in Chapter 3.

The generic product may be the most pervasive issue for the small school. When the word *small* is used, and students are asked to respond to it, the conversation tends to revolve around such words as "personal, close relations, time with faculty." While these responses are not bad, the next words may be "limited, lack of up-to-date faculty," and the issue of being too closed. It is as if the one set of concepts cancels out the other. The institution may end up having to overcome a considerable handicap if it is below the 1,200 mark. That institution is, after all, smaller than many high schools today.

On the other hand, the very large school has to deal with generic images of being impersonal, treating people like numbers, and having faculty members who are not interested in teaching, along with the favorable reputation of having diversity and a better social environment than the small school. In each case, the marketing effort of one type of school may try to take advantage of the perceptions of the other by using these generic beliefs.

It would seem, in either case, that it is important to think through the nature of the generic product before preparing the communication program. The research program for the institution should also try to collect information about the generic product.

PACKAGING.   To cope with the competition, the small school should seriously consider the idea of packaging. By this it is meant that the whole is better than the sum of the parts.

The smaller school will need to have certain majors or be able to speak about its special programs. This is the area that will get the initial attention of many students who need to be attracted to the school. Beyond that, the smaller school will have to organize their offer in such a way that it is perceived as a package that cannot be obtained easily at another institution.

The package usually will consist of a theme and the organization of the elements of the school around the theme in some creative way. The package will also need to be based on a real set of assumptions about how people learn and the expectations of the marketplace. The school will need to convince the market that expectations can be met but that there must be something beyond that. It is creating the "something extra" that causes a great deal of difficulty as the school organizes itself to compete well.

The package will cause some reframing of what is important in the college experience. This may cause shifting of emphasis from the purely academic to developing a sense of the importance of experiential learning, for instance. This shift can give increased emphasis to off-campus experiences, social life, student development services, or the value of time with faculty and staff.

The package also may require focus on something other than knowledge as the outcome of education at the college. The program may become one that focuses on skills and attitudes as the reason to be at the school. For some schools it may be that the attitude developed at the school is the most important part of the educational process. The school would say that by being with these faculty and staff, certain attitudes can be developed that cannot be easily found in other places. Such was the case at the school described here:

> Commitment was the name of the theme developed for Malcomb College. The research had indicated that this was an important element of the experience at this college. The faculty were committed to seeing that students did well. The students were committed to the process of education and to each other. The administration seemed to be truly focused on making the faculty and the students successful. It was to this good feeling that was attributed the extremely low attrition rate and the success that the school was having with new students.

Commitment was the focus for the communication package at Malcomb College. Overall program design, processing of field experiences, the relationship between administration and faculty, the students, and the focus of alumni were all directed at this element.

DATA. In the data area, it is clear that many larger schools have the resources to create the best enrollment databases possible. The personnel, the hardware, the software, and the needs are all present. At the same time, the willingness to collect and apply data may *not* be present.

These schools often have the academic resources to make certain that the research is done and done well. But too often, the schools do not collect the data. The larger school does not feel the pressure as intensely as the smaller school to perform the job.

On the other hand, the smaller institution may lack the resources to get the job done. The personnel and the hardware are not present, nor is there enough time in the day to accomplish the task. The smaller school needs the data, though, and the intensity of this need may cause them to move more quickly than the larger school to obtain the needed information.

COMMUNICATION. The smaller schools may have to deal with awareness problems. This means that the school experiences almost zero awareness—even within its own market area. This is not necessarily a problem as the school can then create its own positive image in each person who is contacted.

The smaller school may only have to deal with the generic image of being a small school. If this is the sole issue, the school can set out to create, with the right communication program, the image that will do the job of moving the student from uninterested and unaware to educated and committed to the school.

The larger school may be better known. The issue to deal with here is the fact that the image may be inaccurate and cause the school to be perceived in the wrong light. For example, a high school senior was heard to say, "I do not want to go to Apple State. The faculty members there are never in class, and there are a lot of drugs and alcohol in the dorms." She did not want to go to the state school that was near her home even though it could offer a good education at a reasonable cost. This student had never been on the campus of the school, and had never talked to a faculty member or a student. The whole perception was gained from word of mouth in the high school from students, most of whom had not visited the school.

The larger school may have to work hard to overcome the generic and real images that are projected. At times, this may be more difficult than trying to overcome low-awareness problems.

MANAGEMENT.   Management in the smaller schools needs to be the best possible. The larger school is often merely trying to overcome the difficulties of keeping up with the flow of work. While this is indeed a serious management issue, trying to process and deal with the total aspects of product, data, communication, and climate can be the issue for the admissions person at the smaller school.

The training and development of staff, the enrollment plan in its totality, the database, the communication program, and the climate of the institution must be very carefully managed to get the job done, especially in the smaller school. Too often, this school must settle for second-rate management from people with little experience or desire to do an outstanding job.

CLIMATE.   The climate area is very critical for the smaller school. The issues are often more visible and closer to the surface at this institution. The package of the institution and the environment of the school are ingredients to the overall success of the enrollment program. This reflects the climate of the institution in terms of information flow, political groups, and overall culture.

It is the culture of the institution that determines what can be done for students. The belief system and the balance of this system exert an impact on the student, which becomes a large part of the product. The beliefs in meeting expectations, value-added factors, flexibility, and belief in experiential learning all combine to make the system either work well for students or fail.

In the larger school, the beliefs are more varied and students may diffuse to areas where the beliefs are compatible. In the smaller school, the student must become immersed in the beliefs and the political struggles. These have an impact that can drive enrollment up or down very quickly.

PROFESSIONAL/GRADUATE SCHOOL

PRODUCT.   In the professional and graduate school, the role of the faculty is critical. In the graduate school, aside from the availability of financial support, the faculty is a major reason for the student to select one school over another. In the essence of the experience, it often is the single faculty member that the student works with who produces the most powerful impact.

In the professional school, the student is more oriented toward the financial and professional outcomes of the experience. The faculty, in this case, can become the main source of mentoring or modeling for the student. In the medical schools, the physicians on the faculty become the models—in the law schools, it is the lawyer. The graduate of these schools will reflect the prevailing attitudes of the faculty as they have practiced their craft with the student.

In the future, it is likely that student services will become more critical for these schools. Areas such as counseling, financial planning, placement, and advising should see increased use. Research with graduate programs has indicated a higher need for career counseling and placement help. This counseling and placement effort can help the student find ways to use skills developed in graduate school in new and creative ways.

Of course, computer resources, excellent libraries, and some form of networking have always been essential in producing an effective graduate experience.

DATA.   Less seems to be available in terms of data at professional and graduate schools. The information needed to develop an effective product or communication strategy is generally very limited. There also may be less feeling of need to move beyond the development of strong attribute databases.

Many professional schools have been able to develop excellent attribute databases. They can identify the trends, where students are going, the percentages of applicants accepted, and other factors related to results in the enrollment area. Yet, they frequently do not know the attitudes and beliefs of their present or potential students. Their strategies are often purely institutionally driven and ignore the consumer or competitors.

The competition for professional and graduate students will become intense, if it is not already. Efforts to recruit students into business programs, other professional areas, and the armed services will provide an environment in which the student will have many choices. The student who before did not question his or her directions will have to do more thinking before committing to a career.

COMMUNICATION.   While the traditional student can be recruited through the high school and the high school counselor, the recruitment of graduate and professional students is much more difficult. No SAT names, limited national college fairs, no sending institution counselors—or at least hard-to-identify contacts—added to the role of teachers in the colleges make it harder to pinpoint the contacts.

Frequently, it is hard to find the addresses and telephone numbers that will make sophisticated contact possible. While they may be more difficult to apply, the same concepts of communication are true in the recruitment of professional and graduate students as are true in the recruitment of traditional students.

Faculty and alumni can play a key role in the recruiting process. The potential graduate student can be heavily influenced by contact with the faculty of the school. Letter, telephone, and personal contacts, both off- and on-campus, should be heavily encouraged.

On the other hand, the alumnus of the professional school may be the most influential contact as the recruitment year unfolds. The successful alumnus represents the picture that the potential students would like to see or experience. While the assistance of school alumni may be hard to acquire—because time is money to most of them—the results of their help make it well worth the effort.

MANAGEMENT.   In professional and graduate schools, the resources needed to develop and implement a strong enrollment management program are rarely present. The school has not had to work at getting the necessary enrollments, and the idea of devoting more resources and energy to this area sometimes does not seem to make sense.

Increases in spending for marketing or managing enrollments will usually need to occur in terms of personnel, publications, the communication effort, and the data that is needed to make the appropriate decisions that will help the institution meet its targets each year.

This increased rate of spending should not, however, be undertaken until the enrollment plan is in place, including goals, tactical strategies, and the operational strategies to achieve results. This will require a large amount of information and the need to link this information with the development of enrollment goals and strategy as an up-front task.

Professional schools have a distinct advantage that should be included in the enrollment management formula. These schools generally have professional associations who can do a great deal to increase the chances that the schools meet with enrollment success. The impact of associations could be exerted in terms of development of image, development of inquiries, creation and maintenance of the enrollment database, and processing and development of people to the applicant stage. A joint venture often decreases the unit rate of spending. It is surprising that more schools do not undertake this type of process as a group.

CLIMATE.   The major area of climate impact on the professional and graduate schools is the area of culture. This is the system of beliefs and values that drives the decision-making of the institution.

Professional and graduate schools usually have strong built-in beliefs that ultimately get played out in decisions on enrollment management. This may include such beliefs as the professional field requiring only people with certain types of characteristics or qualities.

The nature of the field itself also may become a part of the thinking of the development of the enrollment effort. Lawyers, doctors, podiatrists, graduate chemists, may all have ideas about how the enrollment of students should be done. These often come from basic beliefs that people in the organization have about their field.

TRADITIONAL/NONTRADITIONAL STUDENTS

PRODUCT.   In the product area, there are many changes that faculty have had to face in adapting to nontraditional students. These have included a generous dose of flexibility in many dimensions and getting used to having students in class who will challenge and who are committed to the work of education.

Nontraditional students look for classes that are given at different times, places, and in different frameworks than the faculty may be ready to deliver. These students almost always have to have their programs offered in evenings, early morning, or weekend time frames. These are hardly the times that many faculty would prefer to offer their services.

These students also may prefer to have their instruction offered closer to work or home. The adaptations that are needed to launch a successful effort in this area may require a great deal of creativity from the faculty and the administration of the school. The class rarely can be a lecture that will meet every day, but, on the other hand, faculty availability for clarification of lecture material is of key importance, as demonstrated here:

> The focus group was discussing the program in a high school classroom in a midwestern small town. The college had been given the classroom space and the students were all pursuing their degrees in the evenings and weekends. The topic of discussion was the course offerings and the biology professor from the college was being taken to task.

> "Three hours of lecture is just too much. I can't stay awake, and he moves so fast that the majority of us gave up after the first two weeks. It is a shame that the course is required, because most of us would never take it."

> In addition, the teacher was not available before or after class, so the students had no opportunity to take their concerns to him personally. It was their assumption that he did not care and was unlikely to change.

The framework of how class time and content will be done is a major consideration in the product area. The use of a teaching process that will produce involvement is critical. This becomes even more essential when the student must be in class for longer periods of time with fewer times per course.

DATA.   Data is as much an essential here as it is with the traditional student. The enrollment strategy for product and communication must be based heavily on information.

An additional data element for the nontraditional program may be the development of a database for the businesses and organizations in the area of the school. These organizations can have a heavy influence on the willingness of the student to give time.

In addition, the nontraditional student is often working against barriers rather than incentives. That is, the enrollment of the nontraditional student will often require the school to overcome barriers rather than to meet needs. Certainly, the ultimate decision to attend will be based on the program meeting the needs of the student. In the case of the nontraditional learner, however, the individual frequently has to overcome resistance internally and from others before taking the first step. This can include:

- Fear of failure—can he or she do the work?
- Fear of losing time with family and friends.
- Fear of losing the support of family and friends.
- Fearing that there are too many things to do.
- Affording the program financially.

With the nontraditional student, identifying the barriers and understanding them is the link between the data and enrollment success.

COMMUNICATION.   The communication program for the nontraditional student often has to focus on the areas of messages and the use of personal contact. The messages used in the communication program for this market segment is, initially, concentrated on programs but soon has to shift into the management of barriers.

When dealing with the potential barriers to enrolling the student, the school will need to be a problem solver in showing the potential student how the institution can help with some of the more troublesome issues that are on the individual's mind.

The school will need to use examples of other students to show how these people were able to manage. These should be positive examples of how students were able to include their families or how families reacted to the students' involvement in education.

The examples also may deal with issues of finance, success, and how the school is able to assist the student in getting through the first few weeks of the program. Messages may then shift to issues of flexibility and timing in terms of the offerings.

The effort of enrolling nontraditional students also should involve the use of personal contact. These students may want to meet with faculty or staff to discuss their options and to ensure that the needs they have can be met by the institution.

CLIMATE.   The climate for the nontraditional student will have to be one that fosters peer relationships rather than one that simply puts the faculty member in a place of prominence.

The adult student will be very demanding and the belief of the faculty and staff must be that they are dealing with adults—that these people have had a great deal of experience and have many demands being made on their time.

APPENDIX

The Data Used In This Study

The data in this book is, to a large extent, taken from the 1986 National Student Database, a resource developed by The Ingersoll Group. This includes units that cover the basic findings on expectations and perceptions of the "ideal" school, and what the sample respondents felt would be attractive about their "ideal" school. Based on these factors, the students' perceptions are formed of their first-choice school.

This data was analyzed through principle component analysis, generation of crosstabs, and frequency analysis, and it was compared with focus group information and other databases. The process is repeated each year by The Ingersoll Group.

The sample used in the data presented consists of responses to a survey, reproduced below, that was mailed by The Ingersoll Group in October 1985 to twelve thousand high school seniors planning to enter college.[1] The sample was randomly selected within established zip code regions. The areas were established to correspond with the College Board regions.

The students were sent a survey, letter, return envelope, and hanger asking that the survey be returned as soon as possible. The number of surveys returned to The Ingersoll Group was 1,239, a return rate of 18.8%. Nonreturn bias was investigated through analysis of early and late returners.

SAMPLE SURVEY OF STUDENTS' HIGHER EDUCATION PREFERENCES

The following cover letter and survey were used to gather the 1986 data base.

> The Ingersoll Group, Inc., is in the process of gathering information which will aid many colleges and universities in their planning processes. We would appreciate your cooperation in completing this questionnaire.
>
> Please read each question carefully and follow instructions where they are provided. When finished, simply return the questionnaire in the enclosed envelope. No postage is needed. Your name is not requested.
>
> Thank you for your assistance in this important project.

[1] A special sample was collected to develop information about minority students.

An Important Survey of Individuals
Interested in Higher Education

1. Are you planning to attend a college/university within the next year or two?

1 ☐ YES

2 ☐ NO

2. Will your "ideal" school be:

1 ☐ 2-YEAR PUBLIC

2 ☐ 2-YEAR PRIVATE

3 ☐ 4-YEAR PUBLIC

4 ☐ 4-YEAR PRIVATE

3. Please list all colleges/universities to which you applied. Please list these in preferential order and circle either "1" or "2".

Order Of Preference	College/University	Check The One You Will Attend	Were You Admitted? Yes	No
1st Choice	_____	☐	1	2
2nd Choice	_____	☐	1	2
3rd Choice	_____	☐	1	2

4. In regard to your college choice:

	Did You Apply For Financial Aid? Yes	No	Did You Receive Financial Aid? Yes	No
1st Choice	1	2	1	2
2nd Choice	1	2	1	2
3rd Choice	1	2	1	2

5. What will be the total cost of the school you plan to attend?

1 ☐ LESS THAN $4,000

2 ☐ BETWEEN $4,000 AND $8,000

3 ☐ MORE THAN $8,000

6. Where will you live while you are attending college?

1 ☐ PARENTS'/GUARDIANS' HOME

2 ☐ NON-CAMPUS HOUSING

3 ☐ CAMPUS HOUSING

7. What was the ONE factor most important to you in choosing a college?

_____

8. As of now, in what area do you think you will be majoring:

1 MAJOR _____ OR UNDECIDED ☐

2 CAREER OBJECTIVE _____ OR UNDECIDED ☐

9. During the 86-87 academic year, are you:

1 ☐ ENROLLED AS A HIGH SCHOOL JUNIOR

2 ☐ ENROLLED AS A HIGH SCHOOL SENIOR

3 ☐ ENROLLED AS A COLLEGE STUDENT

4 ☐ NOT ENROLLED AS A STUDENT IN HIGH SCHOOL OR COLLEGE

10. What distance from home is the college/university you plan to attend?

1. ☐ WITHIN 20 MILES OF HOME
2. ☐ BETWEEN 20 AND 100 MILES
3. ☐ BETWEEN 101 AND 250 MILES
4. ☐ BETWEEN 251 AND 500 MILES
5. ☐ BETWEEN 501 AND 1,000 MILES
6. ☐ MORE THAN 1,000 MILES FROM HOME

11. What do you feel a college education should do for you? Please circle the appropriate responses.

	Very Important	Important	Not Very Important	I Don't Know
1. PREPARE ME FOR GRADUATE OR PROFESSIONAL SCHOOL.	3	2	1	4
2. PREPARE ME TO MOVE INTO A CAREER WHEN I GRADUATE.	3	2	1	4
3. PREPARE ME TO COMMUNICATE EFFECTIVELY, BOTH IN ORAL AND WRITTEN FORM.	3	2	1	4
4. THROUGH CULTURAL EVENTS, PROVIDE ME WITH AN APPRECIATION OF THE PERFORMING AND/OR THE FINE ARTS.	3	2	1	4
5. HELP ME TO IDENTIFY PERSONAL GOALS AND DEVELOP MEANS OF ACHIEVING THEM.	3	2	1	4
6. TEACH ME TO IDENTIFY PROBLEMS, EVALUATE EVIDENCE, AND PURSUE SOLUTIONS TO THEM.	3	2	1	4
7. PREPARE ME TO BE AN EXPERT IN A SPECIFIC FIELD.	3	2	1	4
8. PROVIDE A VARIETY OF EDUCATIONAL EXPERIENCES BEYOND TRADITIONAL LECTURES AND LABS (INTERNSHIPS, INDEPENDENT STUDY, "HANDS-ON" PROJECTS, ETC.)	3	2	1	4
9. TEACH ME TO JUDGE IDEAS CRITICALLY AND EXPRESS IDEAS EFFECTIVELY.	3	2	1	4
10. PROVIDE AN ADVISING PROGRAM THAT FOCUSES ON HELPING ME MEET MY PERSONAL GOALS.	3	2	1	4
11. HELP ME DEVELOP MY LEADERSHIP QUALITIES.	3	2	1	4
12. ENABLE ME TO MAKE MORE MONEY.	3	2	1	4
13. HELP ME DEVELOP AN AWARENESS OF DIFFERENT PHILOSOPHIES, CULTURES, AND WAYS OF LIFE.	3	2	1	4
14. HELP ME ACQUIRE DEPTH OF KNOWLEDGE IN MY MAJOR ACADEMIC DISCIPLINE.	3	2	1	4
15. PROVIDE AN ADVISING PROGRAM THAT FOCUSES ON ACADEMIC REQUIREMENTS AND COURSE WORK.	3	2	1	4
16. PROVIDE A HIGH QUALITY ACADEMIC EXPERIENCE THAT CHALLENGES FACULTY AND STUDENTS TO DO THEIR BEST.	3	2	1	4
17. PREPARE ME FOR PROBABLE CAREER CHANGES DURING MY LIFE.	3	2	1	4
18. PROVIDE AN ATHLETIC PROGRAM THAT FEATURES INTERCOLLEGIATE ATHLETICS.	3	2	1	4
19. PROVIDE A HOUSING PROGRAM THAT MEETS MY NEEDS FOR A PLACE OF MY OWN ON CAMPUS.	3	2	1	4
20. PROVIDE AN ATHLETIC PROGRAM THAT FEATURES INTRAMURAL ATHLETICS.	3	2	1	4
21. PROVIDE ACTIVE FRATERNITIES AND SORORITIES.	3	2	1	4
22. PROVIDE EXTRACURRICULAR ACTIVITIES SUCH AS STUDENT GOVERNMENT, THEATRE PRODUCTIONS, MUSIC GROUPS, ETC.	3	2	1	4
23. PROVIDE ATHLETIC FACILITIES THAT INCLUDE RECREATIONAL AND CONDITIONING FACILITIES.	3	2	1	4
24. PROVIDE ME WITH THE OPPORTUNITY TO BECOME A BROADLY-EDUCATED PERSON.	3	2	1	4

11. CONTINUED

	Very Important	Important	Not Very Important	I Don't Know
25. PROVIDE A STRONG RELIGIONS ENVIRONMENT WHICH WILL HELP PREPARE ME FOR LIFE.	3	2	1	4
26. HELP ME DEVELOP A SENSE OF CONFIDENCE AND INDEPENDENCE BY LIVING AWAY FROM HOME.	3	2	1	4
27. PROVIDE A PRACTICAL, "HANDS-ON" EDUCATION.	3	2	1	4

We Would Like To Get Your Reactions And Opinions With Regard To Your "Ideal" College.

12. For this question, we want you to deal with the characteristics of your "ideal" college, the college you would most like to attend. We ask you to indicate the <u>strength</u> of each characteristic that would be desirable. Please circle the appropriate responses.

FOR EXAMPLE: In this example, the individual felt that the "ideal" college is "moderately metropolitan". Therefore, the "4" is circled.

	Very	Moderately	Neither	Moderately	Very	
METROPOLITAN	5	(4)	3	2	1	RURAL

	Very	Moderately	Neither	Moderately	Very	
1. SINGLE-SEX	5	4	3	2	1	CO-EDUCATIONAL
2. METROPOLITAN	5	4	3	2	1	RURAL
3. CAREER ORIENTED	5	4	3	2	1	NON-CAREER ORIENTED
4. WELL-KNOWN ATHLETIC PROGRAM	5	4	3	2	1	NOT WELL-KNOWN ATHLETICS
5. SPECIALIZED ACADEMIC PROGRAM	5	4	3	2	1	DIVERSE ACADEMIC PROGRAM
6. LOW ADMISSION STANDARDS	5	4	3	2	1	HIGH ADMISSION STANDARDS
7. LARGE	5	4	3	2	1	SMALL
8. NON-INNOVATIVE	5	4	3	2	1	INNOVATIVE
9. ACTIVE/VIGOROUS	5	4	3	2	1	QUIET/PEACEFUL
10. CONSERVATIVE ENVIRONMENT	5	4	3	2	1	LIBERAL ENVIRONMENT
11. PERSONAL	5	4	3	2	1	IMPERSONAL
12. NEAR HOME	5	4	3	2	1	FAR FROM HOME
13. NON-PRESTIGIOUS	5	4	3	2	1	PRESTIGIOUS
14. ACADEMICALLY RIGOROUS	5	4	3	2	1	ACADEMICALLY EASY
15. COMPETITIVE	5	4	3	2	1	NON-COMPETITIVE
16. LOW PRESSURE	5	4	3	2	1	HIGH PRESSURE
17. HIGH COST	5	4	3	2	1	LOW COST
18. RESPONSIVE	5	4	3	2	1	UNRESPONSIVE
19. POOR FINANCIAL AID	5	4	3	2	1	GOOD FINANCIAL AID
20. GOOD JOB PLACEMENT	5	4	3	2	1	POOR JOB PLACEMENT
21. POOR HOUSING	5	4	3	2	1	GOOD HOUSING
22. THEORETICAL	5	4	3	2	1	APPLIED
24. TEACHING-ORIENTED	5	4	3	2	1	RESEARCH-ORIENTED
25. ACTIVE STUDENT LIFE PROGRAM	5	4	3	2	1	LITTLE/NO STUDENT LIFE PROG.
26. DEMANDING FACULTY	5	4	3	2	1	LENIENT FACULTY

12. CONTINUED

		Very	Moderately	Neither	Moderately	Very	
27.	GOOD REPUTATION	5	4	3	2	1	POOR REPUTATION
28.	HIGH ACADEMIC QUALITY	5	4	3	2	1	LOW ACADEMIC QUALITY
29.	SOCIALLY ISOLATED	5	4	3	2	1	SOCIALLY INVOLVED
30.	UNATTRACTIVE CAMPUS	5	4	3	2	1	ATTRACTIVE CAMPUS
31.	EXT. RECREATIONAL FACILITIES	5	4	3	2	1	LTD. RECREATIONAL FACILITIES
32.	NOT DISTINCTIVE	5	4	3	2	1	DISTINCTIVE
33.	EXT. SOCIAL OPPORTUNITIES	5	4	3	2	1	LTD. SOCIAL OPPORTUNITIES
34.	STRONG CO-OPERATIVE EDUCATION WORK PROGRAM	5	4	3	2	1	NO CO-OP. EDUCATION WORK PROGRAM

13. Would your "Ideal" college be:

1 ☐ WITHIN 20 MILES OF HOME

2 ☐ BETWEEN 21 AND 100 MILES

3 ☐ BETWEEN 101 AND 250 MILES

4 ☐ BETWEEN 251 AND 500 MILES

5 ☐ BETWEEN 501 AND 1,000 MILES

6 ☐ MORE THAN 1,000 MILES FROM HOME

14. Would your "Ideal" college have:

1 ☐ FEWER THAN 700 STUDENTS

2 ☐ 701 TO 1,200 STUDENTS

3 ☐ 1,201 TO 5,000 STUDENTS

4 ☐ MORE THAN 5,000 STUDENTS

15. How attractive are each of the following characteristics in your "Ideal" college? Please circle the appropriate response.

THE "IDEAL" COLLEGE OR UNIVERSITY . . .

		Very Attractive	Moderately Attractive	Neither	Moderately Unattractive	Very Unattractive
1.	HAS A FACULTY WHICH IS CONCERNED WITH HELPING STUDENTS REACH THEIR MAXIMUM POTENTIAL.	5	4	3	2	1
2.	HAS A FINANCIAL AID PROGRAM THAT HELPS MAKE COLLEGE AFFORDABLE.	5	4	3	2	1
3.	HAS AN ACTIVE SOCIAL LIFE PROGRAM THAT MEETS OUT-OF-CLASSROOM NEEDS.	5	4	3	2	1
4.	IS CONCERNED WITH MY RECOGNIZING VALUES AND THE ROLE THEY PLAY IN MY LIFE.	5	4	3	2	1
5.	PROVIDES PRACTICAL LEARNING OPPORTUNITIES (INTERNSHIPS, APPRENTICESHIPS, CO-OPERATIVE EDUCATION WORK PROGRAMS, ETC.).	5	4	3	2	1
6.	HAS A LIBERAL ARTS CURRICULUM.	5	4	3	2	1
7.	HAS FACULTY MEMBERS WHO ARE ACCESSIBLE.	5	4	3	2	1
8.	HAS AN ADVISING PROGRAM THAT CONCENTRATES ON MY ACADEMIC MAJOR AND OVERALL CURRICULAR REQUIREMENTS.	5	4	3	2	1
9.	HAS AN ADVISING PROGRAM THAT FOCUSES ON PERSONAL GOALS AND DIRECTION.	5	4	3	2	1
10.	HAS A RELIGIOUS ORIENTATION.	5	4	3	2	1
11.	HAS AN EXCELLENT STUDENT LIFE PROGRAM TO HELP ME DEVELOP INDEPENDENCE.	5	4	3	2	1
12.	HAS AN EXCELLENT JOB PLACEMENT PROGRAM.	5	4	3	2	1
13.	HAS EXCELLENT ATHLETIC FACILITIES AND SPORTS PROGRAMS.	5	4	3	2	1

15. CONTINUED

		Very Attractive	Moderately Attractive	Neither	Moderately Unattractive	Very Unattractive
14.	HAS FACULTY MEMBERS WHO ARE UP-TO-DATE IN THEIR FIELDS.	5	4	3	2	1
15.	HAS AN EXCELLENT CAREER PLANNING PROGRAM.	5	4	3	2	1
16.	HAS FACULTY MEMBERS WHO ARE EXCELLENT TEACHERS.	5	4	3	2	1
17.	HAS EXCELLENT HOUSING FACILITIES.	5	4	3	2	1
18.	HAS SORORITIES/FRATERNITIES.	5	4	3	2	1
19.	HAS STAFF MEMBERS WHO ARE ACCESSIBLE AND CARING.	5	4	3	2	1
20.	HAS A LIBRARY THAT MEETS THE STUDENTS' NEEDS.	5	4	3	2	1
21.	HAS A STRONG INTERNATIONAL DIMENSION WHICH PROVIDES AN EXCELLENT LEARNING EXPERIENCE.	5	4	3	2	1
22.	HAS COURSES THAT HELP ME DEVELOP MY BASIC SKILLS IN READING, WRITING, AND MATH TO INCREASE MY CHANCES OF ACADEMIC SUCCESS.	5	4	3	2	1
23.	IS HARD TO GET INTO.	5	4	3	2	1
24.	IS THE SAME RELIGIOUS DENOMINATION/SECT AS I AM.	5	4	3	2	1
25.	HAS A PROGRAM WHICH HELPS ME DEVELOP LEADERSHIP SKILLS.	5	4	3	2	1
26.	HAS AN EXCELLENT TECHNICAL CURRICULUM.	5	4	3	2	1

Now We Would Like To Get Your Reactions And Opinions With Regard To Your First Choice College

16. For this question, we want you to deal with the characteristics of the school that is your first choice. Please rate each characteristic as it relates to your first choice school and circle the appropriate responses.

FOR EXAMPLE: In this example, the individual felt that his/her first choice college is "moderately metropolitan". Therefore, the "4" is circled.

	Very	Moderately	Neither	Moderately	Very	
METROPOLITAN	5	(4)	3	2	1	RURAL

		Very	Moderately	Neither	Moderately	Very	
1.	SINGLE-SEX	5	4	3	2	1	CO-EDUCATIONAL
2.	METROPOLITAN	5	4	3	2	1	RURAL
3.	CAREER ORIENTED	5	4	3	2	1	NON-CAREER ORIENTED
4.	WELL-KNOWN ATHLETIC PROGRAM	5	4	3	2	1	NOT WELL-KNOWN ATHLETICS
5.	SPECIALIZED ACADEMIC PROGRAM	5	4	3	2	1	DIVERSE ACADEMIC PROGRAM
6.	LOW ADMISSION STANDARDS	5	4	3	2	1	HIGH ADMISSION STANDARDS
7.	LARGE	5	4	3	2	1	SMALL
8.	NON-INNOVATIVE	5	4	3	2	1	INNOVATIVE
9.	ACTIVE/VIGOROUS	5	4	3	2	1	QUIET/PEACEFUL
10.	CONSERVATIVE ENVIRONMENT	5	4	3	2	1	LIBERAL ENVIRONMENT
11.	PERSONAL	5	4	3	2	1	IMPERSONAL
12.	NEAR HOME	5	4	3	2	1	FAR FROM HOME
13.	NON-PRESTIGIOUS	5	4	3	2	1	PRESTIGIOUS
14.	ACADEMICALLY RIGOROUS	5	4	3	2	1	ACADEMICALLY EASY
15.	COMPETITIVE	5	4	3	2	1	NON-COMPETITIVE

16. CONTINUED

	Very	Moderately	Neither	Moderately	Very	
16. LOW PRESSURE	5	4	3	2	1	HIGH PRESSURE
17. HIGH COST	5	4	3	2	1	LOW COST
18. RESPONSIVE	5	4	3	2	1	UNRESPONSIVE
19. POOR FINANCIAL AID	5	4	3	2	1	GOOD FINANCIAL AID
20. GOOD JOB PLACEMENT	5	4	3	2	1	POOR JOB PLACEMENT
21. POOR HOUSING	5	4	3	2	1	GOOD HOUSING
22. THEORETICAL	5	4	3	2	1	APPLIED
24. TEACHING-ORIENTED	5	4	3	2	1	RESEARCH-ORIENTED
25. ACTIVE STUDENT LIFE PROGRAM	5	4	3	2	1	LITTLE/NO STUDENT LIFE PROG.
26. DEMANDING FACULTY	5	4	3	2	1	LENIENT FACULTY
27. GOOD REPUTATION	5	4	3	2	1	POOR REPUTATION
28. HIGH ACADEMIC QUALITY	5	4	3	2	1	LOW ACADEMIC QUALITY
29. SOCIALLY ISOLATED	5	4	3	2	1	SOCIALLY INVOLVED
30. UNATTRACTIVE CAMPUS	5	4	3	2	1	ATTRACTIVE CAMPUS
31. EXT. RECREATIONAL FACILITIES	5	4	3	2	1	LTD. RECREATIONAL FACILITIES
32. NOT DISTINCTIVE	5	4	3	2	1	DISTINCTIVE
33. EXT. SOCIAL OPPORTUNITIES	5	4	3	2	1	LTD. SOCIAL OPPORTUNITIES
34. STRONG CO-OPERATIVE EDUCATION WORK PROGRAM	5	4	3	2	1	NO CO-OP. EDUCATION WORK PROGRAM

17. Please indicate how strongly you agree or disagree with the following statements. Please circle the appropriate responses.

	Strongly Agree	Agree	Neither	Disagree	Strongly Disagree	Don't Know
1. MY FIRST CHOICE INSTITUTION HAS A FACULTY WHICH IS CONCERNED WITH HELPING STUDENTS REACH THEIR MAXIMUM POTENTIAL.	5	4	3	2	1	6
2. MY FIRST CHOICE INSTITUTION HAS A FINANCIAL AID PROGRAM THAT HELPS MAKE COLLEGE AFFORDABLE.	5	4	3	2	1	6
3. MY FIRST CHOICE INSTITUTION HAS AN ACTIVE SOCIAL LIFE PROGRAM THAT MEETS OUT-OF-CLASSROOM NEEDS.	5	4	3	2	1	6
4. MY FIRST CHOICE INSTITUTION IS CONCERNED WITH MY RECOGNIZING VALUES AND THE ROLE THEY PLAY IN MY LIFE.	5	4	3	2	1	6
5. MY FIRST CHOICE INSTITUTION PROVIDES PRACTICAL LEARNING OPPORTUNITIES (INTERNSHIPS, APPRENTICESHIPS, CO-OPERATIVE EDUCATION WORK PROGRAM).	5	4	3	2	1	6
6. MY FIRST CHOICE INSTITUTION HAS A LIBERAL ARTS CURRICULUM.	5	4	3	2	1	6
7. MY FIRST CHOICE INSTITUTION HAS FACULTY MEMBERS WHO ARE ACCESSIBLE.	5	4	3	2	1	6
8. MY FIRST CHOICE INSTITUTION HAS AN ADVISING PROGRAM THAT CONCENTRATES ON MY ACADEMIC MAJOR AND OVERALL CURRICULAR REQUIREMENTS.	5	4	3	2	1	6
9. MY FIRST CHOICE INSTITUTION HAS AN ADVISING PROGRAM THAT FOCUSES ON PERSONAL GOALS AND DIRECTION.	5	4	3	2	1	6
10. MY FIRST CHOICE INSTITUTION HAS A RELIGIOUS ORIENTATION.	5	4	3	2	1	6
11. MY FIRST CHOICE INSTITUTION HAS AN EXCELLENT STUDENT LIFE PROGRAM TO HELP ME DEVELOP INDEPENDENCE.	5	4	3	2	1	6
12. MY FIRST CHOICE INSTITUTION HAS AN EXCELLENT JOB PLACEMENT PROGRAM.	5	4	3	2	1	6

17. CONTINUED

	Strongly Agree	Agree	Neither	Disagree	Strongly Disagree	Don't Know
13. MY FIRST CHOICE INSTITUTION HAS EXCELLENT ATHLETIC FACILITIES AND SPORTS PROGRAMS.	5	4	3	2	1	6
14. MY FIRST CHOICE INSTITUTION HAS FACULTY MEMBERS WHO ARE UP-TO-DATE IN THEIR FIELDS.	5	4	3	2	1	6
15. MY FIRST CHOICE INSTITUTION HAS AN EXCELLENT CAREER PLANNING PROGRAM.	5	4	3	2	1	6
16. MY FIRST CHOICE INSTITUTION HAS FACULTY MEMBERS WHO ARE EXCELLENT TEACHERS.	5	4	3	2	1	6
17. MY FIRST CHOICE INSTITUTION HAS EXCELLENT HOUSING FACILITIES.	5	4	3	2	1	6
18. MY FIRST CHOICE INSTITUTION HAS SORORITIES/FRATERNITIES.	5	4	3	2	1	6
19. MY FIRST CHOICE INSTITUTION HAS STAFF MEMBERS WHO ARE ACCESSIBLE AND CARING.	5	4	3	2	1	6
20. MY FIRST CHOICE INSTITUTION HAS A LIBRARY THAT MEETS THE STUDENTS' NEEDS.	5	4	3	2	1	6
21. MY FIRST CHOICE INSTITUTION HAS A STRONG INTERNATIONAL DIMENSION WHICH PROVIDES AN EXCELLENT LEARNING EXPERIENCE.	5	4	3	2	1	6
22. MY FIRST CHOICE INSTITUTION HAS COURSES THAT HELP ME DEVELOP MY BASIC SKILLS IN READING, WRITING, AND MATH TO INCREASE MY CHANCES OF ACADEMIC SUCCESS.	5	4	3	2	1	6
23. MY FIRST CHOICE INSTITUTION IS HARD TO GET INTO.	5	4	3	2	1	6
24. MY FIRST CHOICE INSTITUTION IS THE SAME RELIGIOUS DENOMINATION/SECT AS I AM.	5	4	3	2	1	6
25. MY FIRST CHOICE INSTITUTION HAS A PROGRAM WHICH HELPS ME DEVELOP LEADERSHIP SKILLS.	5	4	3	2	1	6
26. MY FIRST CHOICE INSTITUTION HAS AN EXCELLENT TECHNICAL CURRICULUM.	5	4	3	2	1	6

18. Have you visited the campus of your first choice school?

1 ☐ YES

2 ☐ NO

19. On your campus visit, what impression did you have of . . .

	Favorable	Neutral	Unfavorable
1. THE ADMISSIONS STAFF/OFFICE.	3	2	1
2. THE FACILITIES.	3	2	1
3. THE INSTITUTION'S LOCATION.	3	2	1
4. THE FACULTY INTERVIEW.	3	2	1
5. THE STUDENTS ON CAMPUS.	3	2	1

20. Did you meet with an admissions representative of this school? (Check all that apply.)

1 ☐ NO, DID NOT MEET WITH REPRESENTATIVE

2 ☐ YES, DURING CAMPUS VISIT

3 ☐ YES, AT MY HIGH SCHOOL/COMMUNITY COLLEGE

4 ☐ YES, AT A REGIONAL COLLEGE NIGHT OR COLLEGE FAIR

Questions 20 Through 34 Are For Classification Purposes Only.

21. Which of the following best describes your family's total yearly income?

1 ☐ UNDER $10,000   4 ☐ $50,001 TO $100,000

2 ☐ $10,000 TO $25,000   5 ☐ MORE THAN $100,000

3 ☐ $25,001 TO $50,000   6 ☐ I DON'T KNOW

22. Are you:

1 ☐ MALE

2 ☐ FEMALE

23. What is your current grade point average?

1 ☐ (A) 4.0   5 ☐ (B-) 2.6 - 2.9

2 ☐ (A-) 3.6 - 3.9   6 ☐ (C+) 2.1 - 2.5

3 ☐ (B+) 3.1 - 3.5   7 ☐ (C) 2.0

4 ☐ (B) 3.0   8 ☐ (C- OR BELOW) BELOW 2.0

24. What is the highest degree you will eventually seek?

1 ☐ ASSOCIATE

2 ☐ BACHELOR'S

3 ☐ MASTER'S

4 ☐ DOCTORATE

5 ☐ FIRST PROFESSIONAL (FOR EXAMPLE, MD, JURIS DOCTOR, ETC.)

6 ☐ OTHER

7 ☐ UNDECIDED

25. To what race or ethnic group do you belong?

1 ☐ WHITE, NOT HISPANIC

2 ☐ BLACK, NOT HISPANIC

3 ☐ NATIVE AMERICAN OR AMERICAN INDIAN

4 ☐ HISPANIC

5 ☐ ASIAN

6 ☐ OTHER (Please Specify) _____

26. Of what religious affiliation are you?

1 ☐ CATHOLIC   8 ☐ UCC, CONGREGATIONAL, EVANGELICAL

2 ☐ METHODIST   9 ☐ LUTHERAN

3 ☐ PRESBYTERIAN   10 ☐ BRETHEREN

4 ☐ BAPTIST   11 ☐ NAZARENE

5 ☐ EPISCOPAL   12 ☐ MORMON

6 ☐ JEWISH   13 ☐ OTHER (Please Specify) _____

7 ☐ CHURCH OF CHRIST

27. How important will availability of financial aid be in your choice of a college or university?

1 ☐ ESSENTIAL

2 ☐ VERY IMPORTANT

3 ☐ SOMEWHAT IMPORTANT

4 ☐ SOMEWHAT UNIMPORTANT

5 ☐ NOT ESSENTIAL

28. Is your secondary school:

1 ☐ PRIVATE

2 ☐ PUBLIC

3 ☐ PAROCHIAL

29. In making your final decision as to which college to attend, do you think the decision will be:

1 ☐ EXTREMELY DIFFICULT TO MAKE

2 ☐ FAIRLY DIFFICULT TO MAKE

3 ☐ FAIRLY EASY TO MAKE

4 ☐ QUITE EASY TO MAKE

30. Would the fact that a college emphasizes the Christian perspective in its academic and student life programs:

1 ☐ INCREASE YOUR INTEREST IN ATTENDING THE COLLEGE

2 ☐ DECREASE YOUR INTEREST IN ATTENDING THE COLLEGE

3 ☐ NOT MAKE ANY DIFFERENCE IN YOUR DECISION

31. Would the fact that a college is a single-sex school:

1 ☐ INCREASE YOUR INTEREST IN ATTENDING THE COLLEGE

2 ☐ DECREASE YOUR INTEREST IN ATTENDING THE COLLEGE

3 ☐ NOT MAKE ANY DIFFERENCE IN YOUR DECISION

32. Would the fact that a college emphasizes technology in its academic programs:

1 ☐ INCREASE YOUR INTEREST IN ATTENDING THE COLLEGE

2 ☐ DECREASE YOUR INTEREST IN ATTENDING THE COLLEGE

3 ☐ NOT MAKE ANY DIFFERENCE IN YOUR DECISION

33. Would the fact that a college emphasizes the fine arts in its programs:

1 ☐ INCREASE YOUR INTEREST IN ATTENDING THE COLLEGE

2 ☐ DECREASE YOUR INTEREST IN ATTENDING THE COLLEGE

3 ☐ NOT MAKE ANY DIFFERENCE IN YOUR DECISION

34. What is your age? _____ YEARS

35. What is your zip code? ☐ ☐ ☐ ☐ ☐

1986 NATIONAL STUDENT DATABASE: THE EXPECTATIONS OF SENIORS IN REGARD TO COLLEGE

What Should a College Education Do for You?

EXPECTATIONS	1986 RESPONDENTS†	1985 RESPONDENTS
1. Prepare me for graduate school	46.17%	48.27%
2. Prepare me for a career	95.42%	89.45%
3. Prepare me to communicate	59.39%	60.14%
4. Give me an appreciation of the fine arts	17.70%	14.98%
5. Help me identify personal goals	65.50%	68.04%
6. Help me identify problems	61.83%	68.07%
7. Prepare me to be an expert	69.13%	70.97%
8. Provide experiences	63.74%	62.01%
9. Teach me to judge ideas	55.63%	60.31%
10. Provide personal advising	50.05%	63.07%
11. Help me develop leadership	42.95%	45.61%
12. Help me make more money	46.59%	48.36%
13. Help me develop awareness	26.27%	31.44%
14. Help me acquire depth of knowledge	69.83%	73.55%
15. Provide academic advising	33.24%	39.03%
16. Provide quality academic experiences	61.66%	68.26%
17. Prepare me for changes	48.48%	54.33%
18. Provide intercollegiate athletics	21.58%	20.78%
19. Provide on-campus housing	36.75%	40.77%
20. Provide intramural athletics	19.91%	20.95%
21. Provide fraternities/sororities	14.08%	16.39%
22. Provide extracurricular activities	34.69%	33.65%
23. Provide recreational activities	34.38%	—
24. Become broadly educated	74.30%	70.50%
25. Provide a strong religious environment	16.70%	—
26. Help me develop confidence	55.08%	58.88%
27. Provide a "hands-on" education	59.22%	62.96%
Average	47.42%	47.44%

NOTE: Numbers represent the percentage of respondents who felt each characteristic was very important in what a college education should do for them.

* These questions were not asked of the 1985 Database respondents.

† Data for 1986 has been normalized to the 1985 data.

Please Rate the Characteristics of Your "Ideal" College/University.

CHARACTERISTICS	1986 RESPONDENTS	1985 RESPONDENTS
1. Co-educational	4.49	4.49
2. Metropolitan	3.51	3.49
3. Career-oriented	4.42	4.48
4. Well-known athletic program	3.58	3.69
5. Diverse academic program	2.57	2.46
6. High admission standards	3.51	2.57
7. Small	2.81	2.83
8. Innovative	3.92	3.58
9. Active/vigorous	3.66	3.65
10. Conservative	2.69	2.79
11. Personal	4.03	4.05
12. Near home	3.17	-- *
13. Prestigious	3.74	2.43
14. Academically rigorous	3.78	3.78
15. Competitive	3.93	3.91
16. High pressure	3.02	2.93
17. Low cost	3.71	-- *
18. Responsive	4.21	4.23
19. Good financial aid program	4.50	4.42
20. Good job placement program	4.58	4.59
21. Good housing	4.63	4.55
22. Applied	3.63	-- *
23. Good career counseling	4.58	4.59
24. Teaching-oriented	3.61	3.55
25. Active student life program	4.43	-- *
26. Demanding faculty	3.68	3.73
27. Good reputation	4.68	4.66
28. High academic quality	4.59	4.51
29. Socially involved	4.31	4.26
30. Attractive campus	4.57	4.51
31. Extensive recreational facilities	4.23	4.26
32. Distinctive	4.03	-- *
33. Extensive social opportunities	4.32	4.35
34. Strong co-op work program	4.16	4.19
Average	3.92	3.28

NOTE: Characteristics were rated on a scale of 1 to 5, with opposite characteristics being on opposite ends of the scale. Example:

Metropolitan   5 4 3 2 1   Rural

The numbers above represent the means. Therefore, the mean of the Metropolitan/Rural question is 3.51, indicating that respondents felt the "ideal" school was slightly more metropolitan than rural.

* These questions were not asked of the 1985 Database respondents.

Please Rate the Attractiveness of the Following Characteristics in Your "Ideal" College.

	CHARACTERISTICS	1986 RESPONDENTS	1985 RESPONDENTS
1.	Concerned faculty	80.34%	81.27%
2.	Affordable programs	71.34%	75.22%
3.	Active social life	55.59%	85.64%
4.	Concerned with values	47.24%	47.62%
5.	Practical learning	59.06%	56.17%
6.	Liberal arts curriculum	29.06%	26.30%
7.	Accessible faculty	61.16%	60.47%
8.	Academic advising	60.91%	62.63%
9.	Personal advising	52.76%	54.01%
10.	Religious orientation	13.18%	—
11.	Excellent student life	47.16%	57.20%
12.	Excellent job placement	72.73%	72.76%
13.	Excellent athletic facilities	29.87%	30.26%
14.	Up-to-date faculty	82.58%	85.62%
15.	Excellent career planning	70.99%	72.70%
16.	Excellent teachers	8.53%	86.60%
17.	Excellent housing	60.50%	60.36%
18.	Sororities/fraternities	19.77%	19.99%
19.	Accessible staff	73.88%	72.67%
20.	Adequate library	77.46%	78.88%
21.	International dimension	46.45%	47.03%
22.	Develop basic skills	45.96%	48.93%
23.	Hard to get into	8.34%	10.02%
24.	Same religion as me	8.84%	—
25.	Develop leadership	35.11%	33.21%
26.	Technical curriculum	26.82%	25.47%
	Average	50.91%	51.96%

NOTE: Numbers represent the percentage of respondents who felt each characteristic was very attractive in the "ideal" college.

* These questions were not asked of the 1985 Database respondents.

What distance from home is the college/university you plan to attend?

	LOCATION	1986 RESPONDENTS	1985 RESPONDENTS
1.	Within 20 Miles Of Home	23.16%	21.83%
2.	Between 20 And 100 Miles	25.70%	27.94%
3.	Between 101 And 250 Miles	21.46%	21.49%
4.	Between 251 And 500 Miles	15.27%	14.31%
5.	Between 501 And 1,000 Miles	7.72%	7.52%
6.	More Than 1,000 Miles	6.62%	6.90%

What will be the total cost of the school you plan to attend?

COST	1986 RESPONDENTS	1985 RESPONDENTS
1. Less Than $4,000.00	16.47%	19.13%
2. Between $4,000.00 And $8,000.00	48.98%	48.98%
3. More Than $8,000.00	34.46%	31.89%

"FIT" ISSUES

There are implications from each of the major charts for "fit" of the institution to the marketplace. In this case, we will use Levitt's model and look at what this data says about the expected product and the augmented product.*

There are seven primary *expectations* listed by the respondents in this report. These include:

• Prepare me for a career.
• Help me to become broadly educated.
• Prepare me to be an expert.
• Help me acquire depth of knowledge.
• Provide experiences.
• Help me to learn how to solve problems.
• Provide quality academic experience.

Each of these adds a single dimension to the items that should cluster in the area of expectations of the school. It should be noted that preparation for a career is very strong. Even those who see themselves going on to graduate school ultimately perceive this as a career experience.

Many of the follow-up responses also relate to career preparation, including becoming an expert in a specific field. The issues of broad education and in-depth preparation will turn to careers when covered in focus groups. The student expects broad yet in-depth preparation in the major as a part of being able to problem-solve and being perceived as an expert in a field. The broad coverage in a major provides for maximum flexibility in the marketplace.

There are nine items that seem to stand out as the student looks at the "ideal" college. These factors include:

• Being co-educational.
• Being career-oriented.

*Levitt, Theodore, *The Marketing Imagination,* Free Press, 1983. His development of product divides this area into four sections: the generic product, the expected product, the augmented product, and the potential product.

- Having a good financial aid program.
- Having good job placement.
- Having good housing.
- Having an active student life program.
- Having a good reputation.
- Being high quality.
- Having an attractive campus.

Each of these will be an appropriate addition to the expectations cluster of Levitt's product model. It is important to remember that these students will want to know about certain items at certain times. For example, the student may initially want to know more about the programs and cognitive portions of the school. After the student is convinced that the school has the basic essentials, the individual will begin to look at other factors that will make the school feel good. These expectations will become just as important as the primary factors.

The following items were found to be most attractive to students in the "ideal" school:

- Up-to-date faculty.
- Excellent teachers.
- Concerned faculty.
- An adequate library.
- Accessible staff.
- Excellent career planning.
- Excellent job placement.
- Excellent financial aid.

It can be seen in this data that the people at the school play a very large role in meeting the expectations of potential students. The library is also included, along with services that would support expectations such as career-related services and financial aid.

Research has shown the following:

- Students expected to pay a little more for an education in 1986. More students are found in the category that will spend more than $8,000.
- Generally, the student expects to attend within 250 miles from home with over 50% expecting to go within 100 miles.

COMMUNICATION ISSUES

In terms of a discussion of communication issues, we will focus our effort around the communication formulas used in our work with the Enrollment Matrix.

The main areas in which the database information can help us is the use of messages, development of themes, and type of communication. The information in the database can also provide information on image and "fit" about your school.

MESSAGES

It is our assumption that each single communication from a school should focus on only a few messages. It is also our assumption that the messages may change as the student proceeds through the process of deciding about a school. In these cases, the messages we should use are rather clear from the data provided.

We must be able to demonstrate that we can prepare a student for a career and that we have the resources to do so. This will generally include quality, reputation, the services that support careers, practical experiences, and people who can do the job.

People messages have become very important, and the faculty come out very highly. Messages should generally be used, therefore, that support the idea that the individuals know what they are doing, can react well to students, and are ready to work hard to make students successful.

Special brochures should be used that develop profiles of faculty and the fact that they can do the things that students expect. Examples should be used in all of the materials that give a clear indication to the student and influentials that faculty members at your school can meet these expectations.

Services are important and, if your students rate your services strongly, you should talk about them in your literature. It would be wise to discuss the people in your service areas as much as possible.

TYPE

Because of the importance of people, it will be important that many of your messages be delivered by people. The campus visit and special events will become even more important to the student. The professional admission staff and the volunteers become more critical.

Good training of everyone on the staff should be undertaken so that the student can understand your school on his/her terms. Your staff must be ready to deliver and support these messages as clearly as possible.

Use people as much as possible in your program. Have high quality people in contact with the student and reward your staff for this effort.

GLOSSARY OF ENROLLMENT MANAGEMENT TERMS

Administration: The administration includes all people, from officers to those on the clerical and secretarial level. This would normally include, in our thinking, presidents, deans, directors, department chairs, and assistant directors.

Admissions: The status of enrollment programs when there were sufficient numbers of students in the marketplace. The function of the admissions office at that point is to make sure the wrong people do not get into the school.

Attitudes: A key ingredient in being able to influence people. People make decisions based to a large extent on their attitudes.

Attribute data: Purely physical data such as age, sex, income, and place of residence.

Augmented product: The surprises that a student finds on the campus once he or she has enrolled, beyond or contrary to expectations.

Barrier Management: In many cases, particularly with the nontraditional student, the school has to deal with barriers rather then appeals. Lowering the barrier may be accomplished by making the school seem more appealing.

Brochure: A small publication, four to six pages, usually in one or two colors.

Causal: As in a cause/effect relationship, many of the statistics used in matrix work are gained through causal analysis.

Climate: A main ingredient in a successful enrollment program includes information flow and use, political systems, and the cultural systems (attitudes, beliefs, and trust).

Communication program: The sum of amount, messages, type, and quality constituting the ability of the school to communicate with the marketplace.

Competition: Those organizations or groups that compete with the school for students. These may include churches, spouse, the armed forces, or other colleges.

Competition data: Data collected about the competition. This includes such items as mailings, timing, messages, and appeals.

Component analysis: The separation of data using principle component or factor analysis to find what components cluster together.

Consumer satisfaction: A focus of the program from the faculty and staff should be on the consumer. Consumer satisfaction is a major ingredient of an enrollment program.

Content: The right way to do something, as in a career services or advising program.

Convergence: Reliability of information is assumed if similar answers are found to converge from various processes of investigation.

Conversion ratio: The percentage of individuals that move from one status of the enrollment program to another; that is, the conversion of inquiries to applications could be represented by a conversion ratio.

Critical variables: A part of the Enrollment Matrix that proves to be particularly critical for an individual school.

Demographics: Normally thought of as the numbers of individuals in the marketplace at any particular time. Some people also include economic factors.

Diffusion: The movement of information within an organization. One of the critical reasons for a task force is to allow the task force to diffuse information to the organization.

Disturbance term: That term in a causal formulation that includes ingredients not assumed in the model.

Emulators: Individuals who make decisions based on their view of other people. These are individuals who emulate their peers in making enrollment decisions.

Enrollment management: The overall management of enrollment, including all of the key variables associated with enrollment success.

Enrollment master plan: A total plan for the institution in terms of how it is going to meet its enrollment goals. This would include product and climate planning.

Enrollment Matrix: A three-dimensional matrix allowing a unique analysis of the enrollment situation at a given school. These dimensions comprise (1) key variables, (2) critical attributes, and (3) attitudes and beliefs. Demonstrating the Enrollment Matrix (which is depicted on page 13) is the chief object of this study.

Enrollment situation: The particular status of the school in regard to its enrollment efforts.

Environment: The outside world and its impact on the organization.

Environmental data: Data collected in regard to the environment. This includes such information as employment, economy, demographics, attitudes, and beliefs.

Expectations: What students expect from an institution as opposed to generic or augmented products.

Expected product: The school of the future will have to include a minimal commitment to meeting all expectations.

Experiential options: Chances for people to have hands-on experience with a particular program, such as internships and co-ops.

Fit: The way the institution coordinates with the marketplace in terms of expectations—meeting attitudes and beliefs.

Focus group: A small group of about six people gathered to explore a particular topic in a research environment.

Four-box Model: A model used to develop communication systems. Includes rapport, wants and needs, problems, and making the right decisions.

Fundamentals: An enrollment program should have at least the minimum fundamentals. This would include the ability to communicate with the marketplace, a good enrollment management plan, and trained and developed staff members. Fundamental programs should have a good data system.

Future product: What the institution will do in the future in terms of attracting students from the product perspective.

Generic product: What the marketplace thinks about an institution without knowing anything about it, as in the generic image of a community college.

Goal statement: This includes the numbers, type, geography, and other factors that will make up the enrollment goals.

Influence: The ability of the school to change students' minds. The school of the future will have to do a better job at influence.

Influentials: Those who have impact on a student, such as teachers, counselors, or parents.

Inner-directed: Quality possessed by those individuals making decisions based on internal feelings.

Inquiries: Students who actually inquire for information about the school, as opposed to referrals (individuals whose names have been given to the school by another person).

Institutional image: What people in the marketplace think about the institution without prompting.

Management information: This is the data used to manage a program. It normally includes inquiries, applications, complete applications, campus visits, deposits, and acceptances. This usually compares one year to the next.

Marketing: Often thought of as advertising or public relations, in our sense, marketing includes all aspects of the matrix.

Marketing approach: Any approach to enrollment management that includes marketing.

Matrix: A systematic set of variables that impact a particular situation.

Matrix management: The management of the key variables in terms of a particular issue.

Metastrategies: Overall strategies that guide an enrollment program.

Need-driven: Quality possessed by individuals making decisions about enrollment based on basic needs.

Nontraditional students: Those students who are not typical high school seniors, usually designated by age or time out of high school.

Outer-directed: Quality possessed by those individuals who are making decisions about enrollment based on what is happening in the outside world. The opinions and feelings of others will be particularly important.

Packaging: The development of a product that includes many elements. The removal of one element decreases the value of the package.

Peers: Fellow students who have great influence on decision-making.

Process: Those aspects of a situation that generally relate to how people work together.

Product: What the student is purchasing from the institution.

Rapport: This may generally be seen as trust or the ability of an individual to gain a commitment of time and energy from a potential student.

Recruitment: The second stage of enrollment programs after the admission stage. In this stage, the goal is to get as many students to inquire as possible.

Relationship management: The ability of a school to manage its relationships. This will be a key to enrollment success in the future.

Relationships: All aspects of the connection between the school and the student—the ability of the school and people at the school to give time, energy, and commitment to the student.

Resources: Those data aspects of the matrix that deal with the items needed to conduct a particular part of the program.

Segmentation: Dealing with the particular parts of the market. Age, geography, or values may be used to segment.

Services: Those items that support an academic program, such as career counseling, financial aid, and advising. These become a critical part of the package.

Strategy: That plan or package that is designed to allow the school to find its niche or position within the marketplace. The strategies should begin to orient people at the institution in terms of direction and energy.

Tactical strategies: The strategies the institution will use to meet its enrollment goals.

Talent development: The training and development of people involved in the enrollment program.

Task force: A group of people banded together to assist the school in developing tactical strategies and desired states. These individuals are generally grouped together to diffuse information to the environment and to deal especially with climate issues.

Threefold planning: The development of an enrollment program through three steps: goals, tactical strategies, and actions.

Time factors: That part of a causal equation that includes the impact of time.

Traditional: A student who is generally considered to be a high school senior.

Transition states: Those intermediate states that occur between the present and desired states. Knowing these can help one see progress toward the desired state.

Validity: Successfully linking data and information to action.

Values: Those perceptions, attitudes, and beliefs of individuals that may have a key impact on their enrollment decisions.

Viewbook: A small publication (usually 16 to 32 pages) that may be among the first publications the student receives.

BIBLIOGRAPHY

PRODUCT

Apps, Jerold W. *Improving Practice in Continuing Education*. San Francisco: Jossey-Bass Publishers, 1985.

Astin, Alexander W. *Preventing Students from Dropping Out*. San Francisco: Jossey-Bass Publishers, 1975.

Bok, Derek. *Higher Learning*. Cambridge, Massachusetts: Harvard University Press, 1986.

Bolles, Richard N. *The Three Boxes of Life and How to Get Out of Them*. Berkeley, California: Ten Speed Press, 1978.

Boone, Edgar J.; Shearon, Ronald W.; White, Estelle E.; and associates. *Serving Personal and Community Needs through Adult Education*. San Francisco: Jossey-Bass Publishers, 1980.

Bowen, Howard R. *The Costs of Higher Education*. San Francisco: Jossey-Bass Publishers, 1980.

Bowen, Howard R. *Investment in Learning: The Individual and Social Value of American Higher Education*. San Francisco: Jossey-Bass Publishers, 1980.

Bowen, Howard R. *The State of the Nation and the Agenda for Higher Education*. San Francisco: Jossey-Bass Publishers, 1982.

The Carnegie Council on Policy Studies in Higher Education. *Next Steps for the 1980s in Student Financial Aid: A Fourth Alternative*. San Francisco: Jossey-Bass Publishers, 1979.

The Carnegie Council on Policy Studies in Higher Education. *The States and Private Higher Education*. San Francisco: Jossey-Bass Publishers, 1977.

The Carnegie Foundation for the Advancement of Teaching. *Missions of the College Curriculum: A Contemporary Review with Suggestions*. San Francisco: Jossey-Bass Publishers, 1979.

The Carnegie Foundation for the Advancement of Teaching. *More Than*

Survival: Prospects for Higher Education in a Period of Uncertainty. San Francisco: Jossey-Bass Publishers, 1975.

Cetron, Marvin. *Schools of the Future: How American Business and Education Can Cooperate to Save Our Schools.* New York: McGraw-Hill Book Company, 1985.

Chickering, Arthur W. *Education and Identity.* San Francisco: Jossey-Bass Publishers, 1976.

Chickering, Arthur W., and associates. *The Modern American College.* San Francisco: Jossey-Bass Publishers, 1981.

Cohen, Arthur M., and Brawer, Florence B. *The American Community College.* San Francisco: Jossey-Bass Publishers, 1984.

Cross, K. Patricia. *Accent on Learning.* San Francisco: Jossey-Bass Publishers, 1979.

Cross, K. Patricia. *Adults As Learners.* San Francisco: Jossey-Bass Publishers, 1982.

Daloz, Laurent A. *Effective Teaching and Mentoring.* San Francisco: Jossey-Bass Publishers, 1986.

Deegan, William L.; Tillery, Dale; and associates. *Renewing the American Community College.* San Francisco: Jossey-Bass Publishers, 1985.

Delwoeth, Ursula; Hanson, Gary R.; and associates. *Student Services: A Handbook for the Profession.* San Francisco: Jossey-Bass Publishers, 1980.

Derr, C. Brooklyn. *Managing the New Careerists.* San Francisco: Jossey-Bass Publishers, 1986.

Gilligan, Carol. *In a Different Voice: Psychological Theory and Women's Development.* Cambridge, Massachusetts: Harvard University Press, 1982.

Green, Janice S.; Levine, Arthur; and associates. *Opportunity in Adversity.* San Francisco: Jossey-Bass Publishers, 1985.

Grier, William H., and Cobbs, Price M. *Black Rage.* New York: Basic Books, Inc., Publishers, 1968.

Hall, Douglas T., and associates. *Career Development in Organizations.* San Francisco: Jossey-Bass Publishers, 1986.

Handy, Charles. *The Future of Work.* New York: Basil Blackwell, Inc., 1984.

Harris, Norman C., and Grede, John F. *Career Education in Colleges.* San Francisco: Jossey-Bass Publishers, 1977.

Hickman, Craig R., and Silva, Michael A. *Creating Excellence.* New York: New American Library, 1984.

Jenkins, Hugh M., and associates. *Educating Students from Other Nations.* San Francisco: Jossey-Bass Publishers, 1983.

Johnston, William J. *Education on Trial: Strategies for the Future.* San Francisco: Institute for Contemporary Studies, 1985.

Knowles, Malcolm S. *Using Learning Contracts.* San Francisco: Jossey-Bass Publishers, 1986.

Levitt, Theodore. *The Marketing Imagination.* New York: The Free Press, 1983.

Levine, Arthur. *When Dreams and Heroes Died: A Portrait of Today's College Student.* San Francisco: Jossey-Bass Publishers, 1980.

Long, Huey B.; Hiemstra, Roger; and associates. *Changing Approaches to Studying Adult Education.* San Francisco: Jossey-Bass Publishers, 1980.

Martin, Warren Bryan. *College of Character.* San Francisco: Jossey-Bass Publishers, 1982.

May, Ernest R.; and Blaney, Dorothy G. *Careers for Humanists.* New York: Academic Press, 1981.

Mayhew, Lewis B. *Surviving the Eighties.* San Francisco: Jossey-Bass Publishers, 1979.

Miller, Theodore K., and Prince, Judith S. *The Future of Student Affairs.* San Francisco: Jossey-Bass Publishers, 1976.

Mitchell, Arnold. *The Nine American Lifestyles.* New York: Warner Books, 1983.

Noel, Lee; Levitz, Randi; Saluri, Diana; and associates. *Increasing Student Retention.* San Francisco: Jossey-Bass Publishers, 1985.

Peters, John W., and associates. *Building an Effective Adult Education Enterprise.* San Francisco: Jossey-Bass Publishers, 1980.

Peterson, Richard E., and associates. *Lifelong Learning in America.* San Francisco: Jossey-Bass Publishers, 1979.

Porter, Michael E. *Competitive Advantage: Creating and Sustaining Superior Performance.* New York: The Free Press, 1985.

Reich, Robert B. *The Next American Frontier.* New York: Times Books, 1983.

Sitkoff, Harvard. *The Struggle for Black Equality 1954–1980.* New York: Hill And Wang, 1981.

Stadtman, Verne A. *Academic Adaptations: Higher Education Prepares for the 1980s and 1990s.* San Francisco: Jossey-Bass Publishers.

Vermilye, Dyckman W. *Individualizing the System: Current Issues in Higher Education 1976.* San Francisco: Jossey-Bass Publishers, 1976.

Weinberg, Carl. *Education and Social Problems.* New York: The Free Press, 1971.

RESEARCH

Anderson, Scarvia B., and Ball, Samuel. *The Profession and Practice of Program Evaluation*. San Francisco: Jossey-Bass Publishers, 1980.

Argyris, Chris; Putnam, Robert; and Smith, Diana McLain. *Action Science*. San Francisco: Jossey-Bass Publishers, 1985.

ASHE-ERIC Higher Education Research Reports 1984. *Futures Research and the Strategic Planning Process*. Washington, DC: Association for the Study of Higher Education, 1984.

Babbie, Earl R. *The Practice of Social Research*. Belmont, California: Wadsworth Publishing Company, Inc., 1973.

Bell, Daniel. *The Coming of Post-Industrial Society*. New York: Basic Books, Inc., Publishers, 1973.

Bradburn, Norman M.; Sudman, Seymour; and associates. *Improving Interview Methods and Questionnaire Design*. San Francisco: Jossey-Bass Publishers, 1980.

Dillman, Don A. *Mail and Telephone Surveys: The Total Design Method*. New York: John Wiley & Sons, 1978.

Ewell, Peter T. "Recruitment, Retention and Student Flow: A Comprehensive Approach to Enrollment Management Research." National Center For Higher Education Management Systems, April, 1985.

Gallup, George. *Forecast 2000*. New York: William Morrow and Company, Inc., 1984.

Guba, Egon G., and Lincoln, Yvonna S. *Effective Evaluation*. San Francisco: Jossey-Bass Publishers, 1981.

Keller, George. *Academic Strategy: The Management Revolution in American Higher Education*. Baltimore: The Johns Hopkins University Press, 1983.

Kerin, Roger A., and Peterson, Robert A. *Strategic Marketing Problems*. Boston: Allyn and Bacon, Inc., 1981.

Krathwohl, David R. *Social and Behavioral Science Research*. San Francisco: Jossey-Bass Publishers, 1985.

Miles, Matthew B., and Huberman, A. Michael. *Qualitative Data Analysis: A Sourcebook of New Methods*. Beverly Hills, California: Sage Publications, 1984.

Oxford Analytica. *America in Perspective*. Boston: Houghton Mifflin Company, 1986.

Sudman, Seymour, and Bradburn, Norman M. *Asking Questions: A Practical Guide to Questionnaire Design*. San Francisco: Jossey-Bass Publishers, 1983.

Thompson, Ronald B. *Projections of Enrollments, Public and Private Colleges and Universities*. Washington, DC: AACRAO Office, 1970.

Tufte, Edward R. *The Visual Display of Quantitative Information*. Cheshire, Connecticut: Graphics Press. 1983.

Wall Street Journal. *America Tomorrow*. New York: Dow Jones & Company, Inc., 1977.

Yankelovich, Daniel. *New Rules: Searching for Self-Fulfillment in a World Turned Upside Down*. New York: Random House, 1981.

DATA

Botkin, James; Dimancescu, Dan; and Stata, Ray. *Global Stakes: The Future of High Technology in America*. Cambridge, Massachusetts: Ballinger Publishing Company, 1982.

The Carnegie Council on Policy Studies in Higher Education. *Three Thousand Futures: The Next Twenty Years for Higher Education*. San Francisco: Jossey-Bass Publishers, 1980.

Manski, Charles F., and Wise, David A. *College Choice in America*. Cambridge, Massachusetts: Harvard University Press, 1983.

COMMUNICATION

Bandler, Richard, and Grinder, John. *The Structure of Magic: A Book about Language and Therapy,*. Palo Alto, California: Science and Behavior Books, Inc., 1975.

Blyskal, Jeff, and Blyskal, Marie. "PR: How the Public Relations Industry Writes the News." Macmillan Book Clubs, April, 1986.

Dansig, Fred, and Klein, Ted. *How to Be Heard: Making the Media Work for You*. New York: Macmillan Publishing Co., Inc., 1974.

Farlow, Helen. *Publicizing and Promoting Programs*. New York: McGraw-Hill Book Company, 1979.

Goodman, Gary S. *Winning by Telephone: Telephone Effectiveness for Business Professionals and Consumers*. Englewood Cliffs, New Jersey: Prentice-Hall, Inc., 1982.

Hersey, Paul. *Situational Selling: An Approach for Increasing Sales Effectiveness*. Escondido, California: The Center for Leadership Studies, 985.

Maslow, A. H. *The Farther Reaches of Human Nature*. New York: The Viking Press, 1971.

Mitchell, Arnold. *The Nine American Lifestyles*. New York: Warner Books, 1983.

278   RONALD J. INGERSOLL

O'Toole, John *The Trouble with Advertising. New York: Chelsea House, 1981.*

Richardson, Jerry, and Margulis, Joel. *The Magic of Rapport: How You Can Gain Personal Power in Any Situation.* San Francisco: Harbor Publishing, 1981.

Stone, Bob, and Wyman, John. *Successful Telemarketing: Opportunities and Techniques for Increasing Sales and Profits.* Lincolnwood, Illinois: NTC Business Books, 1986.

Walther, George R. "Phone Power: How to Make the Telephone Your Most Profitable Business Tool." Macmillan Book Clubs, September, 1986.

Weight, John S.; Warner, Daniel S.; Winter, Willis L.; and Zeigler, Sherilyn K. *Advertising,* fourth edition. New York: McGraw-Hill Book Company, 1977.

MANAGEMENT

Balderston, Frederick E. *Managing Today's University.* San Francisco: Jossey-Bass Publishers, 1974.

Baldridge, J. Victor, and Deal, Terrence E. *Managing Change in Educational Organizations.* Berkeley: McCutchan Publishing Corporation, 1975.

Bennis, Warren, and Nanus, Burt. *Leaders: Strategies for Taking Charge.* New York: Harper & Row, Publishers, 1985.

Blake, Robert R., and Mouton, Jane S. *The New Managerial Grid.* Houston: Gulf Publishing Company, 1964.

Blake, Robert R.; Mouton, Jane S.; and Williams, Martha Shipe. *The Academic Administrator Grid.* San Francisco: Jossey-Bass Publishers, 1981.

Brown, Arnold. *Supermanaging: How to Harness Change for Personal and Organizational Success.* New York: McGraw-Hill Book Company, 1984.

Cheek, Logan M. *Zero-Base Budgeting Comes of Age.* New York: AMACOM, 1977.

deBono, Edward. *Tactics: The Art and Science of Success.* Boston: Little, Brown And Company, 1984.

Dressel, Paul L. *Administrative Leadership.* San Francisco: Jossey-Bass Publishers, 1981.

Drucker, Peter F. *Concept of the Corporation.* New York: The John Day Company, 1972.

Drucker, Peter F. *The Frontiers of Management, Where Tomorrow's Decisions Are Being Shaped by Today.* New York: Truman Talley Books, 1986.

Drucker, Peter F. *Innovation and Entrepreneurship: Practice and Principles.* New York: Harper & Row, 1985.

Drucker, Peter F. *Managing for Results*. New York: Harper & Row, Publishers, 1964.

Elbe, Kenneth E. *The Art of Administration*. San Francisco: Jossey-Bass Publishers, 1978.

Fink, Steven. *Crisis Management: Planning for the Inevitable*. New York: AMACOM, 1986.

Foster, Richard. *Innovation: The Attacker's Advantage*. New York: Summit Books, 1986.

Foy, Nancy. *The Yin & Yang of Organizations*. New York: William Morrow and Company, Inc., 1980.

Garfield, Charles. *Peak Performers: The New Heroes of American Business*. New York: William Morrow And Company, Inc., 1986.

Greenleaf, Robert K. *Servant Leadership: A Journey into the Nature of Legitimate Power and Greatness*. New York: Paulist Press, 1977.

Gross, Edward, and Grambsch, Paul V. *Changes in University Organization, 1964–1971*. The Carnegie Commission on Higher Education, New York: McGraw-Hill Book Company, 1974.

Harman, Willis, and Rheingold, Howard. *Higher Creativity: Liberating the Unconscious for Breakthrough Insights*. Los Angeles: Jeremy P. Tarcher, Inc., 1984.

Harris, Philip R. *Management in Transition*. San Francisco: Jossey-Bass Publishers, 1985.

Harvard Business Review. *On Human Relations*. New York: Harper & Row, Publishers, 1979.

Heider, John. *The Tao of Leadership: Leadership Strategies for a New Age*. New York: Bantam Books, 1985.

Hersey, Paul. *The Situational Leader*. Escondido, California: Warner Books, Center For Leadership Studies, 1984.

Hossler, Don. *Enrollment Management: An Integrated Approach*. New York: The College Board, 1984.

Houston, Jean. *The Possible Human*. Los Angeles: J. P. Tarcher, Inc., 1982.

Jencks, Christopher, and Riesman, David. *The Academic Revolution*. Chicago: The University of Chicago Press, 1968.

Kanter, Rosabeth Moss, and Stein, Barry A. *Life in Organizations: Workplaces As People Experience Them*. New York: Basic Books, Inc., Publishers, 1979.

Kotler, Philip. *Marketing Management: Analysis, Planning, and Control*, fourth edition. Englewood Cliffs, New Jersey: Prentice-Hall, Inc., 1980.

Laborde, Genie Z. *Influencing with Integrity*. Palo Alto, California: Syntony Publishing, 1984.

Levinson, Harry; Spohn, Andrew G.; and Molinari, Janice. *Organizational Diagnosis.* Cambridge, Massachusetts: Harvard University Press, 1972.

Levitt, Theodore. *The Marketing Imagination.* New York: The Free Press, 1983.

Lindquist, Jack. *Strategies for Change.* Berkeley, California: Pacific Soundings Press, 1978.

Lippitt, Gordon L. *Visualizing Change: Model Building and the Change Process.* La Jolla, California: University Associates, Inc., 1973.

Maccoby, Michael. *The Leader: A New Face for American Management.* New York: Simon and Schuster, 1981.

Musashi, Miyamoto. *A Book of Five Rings: The Classic Guide to Strategy,* tenth printing. Woodstock, New York: The Overlook Press, 1974.

Naisbitt, John, and Aburdene, Patricia. *Re-inventing the Corporation.* New York: Warner Books, Inc., 1985.

Odiorne, George S. *How Managers Make Things Happen,* second edition. Englewood Cliffs, New Jersey: Prentice-Hall, Inc., 1982.

Odiorne, George S. *Strategic Management of Human Resources.* San Francisco: Jossey-Bass Publishers, 1985.

Ohmae, Kenichi. *The Mind of the Strategist: Business Planning for Competitive Advantage.* New York: Penguin Books, Ltd., 1982.

Pastin, Mark. *The Hard Problems of Management: Gaining the Ethics Edge.* San Francisco: Jossey-Bass Publishers, 1986.

Peters, Thomas J., and Austin, Nancy. *A Passion for Excellence: The Leadership Difference.* New York: Warner Books, 1985.

Peters, Thomas J., and Waterman, Robert H. *In Search of Excellence: Lessons from America's Best-Run Companies.* Cambridge, Massachusetts: Harper & Row, Publishers, 1982.

Poster, Michael E. *Competitive Strategy: Techniques for Analyzing Industries and Competitors.* New York: The Free Press, 1980.

Quinn, James Brian. *Strategies for Change: Logical Incrementalism.* Homewood, Illinois: Richard D. Irwin, Inc., 1980.

Satir, Virginia. *Peoplemaking.* Palo Alto, California: Science and Behavior Books, Inc., 1972.

Sayles, Leonard R. *Leadership: What Effective Managers Really Do . . . and How They Do It.* New York: McGraw-Hill Book Company, 1979.

Schutz, Will. *Leaders of Schools: FIRO Theory Applied to Administrators.* La Jolla, California: University Associates, Inc., 1977.

Schwarz, Jack. *Human Energy Systems.* New York: E. P. Dutton, 1980.

Spitzer, Dean. "Five Keys to Successful Training." *Training,* June, 1986.

Steiner, George A. *Strategic Planning: What Every Manager Must Know.* New York: The Free Press, 1979.

Torquato, John. *Why Winners Win! Techniques of Advocate Selling.* New York: AMACOM, 1983.

Woodcock, Mike, and Francis, Dave. *The Unblocked Boss: Activities for Self-Development.* San Diego, California: University Associates, Inc., 1981.

GENERAL SUBJECTS

Ihlanfeldt, William. *Achieving Optimal Enrollments and Tuition Revenues.* San Francisco: Jossey-Bass Publishers, 1980.

Lowery, William R., and associates. *College Admissions Counseling: A Handbook for the Profession.* San Francisco: Jossey-Bass Publishers, 1982.

CULTURE/CLIMATE

Bellah, Robert H.; Madsen, Richard; Sullivan, William M.; Swidler, Ann; and Tipton, Steven M. *Habits of the Heart: Individualism and Commitment in American Life.* New York: Harper & Row, Publishers, 1985.

Berger, Peter L.; Douglas, Mary; Foucault, Michael; and Habermas, Jurgen. *Cultural Analysis.* Boston: Routledge & Kegan Paul, 1984.

Frankl, Viktor E. *The Unheard Cry for Meaning.* New York: Simon And Schuster, 1978.

Goodman, Paul S., and associates. *Change in Organizations.* San Francisco: Jossey-Bass Publishers, 1982.

Kilmann, Ralph H. "Corporate Culture: Managing the Intangible Style of Corporate Life May Be the Key to Avoiding Stagnation." *Psychology Today*, April, 1986.

Kilmann, Ralph H.; Saxton, Mary J.; Serpa, Roy; and associates. *Gaining Control of the Corporate Culture.* San Francisco: Jossey-Bass Publishers, 1985.

Lippitt, Gordon L. *Visualizing Change: Model Building and the Change Process.* La Jolla, California: University Associates, Inc., 1973.

Lockland, George T. *Grow or Die: The Unifying Principle of Transformation.* New York: Random House, 1973.

Naisbitt, John. *Megatrends: Ten New Directions Transforming Our Lives.* New York: Warner Books, Inc., 1982.

Rogers, Everett M. *Diffusion of Innovations.* New York: The Free Press, 1962.

Toffley, Alvin. *Previews and Premises.* New York: William Morrow and Company, Inc., 1983.

INDEX